D1565067

Perspectives on **BARRY HANNAH**

Perspectives on
BARRY

HANNAH

Edited by

Martyn Bone

University Press of Mississippi/Jackson

www.upress.state.ms.us

The University Press of Mississippi is a member of the
Association of American University Presses.

Copyright © 2007 by University Press of Mississippi
All rights reserved
Manufactured in the United States of America

First edition 2007

∞

Library of Congress Cataloging-in-Publication Data

Perspectives on Barry Hannah / edited by Martyn Bone. — 1st ed.
p. cm.
Includes index.
ISBN-13: 978-1-57806-919-4 (cloth : alk. paper)
ISBN-10: 1-57806-919-X (cloth : alk. paper) 1. Hannah, Barry—
Criticism and interpretation. 2. Experimental fiction, American—
History and criticism. 3. Postmodernism (Literature)—United States.
4. Heroes in literature. 5. Masculinity in literature. 6. Southern
States—In literature. I. Bone, Martyn, 1974–
PS3558.A476Z85 2007
813'.54—dc22   2006015723

British Library Cataloging-in-Publication Data available

Contents

CONTENTS

Acknowledgments

This book has its origins in a Barry Hannah special issue of *Mississippi Quarterly* published in spring 2001 (vol. 54, no. 2). The special issue was edited by the leading Hannah scholar Ruth D. Weston, also the author of *Barry Hannah: Postmodern Romantic* (originally published in 1998, and recently reprinted by the University Press of Mississippi). I want to express my gratitude to Ruth for inviting me to turn the special issue into a book, for her ongoing interest in this project, and for the example of her own criticism. The numerous and repeated references to Ruth's work in the essays that follow are an apt testimony to the importance of her scholarship for the rest of us writing about Hannah's fiction.

As this volume has progressed over the last few years, it has moved further and further away from the *Mississippi Quarterly* special issue: only three of the six essays from that issue appear here, and all of them have been revised and expanded to varying degrees. The essay by Ken Millard which opens *Perspectives on Barry Hannah* is significantly revised and extended from the special issue's closing article, "The Metafictional Aesthetic of *High Lonesome*." Thomas Bjerre's contribution to this book is a reworked and much expanded version of "'It was always life intense I was after': Heroes, True and False, in Barry Hannah's Fiction." Finally, my own contribution to the book is moderately revised from "'All the Confederate Dead ... All of Faulkner the great': Faulkner, Hannah, Neo-Confederate Narrative and

Postsouthern Parody." I thank *Mississippi Quarterly* for granting permission to republish material from the special issue in this collection.

Two other essays in this book are based upon previously published articles. James Potts's essay is revised and expanded from "The Shade of Faulkner's Horse: Archetypal Immortality in the Postmodern South," originally published in *Southern Quarterly*, vol. 39, no. 3 (spring 2001). Mark Graybill's essay is reprinted with minor revisions from *Southern Literary Journal*, vol. 33, no. 1 (fall 2000). Thanks to both *Southern Quarterly* and *Southern Literary Journal* for permission to reprint these essays here.

At the University Press of Mississippi, I would like to take this opportunity to thank Seetha Srinivasan and Walter Biggins for their support of and patience with this project and Shane Gong for her editorial guidance in the final stages. Thanks, too, to the Society for the Study of Southern Literature for giving me the opportunity to chair a Hannah panel featuring three of the contributors to this volume (Melanie Benson, Scott Romine, and Matthew Shipe) at its biannual meeting in Birmingham, Alabama, in March 2006.

Finally, I would like to express my—*our*—appreciation to Barry Hannah himself, not least for granting the interview to his old friend and colleague Dan Williams that closes this volume. At this point, Barry has been publishing his hilarious, uproarious novels, short stories, and essays for some thirty-five years—longer than I've been alive. Unlike most of the contributors, I've never met Barry; however, in the nine years since I wrote my MA dissertation on his work at the University of Nottingham in England, I've read enough of Barry's observations on academic criticism of his work to suspect that he will feel—how shall I put it—*ambivalent* about the publication of this collection of essays. Still, it should be clear that the contributors to this volume are united by their deep appreciation for and engagement with Barry's work. We've all heard and enjoyed outlandish stories about Barry Hannah (or Barry and Harry, or Barry and Larry), but ultimately it comes down to the work. Thanks for writing, Barry.

Introduction

   Born in Mississippi in 1942, Barry Hannah is the author of
twelve books (excluding limited editions). His first novel, *Geronimo Rex*
(1972), was nominated for the National Book Award and won the William
Faulkner Prize; his first collection of short stories, *Airships* (1978), won the
Arnold Gingrich Short Fiction Award; his most recent collection, *High
Lonesome* (1996), was nominated for a Pulitzer Prize. Ever since John
Updike reviewed *Geronimo Rex* favorably in the *New Yorker*, Hannah
has garnered reams of praise from writer peers both within and beyond
the United States. *Airships* attracted plaudits from Cynthia Ozick, James
Dickey, and Philip Roth; on the cover of a 1991 British edition pairing
Airships with *Ray* (1980), Julian Barnes declares that "Hannah is a ferocious
and formidable talent." In *Boomerang* (1991), Hannah himself reports that
"[Truman] Capote when he was really drunk called me the maddest writer
in the U.S.A" (114). Another indication of Hannah's standing among fellow
writers is his inclusion in both of Richard Ford's important anthologies:
The Granta Book of the American Short Story (1992) and *The Granta Book of
the American Long Story* (1998).
   It would seem to be clear, then, that Barry Hannah is a major contemporary American writer. Yet few of Hannah's books have achieved anything
resembling popular success. While Hannah's work is taught in universities (and not just in the United States), it does not appear on curricula as

widely or frequently as it might. Though Hannah's prodigious output has generated a number of perceptive articles and two valuable monographs, this scholarly response does not fully reflect the range or power of his work. There is something dispiriting about the fact that the same quotation from Larry McMurtry's review of *Ray* ("The best young fiction writer to appear in the South since Flannery O'Connor") continues to pop up on the dust jackets of Hannah's books: after all, Hannah is no longer a "young fiction writer" but rather (as he puts it in the interview that closes this book) "a geezer"—a geezer, moreover, who has published no less than eight books since *Ray. Perspectives on Barry Hannah* attempts to move beyond the well-worn blurbs and the critical focus on *Airships* and *Ray* to provide a wide-ranging, multi-faceted assessment of Hannah's whole career.

This book is the first-ever collection of critical essays on Barry Hannah's fiction, and the first book to engage with the full range of fiction that Hannah published between 1972 and 2001: taken together, the nine essays cover all of Hannah's twelve books. Some contributors consider the "classics" like *Airships* and *Ray* alongside other, lesser-known novels and stories; other contributors offer the first sustained, essay-length readings of Hannah books from the early 1970s (*Nightwatchmen*) and the last decade (*High Lonesome* and *Yonder Stands Your Orphan*). The thematic and theoretical approaches of the essayists range widely; nevertheless, the volume as a whole brings into focus certain subjects and issues which have recurred throughout Hannah's thirty-five year career: the meaning and aesthetics of language; his interrogation of traditional models of masculinity and heroism; the relationship of Hannah's fiction to postmodern literature and culture; his engagement with southern history, literature, and culture; and his concern with spiritual and moral issues.

In putting the collection together, there was one aspect of some earlier writing about Hannah that I wanted to avoid: a tendency to fall back on juicy anecdotes about Barry Hannah himself. In his introduction to *Perspectives on Harry Crews* (2001), Erik Bledsoe insists that for all the "stories of 'Harry Crews: The Legend' as I've come to call it," such stories should not be allowed to overshadow the fact that, ultimately, it "comes down to [Crews's] work" (Bledsoe x, xiii). I second that emotion with reference to Hannah. Introducing the 1993 University Press of Mississippi reissue of *Boomerang* and *Never Die*, Rick Bass notes that "Much has been made of the bad Barry, the hostage to alcohol, rage, and despair" (viii), but Bass himself cannot resist recounting more "bad-Barry stories" (ix). Bass claims that "[t]hese rumors and acid tales are told here not so much for sensationalism's sake . . . but rather to place the sweet Barry-of-the-Present in context" (x). That may be so, but the stories *about* the man detract from the stories *by* the man: though Bass is ostensibly introducing *Boomerang* and *Never Die*, he glances only briefly at these two relatively neglected novels. To be sure, this seems to have something to do with Bass's reluctance to interpret the novels himself: when Bass remarks that "mumbo-jumbo, deconstruction and explication, is too dry to bring honor to Hannah's work," he is expressing a familiar writer's skepticism toward literary criticism (indeed, it is the kind of view that Hannah himself has been known to express in no uncertain terms). Still, I would suggest that the contributions to this volume do more "honor" to Hannah's work through engaged, inventive "deconstruction and explication" than would another round of bad-Barry anecdotes. *Perspectives on Barry Hannah* does not set out to downplay the oft-remarked autobiographical aspects of Hannah's fiction; however, it does insist on focusing on the work, rather than "Barry Hannah: the Legend."

Readers even vaguely familiar with the course of Hannah's career will be aware that reviewers and critics of his work have repeatedly focused on the virtuosity of his language. David Madden has written of *Geronimo Rex* that "[a]lmost everything that language can do in prose without going berserk in an hysterically experimental way is done well in this first novel" (Madden 316); reviewing *The Tennis Handsome* (1983), Ivan Gold observed that "[l]anguage is made to juggle with its snout, standing on its tail" (Gold 19)—an image Hannah himself might have appreciated. It is appropriate, then, that *Perspectives on Barry Hannah* opens with Ken Millard's analysis of language and aesthetics in works from both ends of Hannah's career. Noting that the themes of "creative energy and emotional honesty" have remained consistent across the entire span of Hannah's writing, Millard considers *Geronimo Rex* alongside Hannah's most recent collection of short stories, *High Lonesome*. Despite their formal differences—the contrast between the single consciousness of Harry Monroe in *Geronimo Rex* and the multiple character-narrators of *High Lonesome*—both books are characterized by a concern with the relationship between language, aesthetics, and identity. Hannah's character-narrators strive for "original and authentic expression of the self" in a contemporary culture characterized by mediation, commercialization, and depletion. Yet despite this yearning for an authentic self, both Harry in *Geronimo Rex* and various characters in *High Lonesome* realize that subjectivity is contingent upon representation—not least the act of narrating or writing one's self. Millard shows how Hannah's narrators meditate upon the production and artistic quality of their own narratives: this process generates the "metafictional aesthetic" of Hannah's fiction. Millard concludes by suggesting that the stories in *High Lonesome* gesture toward a sense of cultural and even spiritual value that exists just beyond language's ability to articulate it.

Where Millard sees Hannah's fiction dramatizing and celebrating "the enigma of the word [and] the mystery of the linguistic referent," Richard Lee's reading of Hannah's overlooked second novel *Nightwatchmen* (1973) identifies a crisis of representation in the gap between language and the "reality" to which language claims to refer. The shift from Harry Monroe's relatively stable consciousness in *Geronimo Rex* to the multiple and conflicting points of view of the characters who narrate *Nightwatchmen* destabilizes the culturally agreed (but actually arbitrary) links between language and "reality." Lee relates this postmodern move on Hannah's part to a generic turn in more recent campus novels by David Lodge, Richard Russo, and others: a rigorously self-reflexive interrogation of the relationship between the "real" and *representations* of the real. Lee echoes and extends Millard's observations on the cultural mediation of authentic experience by explicating the symbolism of glasses and spectacles in *Nightwatchmen*; for Lee, such symbolism suggests how "reality" is mediated by not only language but also point of view.

Reviews and critical appraisals of Hannah's fiction have frequently focused on what Owen Gilman calls "the intense maleness of the central figures in each Hannah story." Gilman adds that "feminist readers find little solace in the way women are represented" (Gilman 219); indeed, Ruth Weston began *Barry Hannah: Postmodern Romantic* (1998) by admitting that "as a woman and a feminist," she had initially been "horrified by his depiction of, and his [male] characters' treatment of, women" (Weston 1). However, Weston's book goes on to demonstrate that Hannah's fiction is far from simply misogynistic; indeed, his male characters' relationships with and attitudes toward women often derive from barely repressed anxieties about their own masculinity. Thomas Ærvold Bjerre's contribution to this volume ranges from *Ray* via *Captain Maximus* (1985) and *Bats Out of Hell* (1993) to *Yonder Stands Your Orphan* (2001) to assess the representation of manhood throughout Hannah's work. Drawing on theoretical and cultural studies of masculinity, Bjerre argues that Hannah consistently interrogates traditional and hegemonic models of manhood based upon action, sex and violence. Echoing Millard's observation that narrators throughout *High Lonesome* become artists by performing or inventing their identities, Bjerre demonstrates how various Hannah characters discover an alternative form of male heroism in "the passionate expression of life through art." For example, Bjerre shows how the U.S. army's defeat in Vietnam and the resulting cultural devaluation of the warrior hero generates a crisis of manhood in Bobby Smith of *The Tennis Handsome*; Bobby eventually finds an alternative model of masculinity in French Edward's peaceful artistry on the tennis court.

Bjerre is explicitly concerned with Hannah's depiction and interrogation of national myths of manhood. The next two essays, by James Potts and Martyn Bone, consider Hannah's work in the regional context of southern culture, and with reference to specifically southern codes of masculinity and myths of military heroism. However, Potts and Bone diverge in their assessment of the relationship between Hannah's writing and earlier southern literature, especially the fiction of William Faulkner. Potts posits that Hannah and two other contemporary southern writers, Cormac McCarthy and Charles Frazier, sustain the southern literary tradition of Faulkner and Allen Tate, and that this continuity is especially evident in Hannah's depiction of horses and horse soldiers. Potts begins by noting that Tate's 1938 novel *The Fathers* presented the Confederate cavalier as a mythic figure from a glorious past, and that Faulkner's fiction repeatedly treats the horse as a symbol of nobility, masculinity, creativity, and religious ecstasy. Drawing on Jungian psychoanalysis, Potts proceeds to show how "the shade of Faulkner's horse" has survived in Hannah's fiction: ideas of art, death, redemption and immortality are linked with equine imagery and the cavalier myth. In a coda, Potts expresses concern at the decline and disappearance of these traditional ideas and myths from contemporary "postsouthern" literature, and suggests that Hannah, McCarthy, and Frazier represent the last gasp of a southern literary tradition that articulated a longing for heroism, transcendence, and immortality. By contrast, my own essay firmly identifies Hannah with the postsouthern turn in contemporary fiction. I read some of the same texts as Potts—Hannah's *Airships*, *Ray*, and *Bats Out of Hell* as well as Faulkner's *Flags in the Dust*—through the lens of what southern literary critic Michael Kreyling was the first to define as "postsouthern parody." I also draw on scholarship by contemporary southern historians to situate the fiction of both Faulkner and Hannah in relation to mythic images and narratives of the Confederacy and its military heroes. My claim is that Hannah interrogates these myths, especially through a recurrent and parodic interrogation of Faulkner's depiction of General J. E. B. Stuart in *Flags in the Dust*.

Matthew Shipe's essay begins by suggesting that *Hey Jack!* (1987) and *Boomerang* (1989) should be read in tandem. For Shipe, these two novels constitute an affirmative and optimistic turn in Hannah's career after the bleakness and even nihilism that characterized his output in the first half of the 1980s. The narrators Homer (*Hey Jack!*) and Barry (*Boomerang*) overcome their suspicion that existence is meaningless and avert the masculine temptations of sex and violence—a theme familiar from Thomas Bjerre's discussion of various other Hannah texts—by taking responsibility for their actions and reconnecting with their families and friends. Like Potts and Bone, Shipe situates Hannah's fiction in a specifically southern cultural context. Reading *Hey Jack!* with reference to Hannah's own relocation to Oxford, Mississippi, Shipe demonstrates how Homer both challenges negative images of the South in popular culture and formulates a revisionary and progressive idea of southern "community" that requires the inhabitants of his hometown (based on Oxford) to acknowledge various individuals who were previously ostracized. Shipe goes on to show how the affirmative turn in Hannah's late 1980s fiction is completed in *Boomerang* through Yelverston's Christ-like ability to forgive and redeem his son's killers.

The next two essays, by Mark Graybill and Melanie Benson, track a spatial turn in Hannah's fiction—especially *Never Die* (1991)—from the South to the West. Graybill reads *Never Die* as a postmodern western: whereas the traditional western novel fulfils reader's fantasies about how the West was "won," postmodern texts like *Never Die* disturb such fanta-sies. Much as Richard Lee's essay teases out Hannah's postmodern rework-ing of the campus novel, Graybill details Hannah's revisionist approach to the generic conventions of the western; much as my own essay fore-grounds Hannah's postmodern use of parody in order to ease the burden of southern literary history, Graybill emphasizes Hannah's deployment of parody to both dismantle and pay homage to the conventions of the western as a literary tradition which "never dies." Melanie Benson is more circumspect about Hannah's adoption of the western, and about critical readings which identify Hannah as a postsouthern writer. Pointing out the paucity of scholarly attention to the Native Americans who appear throughout Hannah's fiction, Benson interprets four texts—*Geronimo Rex, Ray, Captain Maximus* and *Never Die*—as part of a wider white south-ern tradition which romanticizes *western* Indians even while ignoring or diminishing native *southern* Indians. Benson argues that by adopting the legendary Apache warrior Geronimo as an alter ego even while disdain-ing the Choctaws who live in 1960s Mississippi, Harry Monroe displaces Native American identity from the South to the West, and from the present to the past. For Benson, the westward turn of *Never Die* further obscures white southern responsibility for crimes against Native Americans, while the novel's critique of "vicious capitalism" (Hannah's own phrase, from an interview with Graybill) is compromised by its failure to take seriously the devastating impact of westward expansion on the Native population.

Though Matthew Shipe identifies an emphasis on optimism and redemption in Hannah's fiction from the late 1980s, other contributors conclude their essays by noting the darkness (Bjerre) and diminished pos-sibilities for redemption (Potts) in Hannah's most recent novel, *Yonder Stands Your Orphan*. The final essay by Scott Romine offers a thorough and theoretically informed analysis of *Yonder Stands Your Orphan* which inter-sects in interesting ways with many of the preceding essays. Romine's initial suggestion that *Yonder* imagines Eagle Lake, Mississippi, as a redemptive or utopian space seems less in keeping with Bjerre and Potts's takes on *Yonder* than with Shipe's conception of individual and communal redemp-tion in *Hey Jack!* and *Booomerang*. However, Romine relates this redemp-tive or utopian gesture to the novel's problematic attempt to recover "the real" from a degenerate culture defined by mediation, simulation, and consumption. The nostalgia for "the real" of numerous characters in *Yonder* is symptomatic of—rather than an antidote to—the (home)sickness that permeates a hyperreal, hyper-capitalist society. Hannah has written about orphans since he began *Nightwatchmen* with Thorpe Trove's description of his parents' murder; Romine shows how in *Yonder* orphanhood becomes a metaphor for the pathological condition of a whole culture.

Romine's view that Hannah's latest book yearns to recover "the real" from a society saturated by simulation might be fruitfully compared and contrasted with Richard Lee's argument that some thirty years earlier *Nightwatchmen* was ahead of the postmodern pack in dismantling distinctions between "the real" and representations of the real. Similarly, one might reconsider Shipe's suggestion that *Hey Jack!* and *Boomerang* imagine a redemptive reconnection to family and friends alongside Romine's claim that in *Yonder* the family has been replaced by money as the primary force of socialization, a momentous transition that compounds the characters' feelings of alienation and homesickness. At this point, however, I will leave it to the reader to make further comparisons and contrasts between the nine essays that follow. In his preface to *Let Us Now Praise Famous Men* (1941), James Agee wrote that Walker Evans's photographs and his own text "are co-equal, mutually independent, and fully collaborative" (Agee and Evans, xi); Greil Marcus later contended that, au contraire, Agee and Evans are engaged in "an argument, a violent argument" (Marcus 8). At one level, the essays in *Perspectives on Barry Hannah* can and should be read as "mutually independent": in most cases, the contributors wrote and rewrote their essays without reading each other's drafts. In this introduction, however, I have tried to indicate some of the comparisons *and* contrasts, the agreements *and* "arguments" (though hopefully not "violent" ones!), going on *between* the essays. Indeed, if there are fruitful tensions as well as connections between the nine essays, then one might say the same of the short stories and novels that the essays discuss. If certain themes have recurred through the course of Barry Hannah's career, the twelve books he published between 1972 and 2000 are anything but homogenous or repetitive. Ken Millard quotes a line from the *High Lonesome* story "Through Sunset Into the Racoon Night" in which the character Royce describes his own narrative as "a two-headed snake in jabber with itself" (123–24). Replace the image of the two-headed snake with a twelve-headed Barry Hannah, and one has, I would venture, an appropriately surreal metaphor for an eclectic, provocative, and always engaging body of work.

Perspectives on Barry Hannah closes with the man himself "in jabber" with his friend and former colleague Dan Williams. In this interview, conducted in October 2005, Hannah talks about his current work-in-progress, teaching at the University of Mississippi, his conception of Christianity, and the worst interviews he has ever experienced. Happily, Dan Williams's interview does not fall into this category.

—*Martyn Bone*
COPENHAGEN, APRIL 2006

Works Cited

Agee, James and Walker Evans. *Let Us Now Praise Famous Men*. 1941. Boston: Houghton Mifflin, 2001.

Bass, Rick. "Introduction." In Barry Hannah, *Boomerang/Never Die*. Jackson: Banner Books/UP of Mississippi, 1993. v–xi.

Bledsoe, Erik. "Introduction." In Bledsoe, ed., *Perspectives on Harry Crews*. Jackson: UP of Mississippi, 2001. ix–xiv.

Gilman, Owen W., Jr.. "Barry Hannah (1942–)." In Joseph M. Flora and Robert Bain, eds., *Contemporary Fiction Writers of the South: A Bio-Bibliographical Sourcebook*. Westport: Greenwood P, 1993. 211–21.

Gold, Ivan. "Yoknapatawpha County of the Mind." Review of Barry Hannah, *The Tennis Handsome*. *New York Times Book Review* 1 May 1983. 11, 19.

Hannah, Barry. *Boomerang/Never Die*. Jackson: Banner Books/UP of Mississippi, 1993.

———. "Through Sunset into the Raccoon Night." In *High Lonesome*. New York: Atlantic Monthly P, 1996. 97–124.

Madden, David. "Barry Hannah's *Geronimo Rex* in Retrospect." *Southern Review* 19.2 (spring 1983): 309–16.

Marcus, Greil. "The Expanding Vacant Spot." In *The Dustbin of History*. London: Picador, 1997. 119–25.

Weston, Ruth. *Barry Hannah: Postmodern Romantic*. Baton Rouge: Louisiana State UP, 1998.

Perspectives on **BARRY HANNAH**

The Cultural Value of Metafiction

Geronimo Rex *and* High Lonesome

—*Kenneth Millard*

Barry Hannah's *Geronimo Rex* (1972) is a classic coming-of-age novel that exhibits many characteristics of the bildungsroman and works within the parameters of generic conventions to give "a fresh angle on the great American subject of Growing Up" (Updike 124). The protagonist Harry Monroe gives a retrospective account of his childhood and adolescence so that we might better understand the formative experiences of white southern manhood in Mississippi during the 1950s and 1960s and the "unutterable burning filth of a young male's mind" (271). *Geronimo Rex* is above all an uproarious depiction of adolescence, its foibles, absurdities and affectations lending themselves well to Hannah's linguistic originality and candor. Harry's adolescence is theatrical and gaudy, and many of its key scenes have a lurid and camp quality that is appropriate to the exaggerated mood-shifting and self-dramatizing of teen angst. It is a novel of high jinx and total bathos: it may be 1958 and the heyday of Elvis, but Harry is "as ugly as a shotgunned butt of pork," a teenager who "exude[s] an exotic melancholy" (200), and who falls for a redhead because "even the hint of red in a woman's hair makes me gimp around like a pogo stick" (79). One redhead in particular has "the unamused face of an operatic slut" (50), and a mother like "some species of obese dwarf who wore a swath of garbage for a dress" (50). Harry sleepwalks through adolescent infatuation, but his crush on Ann Mick is total and paralyzing because "no man could look at her without becoming a slobbering kind of rutting boar" (60).

As these quotations should indicate, the eroticism of maniacal teenage lust is captured with great energy and fervor in the ludicrous and absurd dark pantomime of Harry's fantasies, and the particular qualities of the novel's language will be a crucial point of issue in his final coming-of-age at the novel's close. The violent assertions of heterosexual desire contain a good deal of misogyny and self-loathing, but for Harry they are a necessary part of his growing up in small-town southern culture because "[t]o be a queer in Dream of Pines was to be like an alligator wearing panties" (229). The novel also has an episodic quality that is characteristic of the bildungsroman, and its vivid dramatic scenes are often written in the present tense to give the narrative an urgency and immediacy that a retrospective might not otherwise have. There is a strong focus on sex, violence, racial politics and southern forms of masculinity, and the narrative structure is almost a series of epiphanies or moments of ludicrous hyperbole and comic exaggeration that give adolescence its proper dramatic intensity. This much is reasonably conventional.

It is notable, however, that Harry also has a strongly developed interest in matters of aesthetics, especially as they are expressed in music and particularly the jazz trumpet which Harry plays in high school and through college. In the novel's first scene, which takes place in Dream of Pines circa 1950, the eight-year-old Harry watches in awe as "a fanatic man named Jones who risked everything to have the magnificent corps of student musicians he had" (11) conducts rehearsals by the Dream of Pines Colored High School Band. Harry invests his rapt vision of the band with powerful qualities of the spectacular that transform the performance into something remarkable and other-worldly:

The way it was affecting me, I guess I was already a musician at the time and didn't know it. This band was the best music I'd ever heard, bar none. They made you want to pick up a rifle and just get killed somewhere. What drums, and what a wide brassy volume; and the woodwinds were playing tempestuously shrill. The trombones went deeper than what before my heart ever had

room for. And I just didn't know what to thin. . . . The band to
me was like a river tearing down a dam when they played (14).

This moment of epiphany establishes a pattern that is repeated
throughout the novel in which aesthetic performance becomes, as
Christopher Griffin has observed, "a powerful metaphor for the experience
of authentic being" (173). Harry's failure as a jazz trumpeter is a significant
event in his adolescence, then, because it causes him to commit instead
to writing, and writing (as Harry knows) is already over-populated with
the textual voices of others. This knowledge gives *Geronimo Rex* a self-
consciousness that marks it out among modern bildungsroman as Harry
wrestles with the problem of whether an original and authentic expression
of the self can still be accomplished. When the mixed-race bandleader and
employee of Harry's father, Harley Butte, declares, "Look here, Harry, I've
put in my *hours*. I *have done my homework* in this university of life. I have
did my time in Ups and Downs College," Harry can only ponder the deeply
clichéd and mediated nature of Harley's words: "was it some scene I had
seen in the movies, or was it something I had read?" (97). The dilemma
of how one might achieve unmediated originality and authenticity satu-
rates Harry's own attempts at self-representation and makes the novel a
significantly original contribution to the bildungsroman genre.

Geronimo Rex is, then, a novel about not only the ways in which subjectivity is a kind of performance (of the theatricality of adolescence as
an act) but also the contingency of the forms of representation to which
acting and writing are indebted. *Geronimo Rex* is characterized by staged
moments of epiphany in which Harry's subjectivity is formed and articulated, but simultaneously qualified by a self-reflexive acknowledgment of
the contingency of self-representation in language. This tension makes
Harry determined to discover that style of art which represents the self
authentically, and committed to a corresponding critical interrogation of
any art which can be exposed as fraudulent, duplicitous, or meretricious.
Harry understands that even his self-awareness is derived in part from his
knowledge of texts: but which texts (he asks himself) and how are they
properly interpreted? For example, Harry recalls his "*love*" for Catherine
being complicated by the contrast between "her words, her voice . . . this
bad whining illiteracy, not even good Alabama English," and his own

aesthetic sensibility, supposedly heightened by reading James Joyce and F. Scott Fitzgerald: "I'd read so much good English poetry and prose and had developed such a sense of the exquisite—I thought—in grammar." The adult Harry, however, realizes that interpreting or mediating his own feelings through literary texts may have hindered, rather than heightened, his quest for self-awareness and for a corresponding aesthetic. He recounts wryly that "I'd read *Ulysses* and knew about a fifth of what was going on, the sentences stuck in my throat, spread like a cold to my ears, and I was diseased by elegant English sentences. Some days I had such a sense of the exquisite I wouldn't speak at all. . . . This is how thudding stupid being literary can make you" (248–49).

Having learned this lesson, the adult author of *Geronimo Rex* strives for a kind of figurative language, often with the hallucinogenic intensity of lyric poetry, that defies rational explication and even the interpretative paradigms that critics might bring to it. This narrative style also redeems the novel from the kinds of self-absorption or self-indulgence sometimes characteristic of the bildungsroman. *Geronimo Rex* is everywhere preoccupied with the nature of true art, and Harry strives in the writing of his autobiographical narrative to become an original and stylish artist. In his attempts to translate a jazz aesthetic into writing, his college pal Fleece accuses Harry of sounding "like Edgar Allan Poe playing the tuba" (337), but *Geronimo Rex* is a coming-of-age novel in which Harry vanquishes creative father figures with great ingenuity and individuality, and its self-reflexive qualities place the novel in the vanguard of the genre for its time.

Harry's story is driven by a sub-plot of violent racial politics that is grimly appropriate to Mississippi in the 1960s and integral to his development as a southern white man. Harry's adolescent identification with Geronimo is a key part of this racial politics, a displacement of anxieties about the racism of his white southern culture onto another field of ethnic difference. For Harry, the figure of Geronimo offers an opportunity to empathize with the underdog, the vanquished, the heroically defeated. Harry does this partly because the defeat of the white southern way of life is, in his view, foreshadowed by the defeat of the Indians at the end of the nineteenth century. Both the Indian wars and the Civil War are part of the United States' coming-of-age as a modern empire, two violent political confrontations in which the identity of the nation was forged by pronouncing

Indian and white southern lifestyles and cultures anachronistic. Harry's coming-of-age is thereby associated with narratives of national identity, with its costs and losses, and its violent transformative energies. Geronimo is a lost figure of heroic defeat, and this appeals greatly to Harry's interest in the association between failure and personal integrity: he is not "your ordinary romantic hero" (160). Furthermore, as Melanie Benson argues elsewhere in this volume, Harry's conception of Geronimo as his wilder and (crucially) western alter-ego contrasts with Harry's appalled response to real Mississippi Choctaw Indians (281). As Benson indicates, this narrative displacement of Native Americans from the South to the West is itself expressive of an anxiety about racial haunting because Harry knows himself to have an "Asian cut of face no one in the family can account for" (43).

The novel's title is worth particular attention here. "Rex" is clearly an allusion to Oedipus, the character from Greek mythology (and the drama of Sophocles) who unwittingly murdered his father and married his mother. Oedipus is also the figure famously employed by Sigmund Freud in his interpretation of the adolescent psychology of the young male. There is no direct correspondence between Harry's story and Oedipus except in his general emotional development; in fact, as Mark Charney has noted, Harry shows "a potential for sensitivity and thoughtfulness in his affection for his father" (18) which is not conventionally oedipal. Indeed, Harry's father simply disappears from the text without serious conflict (as will his wife Prissy at the novel's end): as Harry himself observes, "very little has passed between us except money" (171). By contrast, Geronimo is a persistent image for Harry, one to which he attends repeatedly after discovering two books about Geronimo in Hedermansever College library: Britton Davis's *The Truth About Geronimo* (1929) and Jason Betzinez's *I Fought with Geronimo* (1959). For Harry, Geronimo's very name has a special significance when he first encounters him in Davis and Betzinez's books: "I went for the name. . . . My eyes fell on the word, name, *Geronimo*, again, and I realized that my last name could be found mixed up in it" (159–60). Geronimo is an almost-anagram of Monroe, and Harry derives a special creative pleasure from this knowledge, as if the Indian chief was a unique linguistic progenitor: "Ah, Geronimo! . . . All the letters of *Monroe* could be found in his name" (302–3). From the outset, Geronimo says something important to Harry about language and self-definition; Harry derives great imaginative inspiration from reading about him; he looks in awe at the photographs of Geronimo reproduced in Davis's biography and remarks that "I seemed to be gathering an energy from them" (231). In the novel's dramatic denouement Harry calls on Geronimo to aid him in his hour of crisis: "Help me, Indian!" (377). Geronimo is, finally, a father-figure, but a textual one: though he represents what Scott Romine in his contribution to this collection terms "the bildungroman's requisite search for the 'spiritual' father," it is in the books *about* Geronimo that Harry discovers the Lacanian word of the father and is thereby inspired both to act and to write.

For Harry, Geronimo represents daring, audacity, risk-taking: he is an outlaw, a loner against superior forces, someone reckless and mutable and protean. Geronimo is thus a model for the kind of artist that Harry aspires to be, but he is also, crucially, a man of action, a soldier in the Apache and Chiricahua wars, and war for Harry is a glorious form of unqualified commitment, even in defeat: "what I especially liked about Geronimo then was that he had cheated, lied, stolen ... and was his own man. ... I would like to leave behind a gnashing hoard of bastards" (231). Geronimo becomes an integral part of Harry's attempt to find the appropriate mythology for his own coming-of-age, and, like Oedipus Rex, one that is contingent upon textual interpretation. This is what one critic, Michael Spikes, has characterized as the "postmodernity" of *Geronimo Rex*, an ironic self-consciousness about literary genre and textual allusion—a self-consciousness that distinguishes it from other bildungsroman but which is nevertheless typical of American fiction of the 1960s and 1970s (Spikes 403–5).

The use of the name "Catherine" and the frequent references to Harry's penchant for disguise and costume recall another important textual antecedent for Harry, Ernest Hemingway's *A Farewell to Arms* (1929). In Hemingway's novel the protagonist Frederick Henry's subjectivity is precarious and fragile, and his existential insecurity is compounded by cultural displacement and the threat of death in battle. Henry's frequent recourse to disguise is symptomatic of an acute existential awareness of the contingency of identity. That anxiety is partly assuaged by both a commitment to action and the discovery of a contemporary language that can authentically convey a new sense of self. In both *A Farewell to Arms* and *Geronimo Rex* the central female character called Catherine dies, and in each case her death facilitates the emotional development of the male protagonist. Like Henry with his uniform, Harry adopts a number of disguises that dramatize the theatricality of identity; in a typical example, he recalls how "when my beard was full out, I got myself a pair of cosmetic spectacles from Sears" (267).

This is not a temporary narrative expedient but a fundamental symptom of Harry's consciousness of the mutability of identity. It is also characteristic of Harry's widespread use of the language of the theatre in his account of himself: he is also a "wild pop-up dummy" who revels in "the fame of having ignited this baroque stream of fraudulent melodrama" (247), and who, at the novel's close, must emerge from the painful sense that he is nothing more than a fraud in a lab coat. Harry even acknowledges his own generic confinement: "I was sealed up in a cartoon farce which was bound to explode with me inside it" (373). These psychological insecurities undoubtedly originate in Harry's parental relationships; in particular, "Mother always looked at me like I was not quite real" (25). This sense of his own insubstantiality haunts Harry's account of himself and helps to explain his pleasure in dressing up and acting. At one point, he adopts an alternative persona upon buying "a new coat made out of reptile leather" (196). This surprising garment strongly recalls Tennessee Williams's play *Orpheus Descending* (1958), in which the young man called Val is known as "Snakeskin" on account of his coat; notably, Val laments the passing of his youth. Williams particularly valued this play because he believed "nothing is more precious to anybody than the emotional record of his youth" (Williams 2).

The emotional record of Harry's youth is saturated with references to texts, to the language of drama, and with an acute awareness of the textual indebtedness of his own narrative of self—an indebtedness that he sought to escape through a commitment to decisive physical action. Besides recounting his distaste for Catherine's bad Alabama idioms because "James Joyce and Fitzgerald were my masters then" (248), Harry recalls his particular fondness for Robert Burns ("the only poetry that ever took me in college" [274]) and tells us that because he was making an "A" grade in English at Hedermansever "no sweat" (239), he had aspirations towards grad school at Columbia: "I could imagine those mean bastards up there reading *Finnegans Wake* upside down and beating you over the head with their pipes" (309). It is significant too that his only good teacher in high school was the woman with the figure of a schoolgirl (like his wife Prissy) who teaches English Literature; she taught him Thomas Wyatt and T. S. Eliot's "The Love Song of J. Alfred Prufrock" and inspired his first poem "in a gust of all the culture I had in me" (44).

These literary references constitute the matrix from which the aesthetic style of Harry's narrative is formed. He develops an unspoken theory of romantic epiphany that structures his narrative in terms of abrupt temporal shifts rather than by conventional "development." His account of himself is a series of epiphanies, often managed by subtle temporal sleights-of-hand that are depicted as out-of-time experiences, transcendental romantic moments that are urgent and intense, but which do not occur as part of a conventional teleological progression. This is Harry's interpretation of romantic epiphany, one in which his consciousness is shaped by sudden dramatic episodes that necessarily involve a powerful suspension of conventional temporal perspectives. In this way, Geronimo Rex becomes the recreation of a series of epiphanies by which Harry becomes the writer that he is. Harry's retrospective self-consciousness about serious aesthetic issues is therefore integral to his self-definition from the novel's first scene in which we read about him watching the Dream of Pines Colored High School Band, to his gradual emergence as the mature adult author of Geronimo Rex.

Harry's most significant coming-of-age experience is his early marriage to a very young woman, Prissy Lombardo, and their move from Mississippi to Fayetteville, Arkansas, where Harry has been accepted to graduate school. These events are accompanied by a significant shift in the novel's style as Harry begins to emerge as a writer while simultaneously approaching the temporal vantage point from which his retrospective narrative is constructed. Both aspects of his life (the early marriage, the faltering start to a writing career) run into immediate difficulties, but there is little psychological explanation for this because Harry has not yet (at the time of writing his narrative) properly understood himself; as such, he cannot offer an interpretation of his own emotional motivations. What is more, the move to Fayetteville is accompanied by a series of authoritative male relationships that are characteristic of the novel's period and southern culture, and which culminate in Harry's oedipal showdown with the crucial father-figure of Dr Gregory Lariat, a literature professor who expounds an aesthetic theory that is strongly at odds with Harry's own writing.

Harry's marriage to Prissy is mediated through a nexus of male (and especially father-son) relationships and an accompanying sensitivity to issues of social class. Harry first meets Prissy because she has been procured for his friend Tommy Neicase by Tommy's father, who is then ashamed to feel "like a pimp" (340) and bars Tommy from seeing Prissy (thus opening the way for Harry). Mr Neicase subsequently presses money on Harry "like a playboy"; Harry is impressed by this largesse and regards it as "a weird boon and a new vantage, having money accumulate right on your hip" (343). Meanwhile Prissy's father Ted Lombardo positively encourages Harry's sexual advances to his daughter and finds his pandering place in the unfolding drama of courtship—"to sport around as love's chorus" (342). Back in Dream of Pines, Harry's own father, Ode Elann, boasts to his friends on the golf course of his son's impending marriage (344) and attends the wedding "sharp as a dandy" (345). This matrix of male relationships is crucial to Harry's desire to marry because it represents the social hierarchy within which he expects to find his place as a southern (white) man. Prissy understands this, and her insistence that Harry return after the wedding to shake hands with her father is tacit recognition of the social condescension with which her father has been treated by the other, wealthier men. Still, it is Prissy who gets what she wants: "I was sore all over about getting somebody like you. And now I've got you" (348).[1]

The marriage begins to go wrong immediately, as expressed by Harry's sudden and extreme awareness of Prissy's diminutive appearance: "It was as if I'd assaulted a child. . . . She looked like the eldest urchin in a crowd in Rome [. . .] the dream of a dago high school" (348–49). Harry's social, intellectual and ethnic snobbery is undone by his guilt-ridden desire for someone who has the appearance of a minor. For Hannah protagonists of Harry's age, some conflicts remain unresolved; or, as Ruth Weston puts it, "In the world of Hannah's fiction, all situations involving the opposite sex seem to reduce men to boys" (17). It is also, however, a function of the bildungsroman's generic conventions that there are some things Harry still does not understand at the end of the novel, and the failure of his marriage is one of them. Harry's desire for Prissy and his wish to marry her originate partly in a moment of epiphany on the beach at Biloxi: "she wore silver shoes, and she crossed her legs under her dress and dangled one of her shoes on her toes. The moon was between her heel and her shoe, and I saw the ridges of sand, with the tide out, and I suppose that did it" (342). Harry might not fully understand his desire sufficiently to express it rationally, but Prissy clearly does; on their wedding night in New Orleans she calls to him from the bed, "Kiss my toe, hard!" (348), as if to reprise the moment that she captured him. This combination of desire and entrapment is symptomatic of Harry's emotional immaturity, and *Geronimo Rex* tactfully and shrewdly refrains from revising that youthfulness from a mature adult perspective in a way that preserves an important sense of Harry's naivety and innocence even *after* he is married. As author of the narrative we read, Harry has still not fully come of age, partly because coming-of-age is necessarily a drama in progress that is never entirely complete.

But if Harry's desire for Prissy is as strongly informed by male relationships of social and economic power as it is by his latent foot fetishism, the most important man in this period of Harry's life is not Mr. Lombardo, Mr. Neicase, or his own father, but Dr Lariat. Lariat is originally from Harry's home town, Dream of Pines, and has lost his wife in a tragi-comic accident; Harry recognizes that he is on the verge of losing his wife too. In meetings at his home, Lariat simultaneously threatens to fail Harry in his graduate school class and to bankrupt him by beating him at snooker; more importantly, however, Lariat expounds an aesthetic theory that is strongly at odds with Harry's writing, and at a time when Harry is about to publish his first book of poems. Lariat is, then, a formidable figure for Harry, one he must vanquish or remain abject forever; their social and literary relationship is purely oedipal in ways that Harry's relationship with his father never was, and constitutes the true "Rex" part of the narrative. Even though the final section of the book derives much of its dramatic urgency from Harry discovering the mettle to shoot "Whitfield" Peter Lepoyster, his literary vanquishing of Lariat is even more significant because it is integral to the kind of stylistic tour-de-force that *Geronimo Rex* itself becomes.

Lariat tells Harry that "If you want to get a C in my class, just write about how *energetic* somebody's work is.... And furthermore, if you want to talk about *honesty*. Such a premium on that word" (366). This is a particularly telling exchange because just such qualities of energy and honesty are absolutely integral to Harry's unique and original account of coming-of-age in *Geronimo Rex*. Harry's narrative is singularly character-ized by a willingness to face up to failure and all that is abject and ridiculous in growing up, and to write about these subjects in an uncompromising style that entirely redeems its subject matter with a remarkable linguis-tic resourcefulness and brio. Lariat has already perceived these qualities in Harry's writing, and threatens Harry with failure: "I read your final. I'm giving you a C for the course" (367). This is potentially catastrophic for Harry, but the symbolic castration of the boy statue in Lariat's yard comes to his rescue; upon observing the defaced statue shorn of its "minimalized renaissance pecker" (362), Harry comes to see Lariat not as a threatening authority figure but as "the dickless grown-up version of that cherub out there" (367). As such, Harry is able to laugh at Lariat "right in the face of his stare" (367) and to confront him about the grade. Lariat immediately backs down, agreeing to give Harry the "A" grade he requires. Harry subsequently beats the professor at snooker and tells him the story of his life; not only is this the story that will provide the raw material for *Geronimo Rex*, but he tells it "on the date of my publishing my first poem in a tiny booklet sort of magazine in New Orleans. Which Lariat lauded" (368). Lariat is thus vanquished in a few short paragraphs as the novel approaches its dramatic climax, and Harry's style is exonerated as he nears the end of his uniquely energetic and honest account of coming-of-age.

Though it is notable that Harry still needs Lariat to attend the novel's final dramatic scene, the shooting of Whitfield Peter, the professor is now an emasculated figure, sidelined by Harry's new-found self-determination. Both during and after the confrontation with Whitfield Peter, Lariat is no longer a threat to Harry's sense of (artistic) identity; as Harry puts it, he appears to be "lost in the longest Lariat pause ever" (380). This is a cut-ting reference to Lariat's aesthetic theory of "the pause between impulse and action" (365). Lariat's ineffectiveness in the violent showdown with Whitfield Peter (he disappears and throws up) symbolizes the redundancy and repudiation of his aesthetic theory. Though Lariat is permitted the novel's final word, "Music!" (381), he is now completely extraneous to Harry's emergent artistic identity. Lariat's own disorientation is confirmed by his observation that "We're in the wrong field" (literature, rather than music); by contrast, Harry, has successfully embraced a jazz aesthetic in the writing of *Geronimo Rex* itself, and ultimately it is this that represents his true artistic coming-of-age. A lariat is, of course, a lasso, and one that Harry has sidestepped. In the process of articulating these formative experiences, Harry defines himself both as a man and as a writer, and *Geronimo Rex* is a testament to the particular ability to address that which is abject in a style full of unique imaginative energy. As one of Hannah's earliest and most appreciative critics, David Madden, has argued, "almost everything that language can do in prose without going berserk in an hysterically experimental way is done well in this novel. Language, more than bizarre characters and attitudes, sustains interest" (131).

Hannah's whole career since *Geronimo Rex* has been characterized by a preoccupation with the same themes: the shifts and tensions between youth and age (punctuated by moments of epiphany); sex and violence; and the significance of southern culture and history for his (overwhelmingly male) protagonists. Above all, however, Hannah's entire oeuvre has been marked by a linguistic exuberance and inventiveness that transforms defeat and failure into something memorable and compelling; as Harry Monroe puts it, "What's the point of pain if you can't be eloquent about it?" James Potts has argued that "Many, perhaps most, of Hannah's stories are coming-of-age stories in which a longing for transcendence, the death drive, and *eros* collide. . . . In some of the rest, the adult males seem to be struggling with an identity crisis that requires a new resolution of an earlier adolescent confusion" (238). It is important to recognize the part that aesthetics plays in these psychological resolutions. Hannah's characters are almost always aware of the transformative potential of art, provided it is an art that is authentic and original. But what is it that makes art in the U.S. South at the end of the century original and authentic? This is the fundamental question of *High Lonesome* (1996), published some twenty-four years after *Geronimo Rex*, but still characterized by the classic Hannah themes and by a creative energy and emotional honesty that makes his writing truly inimitable.

Whereas *Geronimo Rex* examines questions of aesthetics through the developing consciousness of a single protagonist, the short stories in *High Lonesome* feature a veritable gallery of artists—musicians, painters, actors and writers—whose artistic performances are integral to the drama of each narrative. These stories about artists are in turn told by narrators who themselves have a fascination with artistic processes, from creative inspiration to the final staged moment of dramatic revelation, often because they seek to discern the secrets of what constitutes good art. In this way Hannah's narrators strive to emulate the aesthetic of each story's creative characters, so that their art too might aspire to the status of performance. The narrators of *High Lonesome* are makers of tales and narratives, creators of myths, and contributors to folklore and legend; their stories aspire to high art, and they use artist characters as vehicles for considering the nature of the aesthetic in the U.S. South at the end of the century. By examining the efficacy of their characters' art, the stories investigate the idea of aesthetic value both in contemporary southern culture and in the very conduct of the story that their narrator offers. This is the metafictional nature of *High Lonesome*, an investigation of what is aesthetically possible and artistically valuable in the particular conditions of a culture where exhaustion and depletion appears (to Hannah's narrators) endemic, and where the invidious incursions of tawdry commercial forms of art has compromised the idea of cultural value. The stories of *High Lonesome* examine self-reflexively their own narrative devices and strategies, and even their valorization of a particular aesthetic. Many of the narrators find subtle and ingenious ways to ask of themselves, "What is the aesthetic that I strive to articulate?" and to conduct a metafictional interrogation of their own concepts of aesthetic value even while telling their stories.

One way in which Hannah's stories accomplish this is by using at key points the particular speech acts of their characters to dramatize the enigma of the word, the mystery of the linguistic referent. The stories in *High Lonesome* show a fascination with language's ability to signify something of value that lies beyond its powers of signification. These speech acts are vitally important, but articulate something that lies just beyond the ability of language to designate it, except in the most enigmatic and oblique terms of reference. Certain verbal expressions in particular dramatize language's ability to refer to that which, paradoxically, cannot be fully articulated by language. This moment of enigmatic linguistic drama is very similar to those corresponding moments in James Joyce's *Dubliners* (1914) where particular phrases or expressions are given a significance beyond language's signifying capacity. In Joyce's stories the word "paralysis" (in "The Sisters" [7], the phrase "Derevaun Seraun" (in "Eveline" [38], and the lyrics of the song "I dreamt that I Dwelt" (in "Clay" [103] are all pieces of language that appear to have a heightened significance for the protagonists that the stories do not fully elucidate. The reader is left with a sense of the value of the word that consists of more than its referential capacity. Similarly, in *High Lonesome* expressions such as "Stomp my grapes" ("Snerd and Niggero" [85]), "Ma'am, I ain't not rogue" ("The Ice Storm" [190]), and "I blow all they heads off" ("The Agony of T. Bandini" [136]) are offered as repositories of a linguistic and cultural value that cannot be definitively elucidated. As with the conclusions to the stories in *Dubliners*, the stories of *High Lonesome* bring the reader to the dramatic moment of revelation and then stop, because it is their function to bring the reader to that moment but not to interpret it: "Well howdy, stranger, I guess" ("Ned Maxy, He Watching You" [96]); "Please take off that apron" ("Taste Like a Sword" [150]); "Well, you were a wolf" ("Two Gone Over" [184]); "Here, sir. All accounted for" ("Drummer Down" [210]). Further, the inability of each story's language to resolve the anxieties about value that it dramatizes often results in a strategic deferral to other textual authorities (be it Sherwood Anderson in "Two Gone Over," Charles Simic in "Carriba," or the contemporary British rock band Radiohead in "Through Sunset Into the Raccoon Night"), and that authority becomes a representation of linguistic value which is simultaneously an expression of the aesthetic that the story itself strives to articulate. This process becomes one of metafictional self-evaluation: in the South at the end of the century, what kinds of art are possible or desirable, and what kind of fiction can interrogate its own creative processes and yet still claim to be authentically "southern"? Each of Hannah's stories addresses this aesthetic question, and simultaneously creates art from disquisitions on it. The oppositions and comparisons between different forms of art that the stories juxtapose establish the problem of artistic value as the central imaginative preoccupation of *High Lonesome*. The Joycean moment of epiphany with which the stories end posits the acquisition of a sacred language as a form of transcendental knowledge beyond language's signifying powers. The drama of the spoken word thus has a unique value in the formation of the aesthetic that *High Lonesome* articulates.

"Drummer Down" is a story that places special emphasis on the use of certain words. Of Paul Smith's attempt at screenwriting in California, the narrator observes that "this work was entirely made up and false. There was no saving it by pure language" (207). Yet a theory of "pure language" is discovered and articulated, albeit obliquely, by the story's conclusion. Smith is furious that his best friend, Drum Drummond, a man with an otherwise strong aesthetic sensibility (Drum once told Smith that "Nothing is unimportant. Every minute is a jewel. Every stroke of pussy, every nail on the board" [208]), has left only an unoriginal and "vile poem" (195) before committing suicide: "so common, so punk, so lost in democracy, like an old condom" (210). Yet in the enigmatic final line, "Here, sir. All accounted for," the narrator attends to Drum's aesthetic and its authority, previously characterized as "keeping the big heart in" (208): the drum-like heartbeat of authentic art that has its origin in a fall from grace, in suffering and in penitential confession. The life-size ceramic bust of "Sarge" that Drum presented to Smith during the depths of the latter's alcoholism, and which is referenced once more in the final paragraph of the story, becomes both a representation of authority and of a *fall* from status ("He'd been busted from sergeant four times" [203]) that is the necessary concomitant of any valuable creative enterprise.

Hannah's stories often seek to redeem, through art, characters who in life seemed worthless; in turn, genuine art comes from an engagement with subjects ostensibly beyond redemption, and this function gives art an incalculable spiritual purpose. In "Taste Like a Sword" the association between the abject and authentic creativity is signaled when the unnamed narrator posits that women "love nothing better than a bad poet who needs all kinds of help and understanding even to finish out a new poem about self-abuse" (147–48). The narrator himself longs to create a language of his own subjectivity through an account of his abjection: "I'm in love with my weakness" (147). The story's multiple characters are failures that the narrator seeks to identify with in order that he might discover and articulate an authentic language of self. The fragmented and displaced subjectivity of the narrator comes closest to being remedied in his identification with the customer who is given the story's last words: "Isn't it time we met. . . . Please take off that apron" (150). This speech act brings the narrator to the verge of self-realization or fulfillment, but the story ends here because—like the equivalent speech act in "Drummer Down," "Here, Sir. All accounted for"—it is about the drama of reaching that point, not the drama of its resolution. These utterances are dramatic precisely because they have been spoken; the speech act thus becomes the moment of epiphany by which consciousness can develop, and it has a spiritual and emotional value over and above that language's signifying function.

This moment is strongly reminiscent of the epiphanies in Joyce's *Dubliners*, which are also characterized by an emphasis on language, and on a sense of a small and particular local culture at a specific historical moment where secularization of the Word gives a sense of the mystery of language, but one which is no longer attached to God. Joyce's stories almost all end at a moment of revelation that the story does not attempt to elucidate but posits as crucially significant because its importance lies precisely in the knowledge of words, in the acquisition of words, and with a sense of the value and importance of particular words that have a totemic quality over and above their signifying value. In "Taste like a Sword," the moment is an invitation to the narrator to discard the costume of a waiter in order to enact a more authentic version of his self, or who he might learn to become if he had a different language through which to narrate and per-form his subjectivity. Similarly, the story's title is an enigmatic phrase, spo-ken by the narrator's father, which has military and phallic connotations, but which is ultimately very difficult to elucidate because of the multiple connotations that are built around it. When the narrator's father tells him "I taste like a sword," it might be a reference to the course of chemotherapy that he is taking as a remedy for cancer, but it is also a warning about how he might taste to others who would consume him: "I give you my heart and lungs to eat thereof. I taste like a sword" (150). But how exactly does a sword taste? What is the significance of the narrator's father's Christ-like offering of his body? And why is this particular verbal utterance given the special authority of the story's title? These are not easy questions to answer, partly because the phrase's real value consists of its mysterious appeal as part of the drama of the spoken word; it says something important about subjectivity that is important precisely because it lies beyond the powers of definitive elucidation. This emphasis on the dramatic significance of the spoken word is crucial to the aesthetic that the stories of *High Lonesome* articulate.

"A Creature in the Bay of St Louis" provides a narrative of the gen-esis of this creative process; the inspiration and the exact circumstances of its operation or function; the sense of identity that accompanies it; and the particular material social conditions from which it is derived. It is a childhood initiation story in which the central experience—the narrator's boyhood battle to catch "a giant stingaree" (49)—is coterminous with the birth of creative imagination; it is a primal scene, one that the narrator will return to "the rest of my life" (51). During the struggle with the stinga-ree, the narrator faces death, but it also constitutes a dramatic moment both of self-awareness ("I was gone, gone, and I thought of the cats watch-ing onshore and I say good-bye cat friends ... good-bye Mother and Daddy, don't weep for me, it is a thing in the water cave of my destiny. Yes, I thought all these things in detail while drowning" [50]) and of accomplish-ment. The exaggerated narration of this accomplishment feeds on and into the local children's "terrible legends" about an "unfortunate girl or boy" who was "turned into half-stingaree" (47) and institutionalized: "I even worked in the lie [that he was wounded by the ray's hook] more and said furthermore it didn't matter much to me if I was taken to the asylum for stingaree children, that was just the breaks" (50). Here we see how the nar-rator wishes above all to join the community of tales and storytellers; this is further emphasized at the end of the story, when he tells us (his read-ers) how he told his schoolteacher back home in North Mississippi of his encounter with the creature in the bay of St. Louis; the teacher doubted him, but more importantly also "congratulat[ed] me on my imagination" (51). Even though the narrator's father scolded him for over-elaboration, the narrator will return to this scene for the rest of his life, for it is the dramatized moment of the birth of his hyperbolic imagination.

Significantly, *High Lonesome* itself returns to this scene of epiphany: the final story "Uncle High Lonesome" includes the narrator Peter Howard's recollection of "the last curious scene when I recall him [his namesake Peter, also the uncle of the story's title] whole" (226), a scene that takes place in Bay St. Louis. Tellingly, Peter's recall of the location ("This was close to heaven, and everybody knew it" [227]) vividly echoes that of the narrator of "A Creature" ("it was heaven" [48]). The return to Bay St. Louis in "Uncle High Lonesome" can even be seen as the textual fulfillment of the narrator's prophecy in "A Creature" that "I would return and return to it the rest of my life" (51)—not only to the proximity of water and fishing, but also to the scene of his coming-of-age. What is more, "Uncle High Lonesome" ends by emphasizing this pattern of repetition in terms of a familial as well as personal legacy, perhaps even as an expression of inevitable historical entrapment or paralysis. Peter confesses that "for years now I have dreamed I killed somebody" (230), much as his uncle Peter once killed "an out-of-towner" during a drunken poker game; he also informs us that "I've talked to my nephew about this," only to discover that the nephew, too, "has dreamed this very thing, for years" (230). Thus the experience of *High Lonesome* is a metafictional one, a self-contained nostalgic memory, trapped in the historical moment of its making.

This cycle of metafiction and repetition may also suggest that the narrator of "A Creature" is also the narrator of "Uncle High Lonesome," and that he is perpetually anxious about the status of his own story-making—or, as he reveals in the earlier story, his ability to lie. Dissembling is crucial to the art of Hannah's narrators, but this does not invalidate their artistic productions: it is integral to their art. The contrived telling of this story gives it a special place in *High Lonesome*; its principal concern is with the production of fiction, and the material circumstances from which narrative is derived. This is a theme that many of the stories return to in one way or another, covertly or explicitly; they often accommodate a tale of how they came to be made and examine the circumstances of that creative moment and its value. Self-evaluation is an integral and necessary aspect of the aesthetic that they promote.

Royce in "Through Sunset into the Raccoon Night" is the most self-conscious narrator in *High Lonesome*. Royce attempts through storytelling to redeem his narrative of failure and loss by creating art from it, and his story is an extended and sophisticated investigation of how art can be inspired by failure; it is a treatise on the particular circumstances and conditions of the value and status of art that is generated from the loss of honor, of grace, and of self-esteem. Royce is infatuated with the idea of defeat, and his story assembles a gallery of the defeated so that it might consider their potential for artfulness and simultaneously create an artful narrative of itself. This store-owner is the Rolls Royce of narrators in *High Lonesome*, comparing at every turn the aesthetic merits of his surroundings with the aesthetic potential of the narrative he has created from them. Royce believes that "eminent creeps" have come from his birthplace, St Louis, "as by some necessity of the environment" (110), and that his own particular circumstances—the trivia of his job and its degraded commercial pointlessness—has the potential for art in its very futility.

In fact, Royce is a thoughtful man who has "come up with some high country epigrams of my own" (104) and aspires to what he terms (after Miles Davis) the "*country hip*" aesthetic of "bluesmen along the river" (110). Royce also identifies an appealing contemporary aesthetic of failure in the song "Creep" by Radiohead, which features the lines: "I wish I was special! But I'm a creep!" (109). Royce is enraptured by the aesthetic that the song, and particularly this lyrical refrain, articulates—"God what freedom in that statement. I just adore it and am terrified too" (109)—and his imagination is inspired by the possibilities for the redemption of losers and creeps that the song holds out. The staged drama of Royce's own linguistic construction seeks to emulate this aesthetic by creating a beguiling and engaging tale of his own high lonesome inflexion of alienated storytelling: Royce refers to his failed spell in New York as an artist of "something I'm unwilling to discuss. All right, painting" (104). The artfulness of Royce's narrative strategies is most tellingly deployed with the direct appeal to his listeners—"Tell me, let's chat. I'll be mostly in the shop' (124)"—and the aesthetic of which is most explicitly defined when Royce identifies people's "willingness to go public with hideous disease"; after all, he asks, "Why else am *I* writing?"(112). Royce's narrative is thus quite explicitly figured as a meditation upon the conditions from which it is generated, a self-reflexive interrogation of (his own) art and its value. This is why Royce characterizes his narrative as "lost like a two-headed snake in jabber at itself" (123–24): his story's self-reflexivity is a parasitical enquiry into its own artistic value in a world where questions of value are deeply problematical, both in the high art of T. S. Eliot and William Burroughs (110) and the pornographic-commercial art of Royce's Jaguar poster featuring a "woman poised in a diaper on the hood, her toes stretched out as just then in the moment of sexual crisis" (121).

There is, in the artful contrivance of the abject, a distinctly end-of-the-century flavour to many of the stories of *High Lonesome*—in their sense of imminent catastrophe, their nostalgic attempts to recuperate a more heroic past, and in the indulgent, even decadent, language they sometimes employ: "he had no will but dragged his heart and blue loins through ruined hours" ("Snerd and Niggero," 82). The fin de siecle atrophy of "Snerd and Niggero," and the elegiac companionship of its exhausted protagonists, captures a sense of depletion and paralysis where creative enterprise often consists of forms of historical recuperation where the only way to go forward is to go back. This sense of an aesthetic that is necessarily pathological (that is to say diseased, moribund or grotesque) is integral to most of the stories of *High Lonesome*, and it is embodied by the character Hood in "The Ice Storm." Hood is a film-maker, of sorts, but one who is "poisoned" when a tree falls on him during the eponymous storm: the accident destroys his creative talent and "his art vision was gone" (191). Hood's pornographic films full of "lively girls" (191) inspire the narrator to make home movies of his wife that are similarly tawdry: "[I] wanted to shoot scenes of my wife naked or nearly so in compromising positions. I know this is the act of an ageing creep who cannot understand his good luck, but I had ceased to care" (190).

This dubious artistic enterprise is a failure, an abject aesthetic that is sterile and without fulfillment or honor, and the narrator admits as much: "I felt like an idiot" (190). Meanwhile Hood abandons movie-making, instead transforming himself into a distinctly theatrical portrait of the artist:

> One afternoon I noticed a man in a cape and beret rolling down
> in a chair. Across the arms, too, he held a cane. This was a lot of
> costume for early fall or I'd not have noticed. Under the beret
> was a long blond face, very surly. It was Hood. Before I knew this,
> I'd had in mind one of the great wounded artists of the fin de
> siecle (191–92).

Hood is, in fact, a charlatan—a nurse tells the narrator that "there is nothing wrong with him" (192)—but he has made his injury into pure performance and so lays claim to the elevated status (high, but lonesome) of the artist. The dissembling of Hood's impersonation of Toulouse-Lautrec is irrelevant: he has made something of his misfortune, and that is an artistic accomplishment worthy of the narrator's grudging admiration. It is an adult analogue to the exaggerated myth-making and self-fashioning of the boy narrator of "A Creature," and its value is emphasized by the narrator's desire to emulate "Hood's peculiarity" (190). The narrator's confession of his failed attempts to film his wife is, in this context, a significant narrative moment: it constitutes his own claim, however misguided, to the status of "great wounded artist."

The transformative and redemptive potential of these kinds of artistic identification is given major significance by the end of "The Agony of T. Bandini," where the character called Cruthers tells the story of his formative experience in Vietnam. Cruthers's account is remarkable for the elusiveness of its references, for the opaque but lyrical intensity of its enigmatic language, and for the heightened significance of its moment. Cruthers tells Bandini how he once shot a group of Vietcong soldiers only to discover that one of them was a teenaged girl. Cruthers then puns on the word "blow" to explain how he had oral sex with the girl's corpse, and ends the story by pronouncing: "That was the best I ever had" (136). It is possible that Cruthers's narrative is entirely phony, a dramatic tall-tale which, like the account of the encounter with the stingaree in "A Creature in the Bay of St. Louis," is invented purely to help create a mythology of the self. But it is the impact of listening to Cruthers's story that is important here. Bandini is impressed to the point of being overawed: "*Feel* the turning and the twistings of all that," he implores the narrator. The story ends by replicating Bandini's astonishment at Cruthers's tall tale in the narrator's own response to Bandini: "I was stunned by the new deep voice of Bandini, and this whole language" (136). The rapture of Cruthers's experience has the power to transform the auditor Bandini, and Bandini's amazement at Cruthers's language astonishes the story's narrator in a parallel moment that dramatizes the redemptive potential of story-telling. It is fidelity to "this whole language," however exaggerated or invented its subject matter, that "The Agony of T. Bandini" itself strives to accomplish. It is a remarkable process of cyclical repetition by which sometimes delusional and self-mythologizing protagonists discover the power to invoke through their art the potential of creative renewal in their audience.

Throughout the stories of *High Lonesome* the importance of spectacle and rapt attention to the forms of art is dramatized in moments of mysterious wonder, and the vicarious nature of the transference is a common experience. For example, in "The Agony of T. Bandini," the policeman who witnesses Bandini's peculiar worship of the Confederate statue in Oxford's town square is a necessary accompaniment to the drama of Bandini's theatrical act; his presence certifies and illuminates the crucial

dramatic moment, much as Bandini himself acts as witness to and inter-
preter of Cruthers's story. Without an audience both Bandini's distinctive
homage to the Confederate statue and Cruthers's Vietnam tall-tale would
be worthless. The fact that Bandini's or Cruthers's sentiments might be
bogus is not important: the moment of artistic performance has the power
to resurrect and to renew. It is precisely this moment that the stories themselves seek to dramatize; the staged moment of theatrical revelation is their
aesthetic purpose. As I have tried to demonstrate, many of the stories of
High Lonesome are packed with such forms of artistic self-evaluation, and
they each find ways to consider their own artistic status as an integral part
of their narrative conduct. Artistic self-examination is an aesthetic defense
against the pressures of commercial degradation and the erosion of value
that accompanies it.

   In "Uncle High Lonesome," the narrator looks back to what he believes
was the simpler referential function of language in that period: "There was
a plainer language then, there had to be" (222). Throughout *High Lonesome*,
the creation of an authentic aesthetic language in the contemporary South
is much more difficult; as such, the language of Hannah's narrators often
seems oblique, unconventional, and even baffling. This is perhaps most
apparent in *High Lonesome*'s opening and most remarkable story, "Get
Some Young." Although the story does not include an artist figure, the language of "Get Some Young" represents a stunning synthesis of styles and
lexicons, and dramatizes in extreme form the intense energy of Hannah's
interest in language for its own aesthetic sake. In "Get Some Young," the
characters' predicament is articulated as much in the language as it is in
the drama of the story; it is a curiously static tale, one of shifting scenes
in a tableaux, a spectacle of language that advertises itself outrageously in
its brilliant one-liners, its remarkable feats of metaphor, its eclectic synthesis of registers. The kaleidoscopic display of languages is a parasitical
exposition of the history of language, one in which the story's plurality of
languages (Biblical, vernacular, literary quotation) feeds on itself with a
voracious creative energy—as one character appropriately puts it, "I am a
vampire I am a vampire" (13)—and creates a narrative of language from its
own self-reference. This contemporary southern metafiction is not dryly
self-regarding; rather, it is grounded in the material circumstances of the
story's origins among "Civil War ghoulments" (25). It is notable too that

"Get Some Young" is centrally concerned with coming-of-age, with an exploration of how boys grow up to be southern white men, and of how southern white men regret the loss of their boyhood. This is the territory of *Geronimo Rex* almost a quarter of a century earlier—a debut novel in which, as we have seen, the parasitical feeding on southern history had a strongly textual dimension in which the past is devoured to keep the future alive. Ultimately, performing a virtuoso synthesis of multiple historical languages is the means by which Hannah creates a contemporary aesthetic that is recuperative, regenerative, and critically aware of the systems of value from which his fiction derives its aesthetic identity.

Note

1. The importance of economics to this matrix of relationships between the Monroe men and Prissy's father is further dramatized at the wedding. Harry reports that his own father "gave [Ted] Lombardo a negligent scan, as if he would never be troubled to learn his first name. I wasn't sure of it myself until we got the checks from him in Fayetteville" (346).

Works Cited

Charney, Mark. *Barry Hannah*. New York: Twayne Publishers, 1992.

Griffin, Christopher. "Bad Faith and the Ethic of Existential Action: Kierkegaard, Sartre, and a Boy Named Harry." *Mississippi Quarterly* 54.2 (spring 2001): 173–96.

Hannah, Barry. *Geronimo Rex*. 1972. New York: Penguin, 1983.

————. *High Lonesome*. New York: Atlantic Monthly P, 1996.

Joyce, James. *Dubliners*. London: Penguin, 1963.

Madden, David. "Barry Hannah's *Geronimo Rex* in Retrospect," *Southern Review* 19.2 (spring 1983): 309–16.

Potts, James B. "Barry Hannah's Anti-Myth Method: Anti-Freudian Plots and Fractured Fairy Tales." *Mississippi Quarterly* 54.2 (spring 2001): 237–50.

Spikes, Michael. "Lee Durkee's *Rides of the Midway* and Barry Hannah's *Geronimo Rex*." *Mississippi Quarterly* 55.3 (summer 2002): 403–17.

Updike, John. "From Dyna Domes to Turkey-Pressing." *New Yorker*, September 9, 1972, 124.

Weston, Ruth. *Barry Hannah: Postmodern Romantic*. Baton Rouge: Louisiana State UP, 1998.

Williams, Tennessee. *Orpheus Descending and Other Plays*. London: Penguin, 1961.

Off with Their Heads!

Nightwatchmen, *Campus Novels,*
and the Problem of Representation

—Richard E. Lee

In any dispute the intensity of feeling is inversely proportional to
the value of the stakes at issue—that is why academic politics are
so bitter.
—Often attributed by paraphrase to Henry Kissinger[1]

It is particularly appropriate to revisit Barry Hannah's
long-out-of-print second novel, *Nightwatchmen* (1973),
in the wake of the devastation wreaked by Hurricane
Katrina. As during the September 2005 storm, so in the novel much of
the Mississippi Gulf Coast is wiped bare by the inscrutable, overwhelming
force of nature. At a central point in *Nightwatchmen*, Hurricane Camille—
whose eye made landfall at Pass Christian on August 18, 1969[2]—eliminates
the safe haven of the narrative's unifying consciousness, much as it destroys
the top three floors of Old Main, the campus locale where much of the
novel's action takes place. Through the voice of one of the novel's multiple
narrators, Hannah writes of the impossibility of returning to a more pastoral world after this apocalyptic event:

> Because the trees, because the great glassy white mansions,
> because the piers, private and public, because the yacht

clubs and sailing marinas, because the seaside seafood houses
and the bars with sand on the floors . . . because Old Main . . .
because the lighthouse, the ancient one at the outcropping of
the pass . . . because . . . they were all gone, never to be the same
again. (178, ellipses in original)

The parallelism of this passage, with its echoes of biblical parataxis,[3] begins with a lost pastoral image ("trees") and takes in emblems of elite social structures ("mansions," "yacht clubs") before isolating by ellipsis the absence of the college building ("Old Main") in which both academic labor and grisly murder occurred earlier in the narrative. I want to suggest that these formal signs of absence in the syntactic structure of the quoted passage also indicate (in suitably elliptical fashion) the core theme(s) of the novel: the impossibility of mimetic representation in narrative form as it is manifested by a focus on—but also an elision of—scholarly work. More specifically, the absence of the "real" of academic labor (administrative work, the mysteries of the workings of the academic job market, and so on) occurs in a campus novel that makes a claim for authenticity in its use of verbal transcriptions of characters' perceptions rather than omniscient narration.[4]

From a post-Katrina perspective, the apocalyptic erasure of mansions, yacht clubs, and bars by Hurricane Camille in *Nightwatchmen* eerily anticipates Christian fundamentalist claims about "God's reasons" for inflicting destruction on the "sinful city" of New Orleans and the casino towns along the Mississippi Gulf Coast. But if the notion of divine retribution is present in *Nightwatchmen*, the novel is just as prescient in its suggestion that the life of the mind is threatened by the changing nature of academic labor and the infiltration of the "real world" into a previously rarified university life. Even more recent postmodern novels that express skepticism towards the notion of an objective, shared "reality" do not deny or dismiss our yearning for the comfort of such a reality. Campus novels, meanwhile, continue to attract critical attention because, "like other closed societies, the campus can function as a microcosm" (Showalter 3). *Nightwatchmen* notably connects the postmodern novel's generic engagement with the nature of "reality" and the campus novel's concern with the acts of reading and writing that are the inevitable concerns of the professoriate.

As *Nightwatchmen* has been out of print since its original publication, a brief summary of its plot and technique is in order. It is also worth situating Hannah's most neglected book in the context of his career as both a novelist and an academic. Although Donald Noble has dismissed the idea that there is an autobiographical component to *Nightwatchmen* (Noble 40), it is easy to read the novel as an indictment of the elitism and isolation that characterizes the kind of college community in which Hannah was working while writing the novel. Even Noble acknowledges that "Hannah wrote [*Nightwatchmen*] under considerable stress at Clemson University, teaching a full load of courses and trying to come out with a second novel soon enough to capitalize on the success of *Geronimo Rex* [published in 1972]" (41). While speaking to Hannah in 1982, John Griffin Jones observed that "in *Nightwatchmen* you kind of stick it to the academic world; maybe the critics, most of whom are involved in academia, didn't like anybody running down their province." Hannah responded, "Yes, you do get that. A lot of the book critics are academics. . . . You know, they hold a position at Yale or Mississippi Southern. Yes, you know, you're insulting their realm. I think that war is over. You know the universities are full of creeps, and that you have to hunt hard to find a good one" (Jones 153). Critics and reviewers often observe that *Nightwatchmen* is the only one of Hannah's books not to appear in paperback. In 1998, Hannah himself admitted during a lengthy interview with Rob Trucks that "I wrote that book in a hurry, some of it in New York, which wasn't very good for me. . . . It probably needs to be thinned down. I think there are too many people in it and too much event." Hannah wryly termed *Nightwatchmen* "Barry Hannah's lost novel" and commented further that "it might deserve to be lost" (Trucks 19). However, in the earlier interview with Jones, Hannah asserted that: "A lot of people liked that book, and I liked it. . . . I think it's a decent book. . . . It was written quickly, but I thought I had some interesting things to say in there" (Jones 152).

It is notable that *Nightwatchmen* features the reappearance of Harry Monroe, the central character of *Geronimo Rex*, Hannah's widely-acclaimed debut novel of the previous year. Mark Charney has observed that, at the end of *Geronimo Rex*, "Harry commits himself to the musical potential within language" (13). Harry seems to posit that poetry, not prose, is the communicative key to understanding and displaying the world. Early in

Nightwatchmen, Harry recounts a conversation with a student, Ned Friend, whose basic attitude is "fuck knowledge," and who hates reading and (especially) writing (64). When Harry tries to instill in Ned some sense of wonder at the world (and of writing's ability to transmit that wonder), Ned observes acidly that "I believe you notice fucking everything." Harry responds that "[a] poet has a license to do that" (66).[5] However, in contrast to *Geronimo Rex,* Harry Monroe is neither the central character in, nor the only narrator of, *Nightwatchmen.* As Charney notes, the structure of *Nightwatchmen* "enables Hannah to emphasize the irony implicit in multi-perspectivism—each character offers a different version of the 'truth' and each version reveals much about the characters being interviewed . . . [it takes] a variety of perspectives to narrate the 'truth' " (Charney 14). If there is one individual who, initially at least, seems poised to dominate the narrative of *Nightwatchmen,* it is Thorpe Trove. For the first thirty-eight pages, Thorpe's first-person account recalls Harry's role as character-narrator of *Geronimo Rex.* However, Trove generates the text's "multiperspectivism" by asking various graduate students and marginal employees at the fictional Southwestern Mississippi State University to speak into a tape recorder so that he can find out the answers to two mysteries: the "knocking" of graduate students and faculty, and the grisly murder of three university staff members—two nightwatchmen and an instructor—in Old Main. The construction of *Nightwatchmen* around the transcriptions of these recordings devolves narrative authority away from Trove and enables Hannah to foreground the (dis)connections between speech, truth, and reality across the novel's multiple perspectives. Indeed, the different perspectives on reality that emerge from the tapes are quite distinctly postmodern in that they reveal the impossibility of discovering or recovering a singular objective reality or truth.

Trove himself is an orphan, a child of violence. Readers learn on the first page of the novel that his parents were murdered when he was young. This opening sequence also anticipates the subsequent narrative focus on the murders in Old Main: "I thought about Mother and Dad when I heard about Conrad [one of the campus nightwatchmen in Old Main]. Conrad was murdered and beheaded, with no money taken from his pants, in 1969. Mother and Dad were slain and thrown in a ditch in 1944" (3). However, it is not until much later that readers and Trove himself learn more about his parents' murders from Howard Hunter, a private detective and *deus ex machina* who provides a different and deeper perspective on the "mysterious murder of a couple in 1944": "[Hunter's] glasses sprayed out those merry twinkles. . . . He was bringing the episode into the room as if it had happened this morning. It was a shattering familiarity to hear his sympathy for the 'poor young couple' and to know that I was in the presence of someone who knew far more about my parents' death than I did" (209). Trove's epiphany underlines Charney's insight that "truth" is only revealed via multiple perspectives on any given event.

Trove has arrived on the Gulf Coast after dropping out of the University of Mississippi and receiving a large sum of money in his aunt's will. He squanders this fortune by buying a rundown seaside mansion, the rooms of which he rents to graduate students. Via the transcriptions of Trove's tape recordings, some of these students also become narrators of the novel. *Nightwatchmen*'s multiple narrators include four graduate students—Harry Monroe, Lawrence Head, William Tell and Didi Sweet—and two non-academic characters: Frank Theron Knockre, a security guard on campus, and Douglas David Lotrieux, a cinema projectionist. Quite early in the novel Lotrieux is revealed as the "Knocker" of graduate student heads in Old Main. He is not, however, the "Killer," who turns out to be an old acquaintance of Lotrieux, one Ralph White. Yet White is almost entirely absent from the narrative: he appears only at the very end, at which point he is stabbed by Trove, shot by Hunter, and buried in a shallow grave. I will return to the significance of White's eerily absent or "indexical" presence later in my analysis.[6]

Despite their increasingly close relationship, Howard Hunter continues to mispronounce Thorpe Trove's first name as "Thrope," which Trove likes because it "had **hope** voiced in it, something to live for" (213, emphasis in original). This serendipitous semantic linkage is taken further in the last line of the novel when Trove remarks that Hunter's "spectacles were on fire with **hope** for me and him" (232; emphasis added). This closing reference to spectacles also recalls Trove's observation, immediately before Hunter shoots Ralph White, that the detective looks "beaten to grayness by the rain, but my glasses acted oddly and enlarged his movements" (224). In these three key lines, the narrative compares and contrasts words as markers for meaning with the mediation of the world through optical filters. Such linguistic signification and visual mediation of "reality" will be central to my reading of *Nightwatchmen*. First, however, I want to offer a brief overview of the ways in which representations of the campus operate in print culture more generally. Such an overview will help us to see more clearly that *Nightwatchmen* is a prescient and signal example of how fictional attempts to capture the "reality" of academic life have often been characterized and compromised by a broader concern with the problem of representation itself. Depictions of teaching faculty and their professional lives operate in campus novels in ways that call into question the relationship between the real and representations of the real. Ultimately, novels about academic institutions—even ones which use the campus setting and its activities as props for other developments—become self-consuming artifacts: they eat the real in the service of narrative effect.

In *Faculty Towers: The Academic Novel and Its Discontents* (2005), Elaine Showalter creates a typology of the campus novel. She observes that "[t]he academic novel is by now a small but recognizable subgenre of contemporary fiction ... [it is] basically satirical." Quoting critic Sansford Pinsker, Showalter notes that " 'the general form is as old as Aristophanes' *The Clouds*. There, Socrates was held up to ridicule as a man riding through the heavens in a basket; and the label of dreamy impracticality stuck not only to him, but also to all the other befuddled academic types who have followed'" (Showalter 2). Showalter's take on the academic novel posits periodic shifts in the genre over the last six decades—from "Ivory Towers" (the 1950s) via "Tribal Towers" (the 1960s), "Glass Towers" (the 1970s), "Feminist Towers" (the 1980s) and "Tenured Towers" (the 1990s) to the "Tragic Towers" of the twenty-first century. Showalter see a movement away from the representation of the self-absorbed academic communities of the early twentieth century to recent texts which are more concerned with the relations between the campus and wider socio-cultural concerns heretofore absent from the groves of academe and the "life of the mind." In this context, Hannah's novel is both of its time and prescient: *Nightwatchmen* reflects both the discomfort that Showalter sees on the part of academics in the 1970s as they become merely workers, and an early postmodern consciousness as it anticipates and (meta-) comments on the inability of the novel form to represent the *real* of academic life.

Campus novels focus attention upon an environment fraught with power relations: for example, between teacher and student, or between rival teachers. As such there is often an overt connection between teaching and violence (be it physical or emotional violence); this violence is frequently visceral and central to the narrative. A prime example of a relatively recent campus novel which explores the link between violence and intellectualism is Robertson Davies' *The Rebel Angels* (1983), in which a member of the Comparative Literature Department at a Canadian university conducts archival research which leads him to discover who is murdering the graduate faculty. Another prominent contemporary case is J. M. Coetzee's *Disgrace* (1999), which folds together sexual dominance and dramatic violence in the changing South African university system. In *Disgrace* a formerly tenured English professor is emasculated as he is demoted and forced to teach basic communications classes, and when he becomes involved in a student-directed affair which causes his dismissal. The professor's progressive daughter is raped by black South Africans amongst whom she has sought to live.[7]

By focusing on violence against academic staff, students, and other university employees, *Nightwatchmen* anticipates these later campus novels of the 1980s and 1990s. Boring professors who seem unable to publish tend to be especially at risk in the novel. However, as Donald Noble observes, tedious professors are not the only academics in danger: "Some feel 'the Knocker' . . . selects his victims because they are the most boring people in the department, but this thesis is shown to be absolutely invalid when the luscious Didi Sweet is 'knocked.' She has never bored anybody" (Noble 41). The sexual and gendered dimensions of power relations and violence are emphasized in *Nightwatchmen*, both on and off campus, and from the very start of the novel, when Thorpe Trove takes the trouble to mention that his dead mother "had not been raped" (4). However, it is the "luscious" Didi Sweet who emerges as the central figure in *Nightwatchmen*'s taxonomy of sexual violence because she is consistently lusted after—and abused—by men. Even before she arrives at Southwestern Mississippi, Sweet is involved in a sadomasochistic relationship with her first husband: they play a game called "Pain" where he struggles but fails to make her moan/speak. At Old Main, she participates in a "dry ugly mimic of the act of love" (60) with a fellow student, William Tell, which is voyeuristically observed by another student, Lawrence Head. Here *Nightwatchmen* anticipates another later text which, while not technically a "campus novel," is set partially at a university and which homes in on the sexual aspect of academic relations: John Irving's *The World According to Garp* (1978). Garp's wife, Helen, an English professor, allows herself to be drawn into an affair with a callow graduate student named Michael Milton. In a notorious scene, Helen's infidelity leads to the castration of Milton, the death by misadventure of one of the Garps' children, and—most importantly for my purposes here—the failure of both speech and writing. Helen had been fellating Milton in his car when Garp's car slams into them; in the aftermath of the accident and the child's death, the grieving Garp is unable to write while Helen's broken jaw symbolizes the failure of speech. In *Nightwatchmen*, Didi Sweet's silence in the face of sexual(ized) pain similarly becomes a marker for an absence of speech in a novel that nevertheless uses speech (in the form of Trove's tape transcriptions) to represent the fictional world. Through motifs like the silencing of Garp, his wife, and Didi Sweet, campus novels like *The World According to Garp* and *Nightwatchmen* call into question the very act of representation itself, despite seeming to offer a "realistic" representation of the academic environment. They do this through a sometimes obvious, sometimes surreptitious engagement with the question of whether writing itself can ever really reflect "reality."

Before developing my analysis of *Nightwatchmen* further along these lines, a brief gloss of several basic issues in theories of representation is required. As a text which, in its representation of academics, anticipates even *Nightwatchmen* by some two hundred and fifty years—and which, as it happens, is being taught by one of the novel's soon-to-be murdered graduate students (41)—it is worth considering Jonathan Swift's *Gulliver's Travels* (1726). During Gulliver's visit to the Academy of Lagoda on the isle of Laputa, Swift highlights and satirizes the assumed connection between words and the things to which they refer that powers realistic representations in general. Gulliver listens with rapt awe as the academy's Professors of Language discourse upon their schemes to systematize their language(s): "The first Project was to shorten Discourse by cutting Polysyllables into one, and leaving out Verbs and Participles, because in reality all things imaginable are but Nouns." Another professor has constructed a scheme for making "concrete" all possible combinations of language. He will construct a "literary engine," not unlike a Japanese *katakana* frame, in which each character or word occupies a discrete square on a machine. Turning tiny handles enables a language "user" to isolate each actual word/symbol and array it in sequence with others so that a finite model of language would be available for display: "Six Hours a-day the young Students were employed in this Labour, and the Professor shewed me several Volumes in large Folio already collected, of broken Sentences, which he intended to piece together, and out of those rich Materials to give the World a compleat Body of all Arts and Sciences" (210–11). Most relevant to my focus here is another scheme based on the premise that words are intimately and inextricably linked to the things to which they refer, and which would allow the "abolishing [of] all Words whatsoever":

> For it is plain, that every Word we speak is in some Degree a Diminution of our Lungs by Corrosion, and consequently contributes to the shortning of our Lives. An Expedient was therefore offered, that since Words are only Names for *Things*, it would be more convenient for all Men to carry about them, such *Things* as were necessary to express the particular Business they are to discourse on.
>   . . . many of the most Learned and Wise adhere to the New Scheme of expressing themselves by *Things*, which hath only this Inconvenience attending it, that if a Man's Business be very great, and of various kinds, he must be obliged in Proportion to carry a greater bundle of *Things* upon his Back, unless he can afford one or two strong Servants to attend him. I have often beheld two of those Sages almost sinking under the Weight of their Packs, like Pedlars among us; who, when they met in the Streets, would lay down their Loads, open their Sacks, and hold Conversation for an Hour together; then put up their Implements, help each other to resume their Burthens, and take their Leave. (211–12)

Swift is, of course, satirizing simplistic ways of understanding and conceptualizing language use. Yet an assumed connection between *words and things* endures in our often uncritical consumption of even satirical or

absurd narrative representations of "reality." We continue to ascribe faithfully to the belief that an accurate, *mimetic*, representation of the real is at
least possible. This residual Platonic reflectionism—the belief that the
things in the world can be mimetically conveyed—remained prominent in
twentieth-century literary theory at least until the emergence of structural-
ism; it was expressed most famously through M. H. Abrams's figure of the
artist holding a mirror up to nature (Abrams 8–14). Ultimately, however—
and as postmodern literary theory has iterated—the relationship between
words and the things to which they refer is arbitrary (and consensual).
Therefore, representations which seek to elide this disjuncture collapse
under the weight of that which they cannot say. In other words, the more a
narrative strives for "realism," the more it displays ambivalence about its
own ability to represent. The conflation of the real and the fictive in
Nightwatchmen highlights and explores precisely this conundrum.[8]

Representations displace the real in literal and figurative ways. The
ways in which we buy into narratives—in this case, narratives about professors of the humanities—are conventions, cultural constructions; they
are not inevitable or "real." Showalter observes that academics who read
campus novels are involved in "narcissistic pleasure" (1); they consume
that which consumes them, reading about the site of their own self-absorption. But because academic readers affiliate themselves with the texts that
most closely subscribe to the world they know, they are confronted with a
significant paradox: they know that fiction is not real, but have to be con-
stantly reminded of that fact. David Lodge wryly comments in his author's
note to *Small World* (1984) that:

> Like *Changing Places*, to which it is a kind of sequel, *Small
> World* resembles what is sometimes called the real world, with-
> out corresponding exactly to it, and is peopled by figments of
> the imagination (the name of one of the minor characters has
> been changed in later editions to avoid misunderstanding on this
> score). Rummidge is not Birmingham, though it owes something
> to popular prejudices about that city. There really is an under-
> ground chapel at Heathrow and a James Joyce Pub in Zurich. . . .
> The MLA Convention of 1979 did not take place in New York,
> though I have drawn on the programme for the 1978 one, which
> did. And so on.

Lodge feels compelled to remind his implied readers—who are presumably fairly sophisticated, and likely fellow academics—that he is not writing a *roman à clef*; indeed, he is not even "basing" his novel on "the real world." Ultimately, it is writing itself that becomes the true focus of numerous campus novels that purport to represent professorial existence; what is more, these novels' perspectives on language almost inevitably point to writing's inability to represent existence of *any* kind, due to the arbitrary nature of representation.

Nightwatchmen has little good to say about the value of literary classics or of scholarly activity. Early on we learn that Thorpe Trove "walked over to William Faulkner's house one evening and wee-weed on his lawn" (5). The English Department chairman is described as a "belligerent old aunt who was a medievalist in the truest sense—that is, he saw life as through a slit in a Norman Castle . . . [and] had been pestering students with the dullest facts about Chaucer for thirty years" (48). To be sure, Trove himself does say that "I felt myself in a community of spirits when I opened a book," and he respects his professors at Ole Miss because they showed up "right on time, to shower us dolts with all that information" (16). But Trove by this point is outside the working world of academia, and he is unaware of what academic work entails. More often than not, the isolated nature of intellectual work described in *Nightwatchmen* is quite the opposite of "a community of spirits": as (soon-to-be-beheaded) junior faculty member William Tell puts it, "When I spread a book out in front of me, I am as much a heedless zombie as anyone around" (42). Tell also speaks the truth about the supposed community of like-minded intellectuals who have read a common canon by admitting he has never read *The Odyssey*: "I had the Ph.D. and had pretended that I'd read it on three or four examinations, but now it was very agreeable to be reading the honored old tale under no pressure" (42).[9] The absence of community and the isolated nature of academic labor is exploited by The Knocker: "Teachers and graduate students would be studying on their offices, and the Knocker would get behind them somehow and knock them out with one blow. He took no money from them" (39). The mysterious method (signaled by Tell's "somehow") and apparent lack of motive for the attacks (which recalls how the murderer of Trove's parents left money in Trove's father's wallet) also highlights the disconnection of the working world of the academic from the larger community.

In Lodge's *Nice Work* (1988), Robyn Penrose, an English instructor struggling to obtain a permanent position, is involved in an exchange with Vic Wilcox, a factory owner, regarding the meaning and truth-value of literature. When Vic asks "What's the point of sitting around discussing books all day, if you're no wiser at the end of it?" Robyn responds "Oh, you're wiser. . . . What you learn is that language is an infinitely more devious and slippery medium than you had supposed" (244). That language is a "slippery medium" becomes evident when one considers various approaches to the problem of representation. Thomas McLaughlin has observed that "[a]ll representation is of someone or something, by someone, for someone," and that there are three basic types of representation: iconic, symbolic, and indexical. Iconic representation is premised upon resemblance to what is being represented; "no matter how feeble," this supposed resemblance "allows us to construct a connection." McLaughlin notes that "realism in the visual arts is the most obvious example" of iconic representation. Symbolic representation, by contrast, "is arbitrary and consensually derived": that is, a symbol only has an abstract value because we agree to that value, such as a river symbolizing life's journey when a character travels upon the water. McLaughlin emphasizes that "ALL literary representation falls into this category." Finally, indexical representation "suggests a relationship between the trace and some maker. For example a footprint presupposes the passage of a human; thus the effect (representation) suggests a causative agent" (McLaughlin 1–5).

All three forms of representation identified by McLaughlin are used in *Nightwatchmen*. Similes and tacit acceptance of a "real world" abound; symbols—especially those related to "glasses" and windows—are frequent; and the prime mover of the novel's ostensible plot—Ralph White, the Killer—is seen throughout only by way of traces or effects: the corpses of his victims. That a refracted, partial and fractured view of "reality" is all that representations can provide is signaled early on in *Nightwatchmen*. Thorpe Trove recalls attending a football game at Ole Miss in 1956, when he was still an undergraduate, and being attacked by a "drunken bald fan": "he began pummeling me, for, as best I can tell, being myself" (4). As Trove was being throttled, a woman offered him "something. . . . As I took it, the man fastened his hands around my neck again. What I had was a piece of broken mirror. . . . So I stuck him. I gouged at him." Readers are hereby invited to recognize that the theory of literature as a "mirror" or "reflection" of reality has been shattered. We are encouraged to attend instead to the recurrence of accidental offers, overheard conversations, purely speculative explanations for absurd behavior, voyeuristic sightings and, most crucially, a world seen only through filters.

The dominant optical economy of the novel—glasses, spectacles, windows, televisions—operates both to sustain and challenge the correspondence of symbols to a consensual or objective understanding of the world. Both Trove and Dougie Lotrieux experience the world at second-hand through television. Trove himself insists that "I know everything about life by watching T.V." (27). Prior to his purchase of the rundown mansion in Pass Christian and the arrival of his various boarders, Trove was a complete social cripple: "I watched television frequently. I am lying. I watched television from the moment I got up until the moment I went to sleep." Tellingly, he even calls television "my university" (23). Similarly, Dougie views the world through the movies he screens at the local cinema: "I have tried in my way to grasp all that I've run through the machine" (52).[10]

Many of the characters in the novel view the world through glasses (though interestingly, Harry Monroe, with his vision of truth through poetry and violence, does not). Describing coeds on the campus, Trove observes that "[s]ome of them wore purple glasses like mine" (31). The murder of Conrad is related by William Tell with an emphasis on (among other gruesome details) the old nightwatchman's spectacles: "he had been shot six times with his own gun . . . the janitor found the head in one of the toilets. The face was turned upward, still wearing its spectacles. In the mouth, pinned through both lips, was the policeman's badge" (40). The glasses and the badge, a symbol of his authority, work together to metaphorize the communicative problem of speech. Whereas the badge stands as a conventional symbol of social (but not natural) authority, the glasses suggest how subjective points of view, or personal biases, mediate social "reality." Indeed, this emphasis on *visualized* perspective through the various characters who wear glasses also (albeit indirectly) calls into question the "true relations" of the *vocalized* transcriptions through which the novel speaks.

Another character who wears glasses is Charles Israel: he is described "in his beard and moon-glinting spectacles . . . like a black ram on fire" (153). Apparently based upon—or at least alluding to—a friend of Hannah's who attended nearby Emory University and is mentioned in the novel's dedication, the character Israel would also seem to provide a link to the "real world." Yet such sly textual references to the "real world" only serve to problematize further the idea of realistic representation. The novel *qua* novel often makes a claim on this kind of correspondence to the "real world" by "locating" itself in familiar settings: the city of Pass Christian, the University of Mississippi, Hurricane Camille, and so on. However, this localized particularity of experience is a part of the *reality effect*, one of the narrative conventions that we tend to uncritically accept as part of the way narratives operate. A campus novel like Lodge's *Small World* meta-comments on this convention of literary realism:

> "Is this where the narratee sits?" [Morris Zapp] enquired.
> Philip [Swallow], gazing absently into the fire, smiled vaguely, but made no reply . . . [Philip tells a story to Morris, adding, after what seems to be a superfluous detail] "That comes into the story."
> "I should hope so," said Morris. *There should be nothing superfluous in a good story.*" [The story continues, and then Philip mentions that] "I was sitting next to an English businessman, a salesman in woolen textiles I think he was . . . "
> "Is that relevant?"
> "Not really."
> "Never mind. Solidity of specification," said Morris with a tolerant wave of his cigar. "It contributes to the reality effect."
> (Lodge, *Small World* 67)

In *Nightwatchmen*, Hannah is a decade ahead of Lodge and other post-modern authors who have foregrounded and challenged such narrative conventions.

I noted earlier that the figure who is at one level the greatest "actual" presence in the novel, The Killer, is only a "trace"; that is, an example of what McLaughlin calls indexical representation. His murders—enigmatic, unjustifiable, like a force of nature—are effects without causes. The Knocker, Dougie, says that The Killer is "an enigma," unknowable. The powers that enable or cripple academic careers—dissertation committees, department

and university administrators—operate just as enigmatically as The Killer
and Hurricane Camille. Despite the repeated emphasis on the isolation of
intellectual academic labor, nowhere in the novel is *administrative* work
mentioned (in contrast, too, to the *physical* labor of janitors, plumbers, and
nightwatchmen). However, striving for academic careers (rather than jobs)
is a subtext of the novel. At one point Harry Monroe wonders if William
Tell might be The Killer, but then he reasons with delicious irony that
"Tell was not The Killer. He would not mess up his dossier by being The
Killer. It was terribly hard to get a position nowadays even with a Ph.D. and
he would not have fouled up his student record by being a homicidal
maniac" (72).[11] Elsewhere, Didi Sweet announces her pride in her academic
accomplishments:

> Have I forgotten to say that at Southwestern Mississippi I've
> made all A's and that I'm a serious student? I read French thirty
> minutes a night. . . . I have written a paper called "Kissing the
> Tyger"—about Blake—which has been selected to be read at the
> South Central Modern Language Association in New Orleans
> next November. Soon I will be Dr. Didi Sweet, just like soon-
> to-be Dr. William Tell, Dr. Harry Monroe, and Dr. Lawrence
> Head (101).

By 1971, Didi has indeed achieved her doctorate, but she has also come
to understand the hierarchy of American degree-granting institutions
and the invisibility of the machinery of employment. She marries a "big
Chattanooga boy from Harvard" who gets "a better job with his Master's
from Harvard than I could with the Ph.D. from Southwestern Mississippi . . .
we moved to Sewanee, where he teaches full time and I have one freshman
class" (186). When Trove reassembles the dispersed community of graduate students in 1971, they have all have become academic workers, but the
mechanisms for employment are elided:

> I wrote letters and arranged a reunion. I wrote Monroe at
> Clemson University, I wrote Bryant and Hill at Millsaps and
> Memphis State; I wrote Israel at South Carolina; I wrote Magee,
> who was still getting the doctorate at Southwestern Mississippi.

I even wrote Weymouth a hopeless note—he was in England,
happily poverty-stricken as a teacher.

I even wrote Head at Trinity University, knowing he never
wanted to look at us or Pass Christian again. (177)

The combined indexical effect of such absences—of work, of explanations, of certainty—is analogous to the indexical traces of the Killer himself. Ultimately, the challenge to representational claims to correspondence
and coherence are the true heart of *Nightwatchmen.*

Wish fulfillment and "affiliation" notwithstanding, narratives which aspire
to portray the professoriate operate by way of a significant absence. Because
campus novels are forced to contend with their own inability to represent,
they will tend to focus on writing itself through either meta-level commentary on the narrative, or an emphasis upon the inability of the characters to write. Themes of violence (physical and psychic) and dominance
(sexual and social) are also prominent because these distracters occlude
the fact that the cultural systems of real colleges and college novels share
a narrative logic. This narrative logic questions the direct transmission
of information (a mimetic conception, an *iconic* construction), but fears
that *symbolic* (arbitrary/consensual) and *indexical* categories—where, for
example, we "exist" only insofar as the traces of our actions are apparent—
are insufficient. Texts "about" the campus are most often about other texts;
externalized, particularized action is prioritized over internal (unrepre-
sentable, passive) work. The pretense of *mimesis* is uncovered by the fact—
on campuses real and fictive—that only indexical, indirect measurements
of the professoriate are possible.

Barry Hannah's second novel deserves reassessment (not to mention
reprinting) because, notwithstanding Hannah's own comments in interviews, it is coherent: the novel begins with a disjunction (the revelation of
Trove's orphan status), builds to the establishment of a community of
"murderous scholars" (164), and then allows entropy—in the figure of
Hurricane Camille and the absent engine of professional career-
building—to dissolve that community. Towards the end of the narrative,
Trove reunites the dispersed tenants of his community and seems poised to
proceed with a life which is more engaged with the world than he (and

readers) could have imagined at the start of the novel. Mark Charney also sees cohesion at the end of *Nightwatchmen*, which concludes with "hope for me and him" (*Nightwatchmen* 232)—what Charney calls "a simple act of humanity" (19). But the search for meaning—of the motives of The Knocker, The Killer, and of the devastation caused by the hurricane—suggests also an absent God who has fled from the scene of creation. That search for coherence is tied to and contingent upon language and a postmodern acknowledgement of fragmentation rather than certainty.

Extending Donald Noble's suggestion that "Hannah seems to be saying we are all nightwatchmen . . . we all stand lonely watches and are hungry for communication with friends," Charney argues compellingly that:

> The lonely vigils experienced by the security guards in the Old Main are shared by almost everyone in the novel: Didi Sweet, who waits patiently for a man who will treat her with respect; Lawrence Head, who looks for a companion with whom to share ideas; David Lotrieux, who knocks people over the head rather than risk alienation; and Harriman Monroe, who realizes that his heart "is a piece of false junk" (*NW*, 68). . . . Ultimately, Hannah's characters violently reexamine the self to discover that the true possibility of salvation lies within man's latent and untapped ability to create new avenues for communication. (Charney 20)

I would say that the novel also *challenges* the possibility of transparent communication—both personal and narrative. Noble's point that "we . . . are hungry for communication and friends" is, to a degree, undermined by the failure of such connections in the novel. It is noteworthy that Harry Monroe's student Ned Friend twice misspells his own name as "Ned Freind" (63) on exam papers; this is a written analogue to Howard Hunter's mispronunciation of Trove's first name as "Thrope." Ultimately, too much of the novel is concerned with the indexical traces of events, the detritus of human activity, to suggest an unambiguously optimistic closure; too much is "told to" (not least the transcribed interviews conducted by Trove that constitute most of the narrative), mispronounced, and misinterpreted rather than *experienced*. Trove does develop into a (more) active participant in his own life, but only after the narrative consumes and ejects all its academic participants: those characters who are linked, as Charney shows, to self-absorption, written representation and abstraction (Charney 15–16). Academic politics may well be vicious, but "politics" presupposes human interaction of a kind that is conspicuous by its absence from Barry Hannah's contribution to the campus novel genre.

Notes

1. Although often attributed to Kissinger (usually as "academic politics are vicious precisely because the stakes are so small"), a website that cites as "a source" *The Yale Dictionary of Quotations* suggests the correct attribution is Wallace S. Sayre, quoted in Charles Issawi, "Issawi's Laws of Social Motion" (1973). See http://lawlibrary.ucdavis.edu/ LAWLIB/Septo3/ 0006.html.
2. Photos of the aftermath of Hurricane Camille, including before-and-after photos of Pass Christian, are available at http://www.geocities.com/hurricanene/hurricanecamille.htm.
3. *The Penguin Dictionary of Literary Terms* (1991) defines "parataxis" as the "[c]o-ordina-tion of clauses without conjunctions. . . . The effect is terseness and compression" (680). A more specific linkage to the cited passage from *Nightwatchmen* can be seen in Frank Kermode's review, in *The New York Review of Books* (20 October 2005), of Robert Alter's *The Five Books of Moses*: "Nor will [Alter] avoid the habitual parataxis of the original [in his translation]—clauses linked by 'and' and not arranged according to the English habit of using subordinate clauses . . . for parataxis 'is the essential literary vehicle of biblical narrative' " (39).
4. In a more limited way, it can be argued that this novel is really about the violence of lan-guage shaping the world of mundane experience; that *Nightwatchmen* itself constitutes a plea for a poetic rather than a prosaic linguistic "capture" of the world.
5. Harriman Monroe, the poet trapped in academia, recalls to the ear and the mind Harriet Monroe (1860–1936), the influential proselytizer for early-twentieth century modernist poetry, especially through her editorial work on the journal she founded in 1912, *Poetry: A Magazine of Verse*. The connection between Harry and Harriet Monroe is established in the novel, albeit indirectly. Where Harriet Monroe was responsible for the first American publication of T. S. Eliot's "The Love Song of J. Alfred Prufrock," Lawrence Head in *Nightwatchmen* castigates Harry Monroe for his poetic pretensions: " 'Monroe, you have a lot of nerve claiming to be a poet after the Poem of the Century has already been written back in 1913. . . . Honestly, do you think you've written anything that comes near 'The Love Song of J. Alfred'?' " (49).
6. This closing sequence also features Monroe finally using the pistol that he has carried throughout much of the story to murder Lotrieux. Having learned of his pregnant wife Fanny's murder by White, Lotrieux insists that he too wants to die: "Monroe shot him in the back of the head, like one of those sage childhood doctors who is putting in the needle while he is explaining there is nothing to it. . . . We took Monroe back to the plane and he got on it like a zombie. . . . He had gone through a haze into another realm and I could not find a relevant word to bother him with" (230).

7. American popular culture provides only a few references to the actual work of teaching humanities at the college level. Three movies that present scenes of the classroom are *Animal House* (1977), *The Eiger Sanction* (1984), and *Wonder Boys* (2000)—this last based on Michael Chabon's 1995 novel. In each case, a scene of classroom instruction is either encapsulated by sexual impropriety and violence, or the classroom is used as a launching pad for sexual impropriety and violence.

8. In *Imagining the Penitentiary: Fiction and the Architecture of the Mind in Eighteenth-Century England* (1989), John Bender suggests that narrative (and art in general) is part of a continuing construction of our sense of the Real, rather than its reflection: "I consider literature and the visual arts as advanced forms of knowledge, as cognitive instruments that anticipate and contribute to institutional formation . . . [narratives] are primary historical and ideological documents; the vehicles, not the reflections, of social change" (1). Bender quotes anthropologist and cultural critic Clifford Geertz, from *The Interpretation of Cultures*, as support for Bender's contention that a proper focus for novelistic analysis is the subtle construction of the Self who consumes narrative representations:

    > Subjectivity does not properly exist until it is . . . organized; art forms generate and regenerate the very subjectivity they pretend only to display. Quartets, still lifes, and cockfights are not merely reflections of a pre-existing sensibility analogically presented; they are positive agents in the creation and maintenance of such a sensibility. (Bender xviii)

    Thus, a focus upon *how* representation operates—not alone upon *what* the representation shows—is necessary and appropriate.

9. Tell's admission recalls the academics' parlor game called "Humiliation" in Lodge's *Changing Places* (1975): the person who can name the most "classic" texts that he or she has *not* read wins the game, but risks his or her professional career in the process (*Changing Places* 96, 136).

10. One might also mention here the sixth victim of the Knocker, an everyman named John Brown. He is one of very few victims of the Knocker (besides Didi Sweet) who is described in any detail. Already dissociated from any putative "reality" by his divorce, Brown "taught his students by televising them and having them see themselves on screen later" (39).

11. Monroe's disdain for students and his own labor as an academic is palpable. Late in the novel Trove informs us that "Monroe had written his dissertation in two weeks and handed it in, and it was approved. I think he thought he was a god now, being a doctor of literature. He was going to take a pistol with him for his defense of the dissertation, in case any of the examiners got smart" (214) The ambiguity of the word "defense"— abstract in the case of the dissertation committee, concrete in the case of Harry's pistol-packing—is an example of a tonal issue that Mark Charney has observed (15–17).

Works Cited

Abrams, M. H. *The Mirror and the Lamp: Romantic Theory and the Critical Tradition.* 1953. Oxford UP, 1971.

Bender, John. *Imagining the Penitentiary: Fiction and the Architecture of the Mind in Eighteenth Century England*. Chicago and London: U of Chicago P, 1987.

Charney, Mark J. *Barry Hannah*. New York: Twayne, 1992.

Coetzee, J. M. *Disgrace*. New York: Viking, 1999.

Davies, Robertson. *The Rebel Angels*. New York: Penguin, 1983.

Gilman, Owen W., Jr. "Barry Hannah." *Contemporary Fiction Writers of the South: A Bio-Bibliographic Source Book*. Edited by Joseph M. Flora and Robert Bain. Westport, Conn.: Greenwood P, 1993.

Hannah, Barry. *Nightwatchmen*. New York: Viking, 1973.

Irving, John. *The World According to Garp*. 1978. New York: Ballantine, 1990.

Jones, John Griffin. *Mississippi Writers Talking*. Jackson: UP of Mississippi, 1982.

Kermode, Frank. "A New Story of Stories." *New York Review of Books* (20 October 2005), 38–39.

Lodge, David. *Changing Places: A Tale of Two Campuses*. New York: Penguin, 1975.

———. *Nice Work*. London: Martin Secker & Warburg Ltd., 1988.

———. *Small World: An Academic Romance*. New York: Macmillan, 1984.

Madden, David. "Barry Hannah's *Geronimo Rex* in Retrospect." *Southern Review* 19.2 (1983): 309–16.

McLaughlin, Thomas. "Representation." *Critical Terms for Literary Study* (2nd Edition). Eds. Frank Lentricchia and Thomas McLaughlin. U of Chicago P, 1995.

Noble, Donald R. "'Tragic and Meaningful to an Insane Degree': Barry Hannah." *Southern Literary Journal* 15.1 (1982): 37–44.

Showalter, Elaine. *Faculty Towers: The Academic Novel and Its Discontents*. Philadelphia: U of Pennsylvania P, 2005.

Swift, Jonathan. *Gulliver's Travels*. 1726. New York: Bonanza Books, 1947.

Trucks, Rob. "A Conversation with Barry Hannah." *Black Warrior Review* 24.2 (1998): 13–40.

Heroism and the Changing Face of American Manhood in Barry Hannah's Fiction

—Thomas Ærvold Bjerre

The fine line between heroic behavior and mere violence is one that Barry Hannah explores in most of his fiction; his characters often veer from one side of the line to the other in a confused quest for meaning. As Hannah's characters search for meaning in life, their pursuit finds expression in foolhardy attempts at heroism and sporadic bursts of violence. Hannah's fiction is full of heroes, both true and false. The narrators or protagonists of Hannah's stories are rarely the heroes, though they try to be. Instead, as Jan Gretlund has pointed out, they find themselves reduced to "seeking redemption through the experience of sex and violence" (1). Their attempts may be noble enough in their earnestness, since any action is better than inaction, but they are not gratified. All the while they strive to reach the level of the real heroes in their lives, those who seem to symbolize some kind of peace and tranquility and who are able to communicate their thoughts through either music or art. Like Hemingway's heroes, Hannah's heroes must display passion for their art, but they also demonstrate a Faulknerian ability to endure suffering. Through their passion, Hannah's male heroes prevail and communicate values to which the confused narrators or protagonists can relate.

As a southerner Barry Hannah grew up surrounded by myths of the valiant heroes of the Lost Cause. Much of his fiction is permeated by characters who, in one way or the other, try to live up to the burden of the Lost

War and the masculine codes of honor and heroism it connotes. Indeed, perhaps the most striking example of Hannah's false heroes can be found in his Civil War stories and especially in the figure of J. E. B. Stuart, "the Confederacy's greatest cavalry officer" (Seib 41). As Kenneth Seib, Mark Charney and (elsewhere in this volume) Martyn Bone have shown, Hannah's portrayal of Stuart debunks the traditional image of the southern hero by a harsh and satiric unmasking of the old myths and values. Hannah's picture of Stuart is one that supports some parts of the Confederate myth, but it is finally a rebuttal of the popular picture of a brave and courageous soldier. As Charney observes, Stuart ultimately "symbolizes for the vainglorious South an almost comic mixture of foolishness, humor, and noble intentions" (27).

In this essay, I consider Hannah's representation of wider American cultural myths of manhood, and the way in which Hannah shows the hollowness of his protagonists' macho actions by juxtaposing them with a more subtle form of heroism: the passionate expression of life through art. The ambivalent relationship between masculinity and art runs like a leitmotif through Hannah's fiction and his characters have problems combining the two without feeling emasculated. This is partly due to traditional views of heroism ingrained in American culture. Hannah's characters fit the pattern of men who, in Mark Gerzon's words, "consume certain images of manhood even though the world from which they are derived may have disappeared—if it ever existed." Gerzon argues that "in comparing themselves to the dashing figure riding off into the setting sun or racing across the goal line, ordinary men in everyday life cannot help but feel overshadowed" (5). What makes life so difficult for Hannah's male characters is their failure to understand that traditional models of masculinity are no longer relevant. Moreover, new or emerging models of masculinity only confuse Hannah's characters further, prompting them to cling to preconceived notions of what a real man should be.

The clash between traditional heroic behavior and a search for something more meaningful takes place in most of Hannah's fiction. His male characters are caught in traditional masculine codes, especially in what sociologists have called "hegemonic masculinity." R. W. Connell posits that hegemonic masculinity "guarantees (or is taken to guarantee) the dominant position of men and the subordination of women," and that "it is the successful claim to authority, more than direct violence, that is the mark of hegemony (though violence often underpins or supports authority)" (*Masculinities* 77). Furthermore, hegemonic conceptions of masculinity do not necessarily correspond "with the actual personalities of the majority of men. Indeed," Connell argues, "the winning of hegemony often involves the creation of models of masculinity which are quite specifically fantasy figures, such as the film characters played by Humphrey Bogart, John Wayne and Sylvester Stallone" (*Gender and Power* 184). This definition fits Hannah's characters extremely well. While Hannah's characters dream of some heroic "macho" ideal, they are at the same time aware that their dream, as Ruth D. Weston observes, "is based on cultural falsehoods they have internalized" (22). This awareness forces them to seek untraditional ways of obtaining masculine power: for example, through art.

In a 1999 essay, Hannah explains his fascination with the art of writing: "The first hit of art is a kick, like junk. . . . I believe I saved myself by way of the bad poems. It was always life intense I was after, life as its own comment when drawn well enough, never much else" ("Mr Brain" 74–75). This statement goes to the core of Hannah's fiction: how does one explore and experience "life intense" without succumbing to the recklessly heroic ideals that society has created? While Hannah tries to capture such intensity in his writing, his characters try to capture it in life. The division between life and writing is the subject of Peter Schwenger's *Phallic Critiques* (1984), in which he looks at traditional notions of masculine and feminine writing styles. Schwenger identifies what he calls "the language of men" (13) formulated by Ernest Hemingway, Henry Miller, Norman Mailer and other members of the so-called School of Virility. However, as Schwenger reminds us, the very act of writing is traditionally considered a feminine activity. A "real man" is supposed to be a man of action; as such, a male writer cannot afford to jeopardize his perceived virility by being too articulate, by showing too much comfort with and control over language (18). Confronted by this tradition, a consciously masculine writer may try to resolve this paradox by selecting not only a manly subject matter but also a style of writing, "a certain toughness of language," that shows without doubt he is in fact a man of action (14). Hemingway's language is a good example of the "tough style" Schwenger identifies: terse and spare, void of the long and elaborate words that became Faulkner's trademark, it reflects the macho ideal of a writer as not *too* articulate. Like Hemingway's fictional world, Hannah's is permeated by the kind of violent and sexual subject matter tradition-ally regarded as the preserve of the masculine writer; arguably, Hannah's frank explicitness imparts his language a "toughness" that exceeds even Hemingway's.

Hannah's characters, if they are lucky, are able to be men of action, but in a peaceful way. They also struggle with ways of depicting life in heroic but serene terms. In the story "Idaho," from *Captain Maximus* (1985), Hannah juxtaposes traditional notions of masculine heroism with an alternative heroism of artistic creation. In this highly autobiographical story the narrator "began drinking and playing pool and winning some money—and his life was bursting with a heroic certainty" (18). Riding his motorcycle, he is "trying to be the hero in [his] leather jacket" (19). But after the death of a poet friend, listening to Jimi Hendrix helps the narra-tor resolve to kick his alcohol addiction on the basis that "the drunk has all the feeling for the miracle and not quite the substance of it" (22). Instead, the narrator finds some kind of fulfillment through sobriety, fuller engage-ment with his family, and writing. When he dreams of Stonewall Jackson it is not the Confederate general's heroic courage that he admires but his ability to refuse liquor "because he liked it too much" (22). At the end of the story the narrator no longer needs to shoot a gun in order to feel mas-culine or heroic; he can pick up the pen and write about his experiences instead: "I look down at my hand. It's not a gun. It's only a pencil. I am not going anywhere" (23).

"Rat-faced Auntie" from *Bats Out of Hell* also focuses on heroism and art. After a successful adolescence as a trombone player in a popular jazz band, Edgar finds himself a former bum and a "gutless lackey at thirty-five" (174) who lives with his vicious Aunt Hadley. Trying to regain his dignity, Edgar seeks the traditional masculine ideals; his aunt, meanwhile, goes out of her way to make him feel inferior. She scorns his alcoholism by com-paring him with the great men of the past: "When men were realler, they drank for good reasons. Look at Grant and Churchill with their great wars. Look at Poe and Faulkner and Jack London and their masterpieces. . . . It seems to me you became a drunkard just for lack of something to do. Just a miserable fad. No direction, no strong legs under you" (176). Hadley uses two kinds of masculine heroes to taunt Edgar: the warrior hero and the artist hero. In a twisted way she makes it possible for Edgar to choose both paths in his search for vindication and masculinity: Hadley gives him not only her diaries and jottings, accumulated over her seventy-three years, but also a BMW motorcycle as a way of bribing him to write her life story.

On his motorcycle Edgar achieves a sense of masculinity, further enhanced by his girlfriend Emma riding pillion with her panties off: "He was sly. Nature was with him. . . . She told him he was a new man, all bronzed and straight, on the motorcycle" (179). To assure himself of his masculinity he deliberately challenges himself: "A weak and dim man could not have her. A dim and weak man could not handle the BMW with this intelligent brunette frightened on the back seat. Deliberately he drove right into the racing ring-road fury of Atlanta traffic, cocky and weaving at seventy-five plus, envied" (180). Thus reassured of his manhood, Edgar considers his aunt's request to have him write her life and realizes that her plea changes the balance of power between the two. Edgar suddenly has the upper hand and enjoys letting Hadley wait. He now becomes an artist hero with a distinct tough language consisting of "grunt-talk" and "a primitive-getting there" which is beyond even Hemingway (183).

Ironically, the macho ideals Edgar strives for are denied him when he is accidentally blinded by Emma. With "only a speck of vision, low in his left eye" (188), Edgar emerges as a Milton-figure, while his aunt Hadley, formerly so vicious, has become dependent on Edgar to tell her story and has thereby turned into a docile amanuensis. Finally Edgar has become his own man, and he is able to let go of his girlfriend and focus fully on defeating Aunt Hadley. Edgar finds himself "happy, so profoundly, almost, delirious" and he is ready to take on that ambivalent masculine and creative act—writing: "Loud and bright and full of jazz, *Rat-Face Confesses*—that would be the title of their book" (190). Thus Edgar chooses a writing style and title that oppose the stereotypical view of writers as effeminate and instead suggest a certain manliness. The book will mark Edgar's final victory in the long battle of power between him and Hadley. Her long life will now be mediated by his narrative authority and through his distinctly masculine style. The title clearly conveys his animosity towards Hadley, depicting her pejoratively as a suspect, someone in need of confession. That *Hannah's* story has a different title than Edgar's suggests an ambivalence on his part towards Edgar's exaggerated masculine mastery over both Hadley and Emma. Ultimately, Edgar's authoritative manhood may boil down to mere self-deception, a condition common to Hannah's male characters.

The search for an alternative masculinity is also embodied in Bobby Smith of *The Tennis Handsome* (1983). Bobby has been ruined by the war in Vietnam. His doubts about the purpose of his being in Vietnam are revealed in a painful self-examination during which he lashes out against the image of the soldier as hero: "I'd killed so many gooks. I'd killed them with machine guns, mortars, howitzers, knives, wire—me and my boys. . . . It seemed to me my life had gone straight from teenage giggling to horror. I had never had time to be but two things, a giggler and a killer" (47). Bobby Smith is a modern-day version of Hemingway's Jake Barnes in *The Sun Also Rises* (1926), but without the physical wounds. Barnes admires the bullfighter Pedro Romero because of his "aficion," his passion: "Romero never made any contortions, always it was straight and pure and natural in line." He displays "real emotion, because he kept the absolute purity of line in his movements and always quietly and calmly let the horns pass him close each time" (171). It is this same trait, the sense of authentic passion, that Bobby Smith admires in the tennis player French Edward. As Bobby explains, "the thing that got me was that he *cared* so much about what he was doing. It made me love America, to know he was in it, and I hadn't loved anything for maybe three years then. . . . It was a man at work and play at the same time, doing his damnedest" (41). Having been emotionally paralyzed by the horrors of the war, Bobby looks to Edward for affirmation that strong feelings like passion and caring still exist. What draws Bobby to Edward is the fact that he cares so much for something that is harmless and serene: "There was such care in his eyes, and it was only a tennis ball, a goddamned piece of store-bought bounce. But it was wonderful and nobody was being killed" (47).

Yet it is not only the passion that Edward displays that attracts Bobby; it is also his peaceful masculinity. As Michael Kimmel points out, one result of the Vietnam War was that the soldier, a previously reliable symbol of American masculinity, became stigmatized for acting out an "excessive and false hypermasculinity"; the popular image of the soldier changed from a figure of "manly virtue" to "a failed man" (263). By contrast, because Edward is an athlete, he is still a legitimate symbol of masculinity.

Connell argues that "sport has come to be the leading definer of masculinity in mass culture. Sport provides a continuous display of men's bodies in motion. . . . It serves as symbolic proof of men's superiority and right to rule." Connell goes on to say that "true masculinity is almost always thought to proceed from men's bodies—to be inherent in a male body or to express something about a male body" (*Masculinities* 54, 45). When Bobby looks at a picture of Edward, he focuses on the athlete's body:

> French had his mouth open and the forearm muscles were
> bulked up plain as wires. . . . French seemed to be hitting under
> a heroic deficiency. You could see the sweat droplets on his
> neck. His eyes were in an agony. . . . And French was a beauti-
> ful man. . . . The way French Edward looked, it sort of rebuked
> yourself ever hoping to call yourself a man . . . his face was curled
> around by that wild hair the color of beer; his chest was deep,
> just about to bust out of that collar and bowtie. (41–42)

French's masculinity and peaceful passion for tennis help Bobby in his quest for remasculinization after the U.S. army's defeat in Vietnam. Tellingly, Hannah's descriptions of the tennis matches borrow heavily from military vocabulary, thus emphasizing the relation between sports and masculinity while exposing the futility and horror of war: "It was a brilliant and har-rying match, a match that invented major calamity and triumph out of a simple furry ball. The contortions, the dives, the retreat, the attack into ruin" (75). On the tennis court Hannah's male characters can engage in a peaceful battle, one that boosts self-esteem and is void of trauma. In this way sport is offered as a surrogate but nonviolent form of war.

The eponymous protagonist of *Ray*, another Vietnam veteran, admires the same masculine traits as Bobby Smith. Ray is an "aficionado" of Mr. Hooch, the father of his sexual partner Sister. Through his poetry and music Mr. Hooch displays much the same passion as Edward does on the tennis court. But Mr. Hooch is not a pure Hemingway character. Unlike a Hemingway hero, Mr. Hooch finds it essential to express his emotions, especially after the murder of Sister by a local priest driven crazy by her beauty (52). As he says: "It's my only goddamn talent. When I quit talk-ing, I'll be as dead as my daughter" (59). When Ray needs to experience a sense of peace and order, he listens to "the tender sorrow coming through the forty-eight reeds" of Mr. Hooch's harmonica (79). Mr. Hooch's garrulous passion is evident in his declaration that "I'll be what my daughter was trying to be! . . . Already got myself recorded. All I need is a drum. I read Sister's diary! Goddamn it, I'm a great old son of a bitch!" (79). In his assertive display of passion for literature and life Mr. Hooch becomes a yardstick for Ray, one by which he can measure his own shortcomings as a human and a poet: "When I think I'm doing good, I have to come over [to Hooch's house] and see that I'm not even in the contest" (111).

Whereas Mr. Hooch finds a separate peace in his poetry and music following Sister's death, Ray seeks release in both sex and violence. Connell states that violence is implicit in "the physical construction of hegemonic masculinity" because it allows a belief in "the superiority of men, and the oppressive practices that flow from it, to be sustained by men who in other respects have very little power" (*Gender and Power* 85–86). Trying to adhere to the masculine code, Ray takes the law into his own hands by slugging a bad poet in defense of southern writing; beating up a juvenile delinquent with a two-by-four; deliberately letting a violent patient die; and shooting another patient in the ribs as a warning. He also asserts his masculinity through (accounts of) sex, be it with his wife Westy, his lover Sister, a woman from the IRS, or Laurie, a casual companion. But Ray is a disturbingly unreliable narrator: like his story about stealing a Learjet and crashing it, his tales of sexual conquests may amount to little more than male fantasies.

Ray justifies his rambling search by stating that "without a healthy sense of confusion, Ray might grow smug. . . . I think it's better with me all messed up" (103). Yet despite his macho assertions of power and attempt to justify his own confusion, Ray still yearns to follow the passionate but peaceful lead of Mr. Hooch. However, when his attempts at poetry fail, violence takes over, and he "kicks over the plants and yells abuses. Mainly, it's because his poems are not going well and he still can't come anywhere close to old J. Hooch" (87). The sad irony is that Ray recognizes the painful split in his character between tranquility and violence, but blames it on history. He tells a class of university students that "Americans have never been consistent. They represent gentleness and rage together. . . . One lesson we as Americans must learn is to get used to the contrarieties in

our hearts and learn to live with them" (51). Though Ray seems here to
be resigned to such supposedly "American" contradictions, his yearning
to live up to Mr. Hooch betrays him. Ray aches for a model of masculinity
that, as Gerzon puts it, points "toward a fuller, more humane understanding of sexuality, reflections of a more loving mutuality between men and
women, other men, and the earth itself" (238). Until he learns to let go
of culturally ingrained masculine ideals, Ray will always oscillate between
moments of insightful tranquility and bursts of violence.

The narrator of "Two Gone Over" from *High Lonesome* (1996) experiences a sense of confusion similar to Ray's. The narrator's life is guided
by obsessive ideals that are almost impossible to match. Trying to save
his doomed marriage, he takes his wife to a reservoir in hope of finding
"woodsy rocks and bluffs with a cold stream down the middle.... I conceived of our eating fish and living off the land, a rebaptism of ourselves."
But his dreams of a pastoral Eden wane when they do not find the place:
"The moment was gone and I was just a fool" (175), he declares. His wife
finds another man, and the narrator gets back together with a former
lover, a girl from Tallahassee half his age who is presently in the process
of divorcing an Air Force pilot. The girl is inscribed with almost mythic
ideals: "She was the one who broke my heart in high school and made
me cry on my pillow. She was the type. Little Anthony and the Imperials
sang about her" (169). However, the first time the two have sex, it leaves
the narrator feeling distinctly feminized: "I became a woman in her, is
what it felt like.... I was sighing as if penetrated and then wrung out."
This is a startling divergence from the usual Hannah narrator boasting of
his sexual exploits in traditionally macho terms; indeed, the narrator of
"Two Gone Over" admits that he felt like "the chew toy of a dog ... a sad
man" (173). The narrator subsequently confesses further that he tried to
raise his self-esteem following the shocking sexual encounter: "For a few
minutes I would recall her beauty and then boast inside, but this went
away fast." He even tried to "attach a profound narrative to myself" based
on his uncle, "a laughing athletic monument of a man" and World War II
pilot (173). This misguided faith in the cultural myth of the war hero dete-
riorates into farce when the Tallahassee girl returns: the narrator tries to
impress her not only by taking on his uncle's World War II pilot persona
but also by dressing in a Confederate cavalry hat: "I have no clear idea why,"

he says, "except I had become also a pilot. I could not refuse the conviction I was a fighter pilot. The hat gave me a certain authority, I felt. The passion of my race ran high in me" (175–76). Blinded by self-deception, the narrator believes the girl is "charmed and amazed," and finds the future "bright now with missy in the house" (176). However, the girl does not share the narrator's clichéd vision of vigorous masculinity; instead she sees the narrator as "a lunatic older version of the very man she had left behind in the air force," and leaves immediately. (Later he receives a letter from her asking, "Who *are* you?" [176].) Like Ray Forrest, the narrator of "Two Gone Over" then plunges headfirst into a drunken search for righteousness, still maintaining the dream of being a pilot, so women will not see him as a fool. His obsession with this masculine ideal becomes even more ludicrously apparent when he attempts to set fire to his car, "which would not fly and was really hot on [his] feet" (178).

"The Vision of Esther by Clem," from *Bats Out of Hell* (1993), is yet another Hannah story featuring a narrator caught up in a dull existence who uses masculine ideals to overcome it. Clem Mestre has reached a point where "he needed saving from nothing." Trying to bring some color back into his life, he turns first to art, painting "at three fixed canvases, wanting passion to come along—perhaps even talent—but his conceptions and executions were vile. They depressed him" (63). He is only shaken out of this dreary void by the news that Esther, a "plain woman he knew," has been raped by several men. Clem and Esther's relationship is somewhat strained since she "had loved him" and "he'd ignored her," simply because she was "plain" (53). The rape of Esther serves as a catalyst for Clem, who begins to see her in terms of an inverted Madonna/whore dichotomy. Instead of being tainted by the rape, Esther becomes almost holy to Clem, a "chattering madonna" (72). Clem begins a quest to restore her honor and undo the wrong he did when he rejected her: "Esther was all at once divine, a treasure that he must hurry to and shower with respect. He must honor her. This was urgent. Terrifying honor was due her because, with his chance, he had slighted her badly. . . . In injury and insult, she seemed a goddess to him now" (54–55).

Clem is secretly fascinated with the rape of Esther. Mental images of the rape keep flashing before his eyes, simultaneously reminding him of his previous marriage with "a lazy nurse," whom he had come to despise so that "he began raping her. She did not know it, but he was raping her, his body in a frenzy like a shark's. His act was one of total control and disgust. In fact, it was good, and his attitude lasted the final year of their marriage" (64–65). According to Roger Horrocks, "for the individual, male rape is often an expression of pseudomasculinity, that stems from feelings of inadequacy, *of not being a man*. Rape is an expression of impotence, not potency" (139). This would explain Clem's reaction against his wife. Not only did he despise her, he also felt sexually threatened by the presence of "her equally lazy and snobbish brother" (64). When he begins courting Esther, Clem gets a "delicious chill" at the "thought of several men taking women sexually, the woman a thing of only slightly resisting orifices, until the animal ecstasy struck her. . . . Writhing orifices, the whimpering, protesting mouth—Esther, my Esther—the amazed eyes, the unbidden hunger" (65). This is Clem's "vision" of Esther and his courting of her, which he sees as an act of heroic honor, is really a way for him to reassert his masculinity; it is the ultimate test of his male powers. Clem considers it "likely that [Esther] hated men at large now, and that Mestre might make her skin crawl" (64). If he can seduce her he will prove that he is perhaps not the "weak slick thing" he feels he is (75). His quest is also born out of jealousy of Esther's scars. Looking at her Clem "marveled at the original hurt, and felt very meager. Her scars were so much beyond his" (75). Clem achieves his goal by conquering Esther sexually, but he is still confused: "Out of strength or weakness—he couldn't figure—he stayed loyal to her through the next months" (76). The couple marry, and Clem continues to act superior to Esther, who "couldn't figure why Clem had married her." Her doubt makes her fragile and subordinate, and this in turn enables Clem to feel that he "loved her" and "felt part of a big thing" (77). Ultimately, Clem's ostensible aim to be a passionate and understanding lover for his hurt companion is debunked by his own vanity and subconscious wish to dominate. Instead of becoming a true hero, he ends up as yet another of Hannah's false heroes.

In Hannah's latest novel, *Yonder Stands Your Orphan* (2001), Raymond Forrest's namesake Max Raymond embodies the typical traits of Hannah's male characters: he constructs his identity through music, poetry, women, and sex, but is wracked by frustration and self doubt. However, Max Raymond is also a further development of the Hannah male in the sense that he is ultimately more spiritual than his antecedents. This can perhaps be ascribed to the fact that during the process of writing the novel Hannah himself "had an intense dream where the Savior appeared very physically." Hannah says of Raymond: "He wants to be a Christian very badly, but he is like me. I needed material evidence" (Bjerre, interview). This newfound interest in Christ does not result in a change of tone for Hannah; *Yonder Stands Your Orphan* is as witty, critical, and violent as any one of his previous novels.

Raymond's ambivalent reliance on his wife, Mimi Suarez ("the Coyote"), and his anxious longing for a more spiritual understanding of himself are both evident early in the narrative: "He needed music, the Coyote and God. And he needed to live close to evil" (36). Raymond is "still doing homework for his soul in his forties" (171), but because he attempts to embrace so many different kinds of masculinity, his life becomes a blurred mess. Waiting for a religious vision, playing the saxophone, and driving around with a gun in his pants are all attempts to reach an understanding of himself. Needless to say, none of these half-serious attempts leads to anything like a coherent or singular sense of identity; on the contrary, they only further confuse his quest for a perfect masculinity.

As a child, Raymond's fanatically religious mother "would grab him by the throat" and say "Love the Lord, you little nit" (89). As an adult, Raymond still "loved Christ, but he yearned for a solid thing to witness, a vision undisputed, because his faith was by no means confirmed" (9). He is "a sort of Christian, but he despised striving, waited for visions. And was a poet. . . . He knew his poetry was not good, like his life, but he waited through the weak words for a vision and an act. . . . He could get higher, higher to God, by his saxophone" (36). Like Ray Forrest, Max Raymond knows his poetry is limited. Instead, music becomes the artistic medium in which he experiences real intensity. In a section of the novel that features his own writing, Raymond ponders John Roman's passion for Chet Baker's trumpet-playing. Raymond writes that "He [Baker] never played the horn loud, never. Never showed off. What an ear. No running around jagged, like me, he was mad for love. To be more like Chet Baker in my heart. My good Christ, give me talent please, no more art" (92). This intense appreciation of music as something honest and passionate places Raymond in a long line of music-loving Hannah characters ranging all the way back to *Geronimo Rex*'s trumpet-playing narrator Harry Monroe who, as Ken Millard notes elsewhere in this volume, develops a "jazz aesthetic" in his writing. Moreover, what Raymond admires in a good musician like Chet Baker is the same trait Bobby Smith of *The Tennis Handsome* admires in the tennis player French Edward: disciplined passion and perfect aesthetic expression. Raymond's plea for "talent" like Baker's captures his yearning for something beyond "art." Raymond clearly distinguishes between a passionate, almost innate musical "talent," like that displayed by Baker, and the more clinical and intellectual term "art," which can be learned but is ultimately limited and inauthentic. Even though Raymond believes himself to be a good saxophone player, he has become so merely "by practicing some dumbish thing over and over"; he has lacked authentic talent and passion. As such, Raymond has tried to find other forms of intense feeling: alarmingly, he has even become dependent on "the evil" he feels "close at hand to know [he is] alive" (94). Indeed, Raymond plays in a band at the casino because, to him, the casino is a symbol of evil.

Raymond's good fortune in being married to the beautiful jazz singer Mimi Suarez only baffles him; he knows that by all traditional measures he does not deserve Mimi. Because Mimi is genuinely talented, Raymond begins to see her "as the cause of his despondency" (37); he wants "evermore an answer to her easy talents, her simple life" (171). Furthermore—and recalling the case of the narrator in "Two Gone Over"—Raymond begins to feel "unmanned by their lovemaking.... He was both voyeur and actor when he took her, in all her spread beauty, but the part of voyeur was increasing and he knew he was a filthy old haint, as far from Christ as a rich man" (37). Laura Mulvey points out in her discussion of voyeurism that "at the extreme, it can become fixated into a perversion, producing obsessive voyeurs and Peeping Toms, whose only sexual satisfaction can come from watching, in an active controlling sense, an objectified other" (60). However, Raymond's increasing voyeurism undermines not only his direct sexual control over Mimi but also his own masculine self-possession. Raymond is emasculated or "unmanned" because he no longer simply "acts" upon Mimi's body; he watches, the passive nature of which threatens Raymond's conception of his own virility. In an attempt to bolster his traditional masculine identity and authority, Raymond buys a gun; however, his use of the weapon as a phallic substitute is laughably obvious: "*Be a man,*" he tries to convince himself, "*use your new long-barrel .38, stuffed in the trousers*" (178).

Raymond's insecurity largely derives from his fear that Mimi's ex-boyfriend Malcolm will return. Raymond had Malcolm put into a coma when he was a doctor, but he is now walking the streets again, and the threat of vengeance haunts Raymond. Even though carrying a gun is supposed to boost Raymond's sense of masculinity, it does not have quite that effect. Convinced that he is stalking Malcolm, Raymond instead ends up facing the killer Man Mortimer. When Raymond tries to walk away from the confrontation, Mortimer stabs him in the back with a penknife; as Raymond scurries towards his car, his gun slips "into the crotch of his underwear. . . . sinking lower even then and trying for his ankle." This abject humiliation leads Raymond to reconsider his quest to become a poet warrior since "his interest in the avocation of gunning was on the wane" (185). After the humiliating encounter with Mortimer, Raymond lays down his guns even though "his disgrace, the stab wound . . . still throbbed in his buttock when he walked or played the sax" (225). Raymond still yearns for revenge, to be "taken into a different room of heaven with Mortimer's blood on his hands" (309), but the wish remains a male fantasy even though he believes that he "could stand being a coward only just a little bit longer" (227). Ultimately, Raymond knows he does not have the courage to live out his revenge fantasy.

Raymond instead tries to achieve a stable sense of self by focusing on the spiritual, and he hopes for a vision that will guide him. At a funeral Raymond experiences an epiphany: he suddenly "knew his vision would come at the end of his life and not a moment before. He was nearly blinded by the realization that he was a nuisance to both God and man. He repented. He would act" (311). Raymond forms a friendship with the Native-/African-American war veteran John Roman, another victim of Man Mortimer's knife. The two men fish and talk "of cancer, music, the history of Roman's Indian tribe, Jesus Christ as a man of the whip, taking time to make it right there in the temple. Raymond had not known a black man since the days of southern apartheid, although he called their names" (323). On the last page we are told that "John Roman and Max Raymond drew closer together" (336). Their relationship is reminiscent of that of the two men in Hannah's "Water Liars" who were both "crucified by the truth" (7). It seems that, for once, a male character in Hannah's fiction has found some sort of closure to his confused quest for identity. Though he is reminiscent of Ray Forrest and other, earlier Hannah protagonists, Max Raymond's spirituality ultimately allows him to reject culturally idealized notions of excessive masculinity.

According to Frank Pittman, men's sense of masculinity changes as they grow older. Their preoccupation with traditional macho assertions of masculinity is replaced with a concern for "emotional control and strength of character" (9). This is not true for all of the old men in Hannah's fiction. Some are determined to rage on. They may be slowed down by various diseases, but they are just as foolhardy as Hannah's adult males. *Yonder Stands Your Orphan* returns to Farte Cove and some of the characters from the *Airships* stories "Water Liars" and "All the Old Harkening Faces at the Rail" (1978), as well as "High-Water Railers" from *Bats Out of Hell.* In "Water Liars," "the old liars" were "snapping and wheezing at one another" at the end of the pier (*Airships* 3) whereas in "High-Water Railers" "almost all the old loved each other at the end of the pier" (*Bats* 4). In *Yonder Stands Your Orphan*, however, old Ulrich complains that "We don't love each other as much as we used to" (46). The old men at the pier have all been affected by the evil that Man Mortimer springs upon the community. As Hannah explained in an interview with Dan Williams, "there is more direction to the people on the pier now. They're animated . . . looking more straight ahead at evil or more up close at it in the presence of casinos and this strange orphanage" (263). We get proof of this early in the novel when the senile, emphysema-stricken, and animal-loving Ulrich attacks a teenager for displaying a shot deer on the front of his car. Ulrich leaves his walker and tries to choke the teenager with his bare hands, "squeezing to kill him," before beating "the vehicle violently with the gun" and driving "over the leg of the hunter" (17–18). As one of the other teenagers exclaims, seeing Ulrich's walker left behind: "Damn. The man can't hardly breathe. This is one old sonofabitch who changed his life in fifteen seconds" (18). Ulrich's rage has filled him with a power strong enough to lash out violently, without consideration or thought. Indeed, this is not the first time that Ulrich's actions have betrayed his frail body. Two years previous he "had bought a used Jet Ski and had gone airborne with it on the other side of the cove. . . . He could not recall what he was trying to prove" (21). Although Ulrich cannot identify it, he is—like so many other Hannah males—"raging against the dying of the light."[1]

To avoid going to a retirement home, Ulrich runs off with his animal-loving friend Carl Bob Feeney. Together, the two behave like children by spying on Mimi Suarez; they also act as wayward missionaries, preaching to everyone about animals' superiority over mankind. Ulrich longs for a way to express all his welled-up emotions: "He wished he could sing all out, in a long exquisite howl for the animals and flight, but he was just croaking here and taking a nose hit now and then from his oxygen bottle" (207). Ulrich's engrossing love for animals and his yearning to express his welled-up emotions suggest once again a need on the part of a male Hannah character to transcend the constraining cultural patterns of masculinity. Animals figure as a sanctuary in Hannah's fiction, a refuge from the complications of human (and especially masculine) life. In the Civil War story "Dragged Fighting from His Tomb" (from 1978's *Airships*), Captain Howard has lost his trust in people and places his faith with horses, the only thing to keep him sane in the midst of the horrors of war: "We are all overbrained and overemotioned. . . . Compared with horses, we are all a dizzy and smelly farce" (53). Similarly, the narrator of "Taste Like a Sword" loves his cat because "[s]he reminds [him] there is not much to it, only the noise, and sleeps three quarters of the day" (*High Lonesome* 143). The animal-lover Ulrich feels out of place in the human world, but he still desperately longs to communicate his emotions: "So much so long in his bosom that could have been shared and vented to his auditors through the years." Ulrich, like Ray Forrest, embodies gentleness and rage together. He wants to sing, to be "a bird with a deep throat" (*Yonder* 207), but when he fails to communicate he falls back on macho ideals that are violent, foolish, and ultimately hazardous to his health.

With *Yonder Stands Your Orphan* Hannah has come full circle in his writing. Using characters and themes from his earlier works, the novel links back to and ties together his work from the past three decades. It ends, however, with a coda that is much darker and more bitter than any of Hannah's previous works. Though in many ways the novel seems a feverish amalgamation of *Ray* and *Never Die* (1991), those two earlier books ended on a note of optimism in the face of hardship that seemed to confirm Hannah's belief in the power of mankind to endure suffering and then

endure it again. The ending of *Ray* echoes the novel's recurrent proclamation "Sabers up, gentlemen!" while *Never Die* closes with the would-be
hero Fernando Muré vowing to start his life over: "Maybe this time I'll have
a whole lot better chance" (152). It is this Faulknerian belief in man's ability
to endure and prevail that informed all of Hannah's fiction before *Yonder*,
and he explained this philosophy in an interview with Larry McCaffery:

> Life *is* a lot of confusion and pain and death, and the only way to
> deal with it is to face it with the attitude that there's no place to
> go but up. "Sabers up, gentlemen!" is the way I end *Ray*. That's all
> I know. Straight ahead. Hit 'em high. Let's go get 'em again. . . .
> There's too much depression and confusion and death to allow
> any *real* hope. We don't have a fucking chance. But "Sabers up!"
> (McCaffery and Gregory 125).

It is the same philosophy that pervades Hannah's male heroes, true and
false, and which underpins their refusal to give in or give up, despite the
many mistakes they make in their ongoing quest to make sense of life.

In *Yonder Stands Your Orphan*, however, the darkness seems to be
encroaching much too fast on the despairing characters. The novel ends on
a note of resignation and sufferance: "Harvard and Melanie were married
by Peden on the pleasure barge. Their marriage was that of pals after a fight
and long silence. It had become too late in time for fights, and often even
memories. They clung" (336). This new tone of desperation is perhaps the
most significant development in Hannah's thirty-year career; yet until the
novel's dark coda, the characters have followed the established patterns of
his true and false heroes. The codes of traditional heroism and masculinity
embedded in American society become both the target of and the obstacle
to the characters' quests for meaning. Unable to let go of ingrained models
of masculinity but also afraid of modern alternatives, Hannah's characters
are caught in limbo between peaceful expressions and violent assertions
of identity. The passion displayed by Hannah's true heroes—the tennis
player French Edward, the poet and musician Mr. Hooch, and the spiritu-
ally inclined Max Raymond—serve as a model for other more confused
characters—the machismo-driven Edgar, the rambling Raymond Forrest,
the vain and dominating Clem, and the raging Ulrich—who all strive for

an outdated hyper-masculinity through foolhardy acts of random sex and violence. While many of Hannah's characters have recourse to obsolete visions of masculine heroism in their search for fulfillment and meaning, they secretly long for the courage to achieve the peaceful passion of their true heroes.

Note

1. I am alluding, of course, to Dylan Thomas's poem "Do Not Go Gentle into That Good Night" (1952).

Works Cited

Bjerre, Thomas Ærvold. Personal Interview with Barry Hannah, conducted at Ohio University Inn, Athens, Ohio, May 11, 2001.
Connell, R. W. *Gender and Power: Society, the Person and Sexual Politics*. Stanford: Stanford UP, 1987.
———. *Masculinities*. Berkeley: U of California P, 1995.
Charney, Mark J. *Barry Hannah*. New York: Twayne, 1992.
Gretlund, Jan Nordby. "Barry Hannah: Beyond Sex and Violence," Prepublication of the English Department of Odense University, 35 (November 1985).
Gerzon, Mark. *A Choice of Heroes: The Changing Face of American Manhood*. Boston: Houghton Mifflin, 1982.
Hannah, Barry. *Airships*. 1978. New York: Grove P, 1994.
———. *Bats Out of Hell*. New York: Grove P, 1993.
———. *Captain Maximus*. New York: Alfred A. Knopf, 1985.
———. *High Lonesome*. New York: Atlantic Monthly P, 1996.
———. "Mr. Brain, He Want a Song," in *The Eleventh Draft*, ed. Frank Conroy. New York: Harper Collins, 1999, 67–75.
———. *Never Die*. Boston: Houghton Mifflin/Seymour Lawrence, 1991.
———. *Ray*. New York: Alfred A. Knopf, 1980.
———. *The Tennis Handsome*. 1983. Baton Rouge: Louisiana State UP, 1995.
———. *Yonder Stands Your Orphan*. New York: Atlantic Monthly P, 2001.
Hemingway, Ernest. *The Sun Also Rises*. 1926. New York: Scribner's, 1995.
Horrocks, Roger. *Masculinity in Crisis*. New York: St. Martin's, 1994.
Kimmel, Michael. *Manhood in America: A Cultural History*. New York: The Free P, 1996.

McCaffery, Larry, and Sinda Gregory, *Alive and Writing: Interviews with American Authors of the* 1980s. Chicago: U of Illinois P, 1987. 109–25.

Mulvey, Laura, "Visual Pleasure and Narrative Cinema." In *Feminism and Film Theory*, ed. Constance Penley. New York: Routledge, 1988. 57–68.

Schwenger, Peter. *Phallic Critiques.* Boston: Routledge & Kegan Paul, 1984.

Seib, Kenneth. " 'Sabers, Gentlemen, Sabers': The J. E. B. Stuart Stories of Barry Hannah." *Mississippi Quarterly* 45.1 (winter 1991–92): 41–52.

Weston, Ruth D. *Barry Hannah: Postmodern Romantic.* Baton Rouge: Louisiana State UP, 1998.

Williams, Daniel E. "Interview with Barry Hannah: February 6, 2001," in *Mississippi Quarterly* 54.2 (spring 2001): 261–68.

The Shade of Faulkner's Horse

Cavalier Heroism and Archetypal Immortality in Barry Hannah's Postmodern South

—*James B. Potts III*

In "The Future of Southern Writing," the closing essay in the *History of Southern Literature* (1985), Donald Noble declared the question of whether a unique southern literature still existed "shopworn," and directed critical attentions to finer definitional concerns. Yet Noble also ventured the opinion that the distinctive qualities of southern life and literature "will be a very long time in the erasing" (578). In the twenty years since Noble's essay appeared, southern male writers have demonstrated a marked continuity with their forebears. This continuity is especially apparent in the ubiquitous use by contemporary southern male writers of seemingly anachronistic images of the horse and horse soldier. In both the high modernist novels of the Southern Renaissance and recent southern fiction such as Charles Frazier's enormously popular *Cold Mountain* (1997), Cormac McCarthy's "westerns" of the 1980s and 1990s, and Barry Hannah's *Airships* (1978) and *Ray* (1980), the horse and the horse soldier still embody myths of creativity, purity, even immortality.

Near the height of the Southern Renaissance, before "cavalier myth" became a trite phrase, Allen Tate's *The Fathers* (1938) helped make the South's most cherished icons, the old Colonel and his cavalier soldier, into images of deluded nobility leading the region blindly to catastrophe. The cavalry soldier in the South once carried with him all the mythos of man elevated to horsebound nobility, but over time he has become the icon of an ideologically flawed Light Brigade, a doomed romantic fool. In *The Fathers*, Tate employs the figure to demonstrate cataclysmic disorder and change in the Civil War South. Michael Kreyling has observed that, in traditional readings of *The Fathers*, the "modern" hero George Posey is said to symbolize the "proto-capitalist" and "machine-age man", as opposed to Major Buchan, who serves as "the civilized man of doomed tradition" (200–203). Posey first appears in the novel riding a horse that he has purchased by selling an intelligent Virginia slave for brutal field labor in Mississippi. Major Buchan represents the old order, but he bears the title of Major only by "grace of the county militia that had not fought since 1812" (Tate 11). Yet Buchan had been a fine horseman in his youth and might even have qualified as "Master of the Horse." The narrator, Lacy Buchan, makes it seem that his father failed to consolidate the aristocratic image because he was "perversely democratic" (11). Still, the Buchans are associated with the lingering icons of chivalric idealism, and they at first demand observance of its rituals. Posey rises to respectability first by buying a worthy horse, then by mimicking battle in a ritual game. The Buchans barely deign to notice him until he wins a mock knight's tournament, without jousting but complete with lances and rings and a Parade of Chivalry to celebrate the "manly arts of Nimrod and Mars" (62–64). However, Posey soon chafes at the demands of such anachronistic behavior. When Margaret wants him to court Papa Buchan's permission for them to marry, Posey says, "No, damn it," and gives in only so far as to present the marriage to Buchan as an inevitability that does not require his blessing. When John Langton drunkenly demands a duel, Posey demonstrates contempt for the etiquette of code duello by cold-cocking Langton and walking away. By contrast, Major Buchan's traditions and mythology accentuate Posey's rationalism. The Buchans worry whether he will ever be "an elegant gentleman"—the essential goal of all this rigid ritual (23). Because definitions of status and masculinity hinge upon the sale of a slave and participation in an archaic tournament, Tate exposes the tarnished vision of the Old South tradition. The narration relies upon the tension created by Lacy's suspended understanding of the true nature of Posey: he is not merely the "horseman riding off over the precipice" into stoic annihilation, but also the harbinger of modernity. Lacy, however, learns this only gradually (179). Tate's novel uses the Buchan family's crisis to demonstrate a gradual unraveling of the core myths of the South itself, and the dominant impression is of the (final) hurrah heard as the horseman rides over a cliff. It is as if the Buchan's fantasies have been decoded and reduced, so they may now be dispensed with.

On a greater scale, William Faulkner also employs the horse as an embodiment of dreams of nobility, as a measure of manhood, and as a wedge between the past and the present generations. As John Flanagan explains, the classic mythos of the mounted man retained strength even into the early twentieth-century South. The power that accrued to man when he mounted a horse in myth led Bellerephon to think himself a demi-god ready for Mount Olympus; to medieval men it represented potential knighthood; to Faulkner's farm boys it represents "power and wealth" (Flanagan 137–39). But where Lacy Buchan's conception of the horse rider Posey is in the high-tragic mode, Faulkner's "Spotted Horses" ridicules the "puerile folly of the farm boys longing to buy mounts they cannot control" (Rankin 143). And yet, as Thomas L. McHaney points out, when a character's ambition or creative impulse contends against the sort of domesticizing compromises most men make to ordinary living as they mature, Faulkner's fictional horses often serve as icons of that drive or impulse. Faulkner's own struggles to form an artistic vision found him caught between the romanticism of his youth and "post-war nihilism"; tensions between idealism and mature acceptance of a lesser world in his art often involve horses as symbolic images of a pure ideal (McHaney 72). Even the humorous treatment in "Spotted Horses" of the wild horse's chaotic flight intimates a sense of the unpredictable, innumerable, virtually uncontainable meanings of this archetypal figure that men—and poets—wish to ride, tame, and master. Ultimately, then, Faulkner's horses represent much more than an anachronistic vision of the Old South; to master the horse requires more power over natural forces, more primal strength, than Faulkner usually grants to ordinary men.

Even when Faulkner treats the myth that he and Tate inherited from their southern forebears most conventionally, Faulkner uses his horse-soldiers to suggest other complexities deep in the (white) southern psyche. In *Flags in the Dust* (the uncut version of *Sartoris*, first published in 1973),

Bayard Sartoris accompanies the fabled Confederate cavalry commander J. E. B. Stuart on his invasion of Union general Pope's private commissary tent. Living out the fantasy of the cavalier soldier, they are superhuman amongst mortal men. In this inner sanctum of the enemy, a coffee pot is shot out of Bayard's hand, but Stuart remains unhurried, maintaining his courteous tone to a captured officer: "Be pleased to mount, sir." As she narrates the fabled raid, Aunt Jenny refers to Stuart as a "consuming flame" and to his flowing locks as "gallant flames" (*Flags* 18). Bayard captures a horse and swings on top of the "splendidly uncontrollable" animal with a coat like "quivering tongues of flame" as it takes off, "unfolding like bronze wings" (140). The use of fire as a symbolic representation of a deity predates Judaeo-Christian rhetoric, but Faulkner certainly would have been familiar with the religious connotations of his language: employing expressions like "consuming fire" and "tongues of fire," he appropriates images of divine visitation and holy ecstasy (see for example Deut. 4:24, Acts 2:4). Hence, for all that Faulkner's tales imply that the cavalier and his horse are important to an understanding of the South, his images also probe into that deeper consciousness where religious ecstasy resides. The southern cavalier astride his horse comes to symbolize a broader human desire for the sacred and for immortality.

Stuart's horsemen press the point of their own mortality: they are deluded about their cause and their invincibility. Aunt Jenny's narrative implies that Stuart's raid comes from his whimsical desire to steal the Yankee's stock of "anchovies"; significantly, the captured Yankee officer tells him that anchovies are an "anachronism," like "gentlemen" in war (*Flags* 21). Displaced in time, shielded by their cloak of delusion, they seem invulnerable because of a quaint certainty that courage alone will deliver them. After World War I, a descendant also named Bayard Sartoris becomes addicted to this myth. Tate's famous observation in "Remarks on the Southern Religion" that "the modern mind sees only half the horse" when it is confronted by mechanized horse*power*, is useful here ("Remarks" 157). Because cavalry charges are no longer available to serve his romantic death wish, Bayard substitutes the horse with horsepower by driving an automobile to its limit; however, he appears less heroic than foolish, even debased, for doing so (107). Nor can Bayard resist trying to ride one of the spotted wild horses, despite onlookers warning that it will kill him. McCallum suspects that Bayard has an equine fixation and a death wish: "that's what he wants" (139). Certainly the Sartoris line passes down a conception of horses with names and powers out of mythology—such as the clan patriarch's horse, Jupiter. In his turn, Bayard feels an affinity for the "whole horse" (Tate, "Remarks," 156), an association between horses, mortal risk and immortality that gives them a larger meaning for him than they have for the farm boys in "Spotted Horses." In other words, Bayard teases death in order to regain not merely the legacy of Confederate chivalry, but mankind's lost Olympian status.

The meaning of the horse to the cavalier in fiction becomes even clearer when the horse and the man are again separate. When not degraded by human foolishness, horses in Faulkner's work often symbolize sex and masculinity, death and immortality, creativity and divinity. Much of the psychological or archetypal significance imputed to horse visions derives from Carl Jung. According to Jung, at unconscious levels even those primal forces that seem to oppose one another are united in visions of horses and other archetypal images. Moreover, the longing for resolution of such oppositions is crucial to integration of the personality, to "a unification of primal psychic opposites: male/female, living/dead, spirit/soul, hot/cold" (Smith 111). In *Modern Man in Search of a Soul* (1933), Jung theorizes that in some dreams the symbols for "horse" and "mother" are equivalent, standing for creativity and the life instinct, and involving some "hidden, nature-bound life of the body" (24). The horse image has sexual connotations because it represents the lower part of the body and the drives that rise there; "moreover . . . it carries one away like a surge of instinct" (24). The horse especially "represents the non-human psyche, the non-human, animal side and therefore the unconscious. This is why the horse in folktales sometimes sees visions, hears voices, and speaks" (24). These internal strivings—between sexual desire and a longing to be "carried away," for control over natural forces, for the will to create, and even within a quasi-religious longing for transcendent immortality—emerge in Faulkner's work as he describes horsemen who want to touch greatness despite their humble origins.

Although Faulkner clearly saw the humor in the mythmaking propensities of southern white men, he nevertheless treats their powerful longing to be something grander than they are, to make something more meaningful of their world, with respect bordering upon reverence. When the impoverished farm boy Jewel Bundren buys a wild horse from Lon Quick in *As I Lay Dying* (1930), the intensity of his desire and the magnificence of the struggle seem to amount to more than the "puerile folly" that Elizabeth Rankin identifies in the farm boys of "Spotted Horses." Faulkner's language in *As I Lay Dying* evokes the mystical realm of sacred fire; Jewel's brother Darl describes the horse's coat as "bunching, swirling like so many flames" (*As I Lay Dying* 9). Darl sees Jewel's frantic struggle to master the horse as one of titanic proportions: "they are like two figures carved for a tableau savage in the sun" (9). Jewel desperately but eagerly tries to contain the horse as the embodiment of his elusive dreams and amid a cluster of suggestive images. Later in the narrative, there is again an "illusion of wings" (as Darl describes it) when Jewel once again tries to mount the horse (9). For Jewel, the horse invokes not only the fantasy of "mobility," but also his deepest desires—for erotic experience, for freedom and for transcendence. By contrast, Jewel's family senses in the frantic struggle something inappropriate because it seems incompatible with the presence of death, and because it is sexual. They see the horse come "kittenish and alert" (9) when Jewel whistles, and this seems all the more offensive because his mother Addie's corpse is nearby, "not cold in her coffin yet" (68) as Anse puts it. In Jungian terms, Anse responds here to the horse's suggestion of desire: he is shocked because Jewel has brought such a powerful symbol of the sexual drive before them in the presence of the mother, which is already improper, and which seems particularly inappropriate during the family's mourning for Addie's death. Moreover, the possibility that the horse serves in some way as a substitute for Addie may occur to Anse, as it clearly does to Darl, who notes that now "Jewel's mother is a horse" (61). From a Jungian perspective, then, the mother's body, death, Jewel's desire for adulthood—and hence escape from his parents—and most importantly, the realm of sacredness all merge in language about Jewel's horse.

Perhaps most vivid of all of Faulkner's evocative "horse passages" is the poetic vignette "Carcasonne," which McHaney calls a "parable of creativity" in which Faulkner merges the multiple meanings of the archetype (McHaney 78). As with other equine references in Faulkner's fiction, the language used to describe the horse is vaguely sexual: there are references to the "taut roundness of its belly" and the horse's legs "rhythmically reaching and overreaching." More than that, though, this dream sequence, like other passages in Faulkner's fiction, melds sexual referent and religious ecstatic language: the animal gallops "with its tangled welter of tossing flames" (*Collected Stories* 896). Ultimately, "Carcassonne" evokes immortality and the Godhead. The horse is undying; it reminds the dreamer of "that rider-less Norman steed which galloped against the Saracen emir," and even when severed in two "thundered on through the assembled foes of our meek Lord . . . not knowing it was dead" (896). Contrasted with wood and bones, the horse embodies dynamic, transcendent forces; it calls together fleeting images of battles, sex, death, and resurrection as constituent parts of the act of creation.

Faulkner seems to call out to the freedom of this innate unconscious realm to give his art eternal life. The creative voice in "Carcassone" speaks of its bed as spectacles "pinned to the deep bosom of the mother of dreams" (895). He does so because, in the end, the only immortality he proposes is within the memories of the living, or the memory of all living: the collective unconscious. The narrator's desired immersion in the "deep bosom of the mother of dreams" implies faith in the creativity of the unconscious in much the way Jung describes it: "the psychic depths are nature and nature is creative life" (*Four Archetypes* 215). Faulkner suggests this image of the creative spirit against the silent void of death: "Steed and rider . . . thundered punily diminishing, a dying star against the immensity of darkness and of silence within which, steadfast, fading, deep-breasted and grave of flank, mused the dark and tragic figure of the Earth, his mother" (*Collected Stories* 900). The human longing to endure, like the horse that gallops on to victory after the rider is dead, takes the form of art so powerful that it might affect, and survive within, the collective unconscious.

I do not suggest that these are the only meanings of Faulkner's ubiquitous horses. John M. Howell says that Faulkner's horses symbolize "the male principle . . . the life force, mana, and sexual abnormality" (213), while McHaney identifies Faulkner's horses with idealism, creativity and sexual desire (84–85). Others would no doubt add to the list, and Faulkner's variety is not easily containable, particularly in an image he used so widely. But clearly, in Faulkner's work, the more static perception of the horse and horse soldier as an embodiment of southern (white) male "gallantry" in a changing social and cultural order became a more fluid, sometimes contradictory, and multiplying vision. Usually the potent, intense, dynamic of Faulkner's texts suggests primitive psychic forces; the dominant impression is the proximity of chaos rather than the gradual decay of social and cultural order seen in *The Fathers*. In particular, the equine image represents a sexual instinct, a life-instinct as well as a death-instinct, a longing for immortality, and a need for individuation that is crucial to creativity. The achievement of this irreducible imagery reflects Faulkner's mastery of a "dialogic" fiction that maintains multiple tensions (Gray 12); indeed, Faulkner's fiction is at its best when "it is never this or that, but this *and* that" (Jung, *Modern Man* 21).

I have argued that Faulkner's images—and especially his equine images—probe into subconscious chaos for wisdom. I now want to demonstrate that the legacy of this "*tableau sauvage*" has continued into distinctively masculine southern literature long after horses have left the streets and battlefields, long after the end of the Southern Renascence, and long after they have largely disappeared from other literature. In particular, this Faulknerian legacy endures in the fiction of Barry Hannah.

Surely it is peculiar that certain archetypes persist in the work of the major figures of contemporary southern literature. It may be that, despite the huge popular success of *Cold Mountain*, Charles Frazier's reputation has not yet established him as a major contemporary southern writer, but both Cormac McCarthy and Barry Hannah seem at least tentatively canonized, and their work features vivid scenes with horses, rich with suggested symbolic content. In particular the shade of Faulkner's horse and horse-soldier hang over Hannah's stories, which sometimes seem to take up where Aunt Jenny's storytelling left off in *Flags in the Dust*. At the core of Hannah's texts are men from Mississippi and Alabama who behave like remnants of a warrior cult as they struggle to come to terms with primitive impulses toward sex and violence that have been the traditional modes of definition for southern white men. As Ruth Weston has noted, Hannah's stories describe "symptoms of a contemporary and particularly masculine disease" (Weston 412). Of the religious and cultural myths that once contributed so much to definitions of southern (white) masculinity, Hannah says he proceeds from the premise "that there has been a great lie to me, from the word 'go,'" and that he contends against the "whole lying opera of it" (Weston 411). Hannah's contemporary protagonists attempt to reconfigure a sense of self despite the heavy and omnipresent burden of southern history and myth. Hannah's stories are loosely tied together by the theme of reincarnation as present-day warriors relive the tribulations of their ancestors, but with a heightened sense of betrayal by their own generation—a generation that has become indifferent along the way to their ancestors' sacrifice and to grandeur (Noble 579).

Accordingly, Hannah's stories also revise the cavalier myth, but they do so in postmodern ways that consistently defy reduction. Weston notes that Hannah's fiction debunks "the unitary self and story," while Allen Shepherd observes that it shatters moral and cultural expectations by positing a "final meltdown of values" (38). As Weston observes, Hannah's heroes do not attain any religious expiation (426); and yet, despite the violence and profane language, Hannah's rhetorical flourishes sometimes still appropriate the language of the sacred. To take a typical example, the beginning of *Power and Light* (1983) describes a waterfall as "holy" and as a "glorious pulpit of rocks" (1). Such sacred language encouraged reviewer Terence Rafferty to describe Hannah's "almost mystical belief in the manipulation of language—as if exact combinations of words and images will induce visions, like a prayer" (qtd. in Weston 426). However, it may be more plausible to say that Hannah's fiction exhibits a love for words without assuming or asserting that words contain certainty or wisdom. Instead, Hannah's language subtly gestures toward elusive and subliminal visions of truth that mankind usually struggles to perceive, much less interpret.

At the heart of these visions are the same memories of battles and horsemen that appear in Faulkner. As Martyn Bone observes in the essay that follows, Hannah's early short story collection, *Airships*, contains a core of cavalrymen tales featuring Jeb Stuart that seem to be responses to scenes in *Flags in the Dust*, especially the "anchovy raid." Another such response is the grim "Bats Out Of Hell Division"—from Hannah's later volume *Bats Out of Hell* (1993)—in which ghostly, emaciated Confederates troops throw themselves against the well-fed Union soldiers to the strains of Tchaikovsky until the Union commander can stand it no longer and surrenders. Partially, these visions are important because they make nonchalant gallantry (despite suicidal odds) the nearest approximation to transcendent heroism and an extension of the cavalier ideal. Like Stuart's battlefield manners in Aunt Jenny's tales, they can only be fantasies. At the story's end, the victorious "specters" feast upon oysters from the Union army's stores—as an unlikely and perishable delicacy, the oysters recall the anchovies in Aunt Jenny's account of Stuart's raid of the Union camp. Hannah's burlesque of the southern fantasy of war by bravado alone and its grand, semi-religious rhetoric is evident in the exultant cry of the Confederate division's general: "Thought I'd never live to see it! There *is* a God, and God is love. . . . Brother against brother! Can Providence truly be this good?" (*Bats* 45).

But though Hannah undermines the cavalry myth in many ways, the southern tradition of valor alongside honor at arms still resonates throughout his stories. Like Faulkner, he is not simply mocking the romantic illusions of the Old South. Stuart may be flawed, but one cavalryman who follows the charismatic and fearless Stuart, Corporal Deed Ainsworth, declares in the story "Knowing He Was Not My Kind Yet I Followed" that the world is diminished without him: "This earth will never see his like again" (*Airships*, 55). In another story from *Airships*, "Dragged Fighting from His Tomb," Captain Howard came into the war with visions of honor that he is loath to sully. His idealism emerges in his reverence for horses. He praises his horse Black Answer, which dies in battle but retains its "deliberate and pure expression . . . even in death" (52). He contrasts the purity of his horses with humans who accept compromise and corruption. He is disillusioned that the Confederates have diluted their moral claim of self-defense by invading Pennsylvania; however, his political concerns are ultimately subordinate to an amorphous longing for cavalier adventure and to his anger over the killing of horses. After recounting how he killed Stuart in a moment of disillusionment, Howard adds flippantly: "Then Booth shot Lincoln, issuing in the graft of the Grant administration" (*Airships* 59). Ultimately, it is the inadequacy of human reality, not the surrender of his ideals, which causes Howard's existential crisis.

Hannah revises the cavalier myth with both humor and grandeur, offering vivid images of comedy, mystery, and terror as he resituates the southern horse-soldier in the Vietnam war. "In Testimony of Pilot," the unusual hero Quadberry achieves his first ambivalent glory as a high school saxophone player when he leads the band at a competition after the sudden, traumatic death of the band director. Standing ready to lead the band's figurative charge, Quadberry responds to the order of the judges: "Quadberry's hand was instantly up in the air, his fingers hard as if around something something like a torch" (*Airships* 28). The narrator fails here to see Quadberry's imaginary saber, but as the narrative proceeds Quadberry more clearly becomes the reincarnated horse-soldier. He goes to war against the Viet Cong from the flight deck of the U.S.S. *Bonhomme Richard* having sent home by telegram his own surreal update of the fanatical soldier's rhetoric: "I am a dragon. America the Beautiful like you will never know" (37). This modern cavalier barely escapes drowning when his Phantom jet flames out at the edge of the aircraft carrier; sinking in the green water, looking up at the surface illuminated by the ship's lights, Quadberry waits for his rebirth—a nightmare out of primal consciousness. Ejecting from the submerged plane, "he woke up ten feet under the surface swimming against an almost overwhelming body of underwater parachute" (41). Despite America's growing cynicism about the war in Vietnam, Quadberry's bravado is not ironic or self-aware: his purity as a soldier is not mixed with cynicism and, like Bayard, he is not in control of the glory he courts.

The running theme of men trying to understand themselves through their history as soldiers pervades other Hannah texts. Perhaps most notably, the short novel *Ray* follows in the vein of the stories in *Airships* by featuring further reminiscences from Confederate cavalry raids spliced into a fragmented text—the first-person narrative of Ray Forrest. Ray's friend Charlie Desoto also seeks to find himself in his spiritual ancestor, Hernando de Soto, by reading Rangel's original expedition diaries. Charlie thus learns that the conquistadors' explorations were full of slaughter and death, and that his home city, Tuscaloosa, is built upon the graves of the original natives (*Ray* 14). Yet despite reading about the senseless killings, Charlie wonders obtusely, "[w]hat was the *it* that fellow [Rangel] was talking about he said he couldn't take any more of?" (15). It is, of course, death and death-seeking, and, unlike Charlie, Ray seems to know this, as if he and Rangel are the reincarnations of earlier soldiers from bloody campaigns. Ray, who bears the surname of another of the South's most famous cavalrymen, Nathan Bedford Forrest, is driven by the same demons of the warrior cult that made this history of carnage a part of the southern inheritance.

Ray's friendship with Charlie is largely based upon their shared warrior experience, and their obsession with the past; Ray too, looks into the past for "my best mind" (95). However, Ray's engagement and obsession with the past goes much farther than Charlie's; he has "memories" of his earlier incarnations. Between his flights in Learjets and performing surgery, he drifts into recollections of past cavalry raids with Stuart:

> We wear gray in the big meadow and there are three thousand enemy in blue, much cannon and machinery behind them. The shadow of the valley passes over our eyes, and in the ridge of the mountains we see the white clouds as Christ's open chest. Many of us start weeping and smiling because we will die and we know. Last week we thought we were immortal. (65)

In Ray's vision the cavalrymen's charge and the grimly pyrrhic quality of this charge makes up part of the demands of manhood, an insistence that no matter how near death looms, one must keep his "saber up" (109). For Ray, contemporary life as an American male reflects an inherent, relentless contradiction between obligations to "gentleness and rage together" that Americans must "learn to live with" (51). Ray's internal struggle for individuation is terribly harsh: on the one hand he misunderstands *eros* and interaction with women, which he reduces to "fucking," and on the other hand he is drawn to *thanatos*-slaughter. In his chaos, there is little in between.

In Ray's dizzying world, juxtapositions of "gentleness and rage"—love and violence—do not so much express the emergence of ecstatic, revelatory peaks in language as comprise the entire surface of his narrative. In another of his battle reveries, Ray relives his own swaggering panache during an intercom conversation with a Vietnamese pilot conversant in English: "I want to know your name and how old before I kill you" (63). Ray's conversations with the enemy recall the performance of poise under pressure by Stuart and Bayard according to Aunt Jenny's account in *Flags in the Dust*, and by Stuart and Captain Howard in "Dragged Fighting From

His Tomb." But in the stillness after the battle, Ray muses more circumspectly: "It's so easy to kill. Saw him make the big white flower. It's so fucking hard to live." Ray discerns the terrible truth of his many reincarnations as a killer: "It was the start of what I've got, and no nooky, no poem and no medicine or nothing will make it go away. Jesus, my head!" (64).

Ray finally turns to art in order to create something enduring: he becomes a poet. The sensory overload and the verbal assault of his narrative maintain the proximity of death and sex, of lust and immortality, so insistently that examples are not difficult to find. Ray's icon of individuated artistic maturity is divided between a local woman, Sister, and her father, Mr. Hooch. Sister is not quite the "incestual sister" vision associated by Jung with a developing creative personality, but she might as well be; Ray calls to her, "My heart, my desire. Sister!" (5). He reveres Mr. Hooch, a man of "pornography, medicine and the love of art—which is Mr. Hooch's poems" (94). Ray's interior dialogue (with his own multiple selves) reveals his frustrated longing to become a poet; his growth as a poet follows Sister's death and his participation in Hooch's recovery. Ultimately art and memory immortalize Sister. Ray recites Hooch's poem about the death of his promiscuous but beloved daughter: "and when I put my ear to the grass/I can hear her, I can hear her, I can hear her/And when I stand up I am dirty in my veins." Ray confesses that "I was humiliated in his poetry. I had to go to the bathroom to cry loud" (110). Hooch and Sister represent the most incontestably positive influence in Ray's fractious life. With their help, he grows poetically and personally, developing his own clumsy but more humane poetry even as he concludes the narrative with an exclamation of his residual feeling for the traditional military bravado of white southern masculinity: "Sabers, gentlemen, sabers!" (113).

Of all Hannah's stories to date, "Dragged Fighting From His Tomb" makes the most of the horse as a significant image from deeper consciousness. At the start of the story, Captain Howard thinks he has been mortally wounded in the neck during a battle at Two Roads Junction in Pennsylvania; however, his horse, Mount Auburn, carries him away, semi-conscious, to survive. The story then proceeds to a cavalry scene in which Howard charges on horseback right into the enemy commander's tent while firing pistols with both hands. With cavalier gamesmanship, he demands "wisdom" at the point of a gun from a frightened, unarmed Union soldier. The aged Yankee sputters: "We're not simple animals. There's a god in every one of us. . . . My mouth can't do it. But there's something here." Howard dismisses the answer as inadequate, as maundering towards subjective "beliefs" rather than the essential "truth" he has demanded. Finally, the old man offers an observation that that Howard accepts: "There is no wisdom, Johnny Reb. There's only tomorrow if you're lucky" (53, 55). Meanwhile a couple copulates under the commander's desk, and a man who looks like Howard dies nearby (55). Here we see human longing to defuse the fear of death, that unknown realm beyond human experience, by entering into a religious eternity or by the reproductive act. For Howard, the sight of his double dying nearby makes the conflict that much more pressing. Hannah thus mingles sex, death, immortality and the longing for a deity in a scene which, significantly, is presided over by a cavalier and his vehicle into Olympus, the horse.

"Dragged Fighting from His Tomb" is also the Hannah work most reminiscent of "Carcassonne." It has Howard carried beyond his expectation of death by a great warhorse (Black Answer) that, like the mythic horse in Faulkner's story, was cut in two during battle and replaced by an equally great horse with identical qualities (Mount Auburn). Howard suggests that Black Answer shared his own bemusement at petty men playing at war. Indeed, Howard repeatedly associates horses with a higher ideal, and he alludes approvingly to the intellectual Houyhnhnms in Jonathan Swift's *Gulliver's Travels* (1726). According to Howard, humans are a "bog and labyrinth . . . overbrained and overemotioned"; compared to horses, they are "a dizzy and smelly farce" (53). Howard's reverence for horses elicits praise for Black Answer in particular: "What a deliberate and pure expression Black Answer retained, even in death" (53). By contrast, a man "even inspired by death . . . simply foams and is addled like a crab" (53). Howard also has a special relationship with Mount Auburn, and represents this second magnificent horse as a paragon of pure, fearless perfection. All told, Howard's beloved horses create a powerful, masculine, and radically *physical* presence; they are not cheapened as their human counterparts are by the phony rhetoric of confused "beliefs."

In Howard's narrative, the mysteries of love, death and immortality are also embodied in the purity of horses. It is the death of Black Answer that first infuriates him "about the war" (55), and when a frightened Union soldier fires a bullet into Mount Auburn, the furious Howard "overmurders" him. Ultimately, Howard defects-and kills his own commander, Stuart, not because he questions the invasion of the North ("You shit! What are we doing killing people in Pennsylvania?"), but because of Stuart's intolerable advice after Black Answer's death: "Use your weeping on people, not on animals" (58). At the end of the story, the aged Howard takes the "grandchild" of his beloved horse for a ride. Howard's last attempt to unify his ideals atop the running pony again both recalls the fluidity of the Jungian archetype and evokes the ultimate Christian icon of purity and redemption for man's depravity: "The beauty I sat on ran to the verge of his heartburst. I had never given the horse a name. I suppose I was waiting for him to say what he wanted, to talk. But Christ is his name, this muscle and heart striding under me" (60). In "Dragged Fighting From His Tomb," Hannah's cavalier and especially his horses mutate from Faulkner's in a postmodern meltdown; whether this is a response to Faulkner specifically or to now-embedded southern mythology hardly seems to matter. Yet Hannah's rhetoric still echoes the language of sacredness and mystery, of idealism merged with sensuality, that Faulkner articulated in "Carcassonne." Although Hannah's story is not ostensibly a "parable of creativity," it demonstrates a familiar philosophical perspective on time, manhood, and the virtual immortality of the pure ideal.

As we have seen, the desire for transcendence that drives mythology and that gives rise to archetypes still exists in the late twentieth-century southern literature of Barry Hannah; it can also be found in the work of Charles Frazier and Cormac McCarthy. However, a nearly opposite trend drives what has been called "postsouthern" fiction. At least since the deaths of Walker Percy and Peter Taylor, with the resulting disappearance of the last vestiges of the gentleman's class (and arguably even of a middle class) among contemporary southern writers, formerly pervasive ideals of glory, glamour and *gravitas* have receded from southern literature to be replaced by something not larger than life but smaller. In much contemporary southern fiction, myths have become reduced beyond the absurd to the merely contemptible; a poisonous and perverse vulgarity rules; and conceptions of how to achieve transcendence have become shriveled and deformed. In effect, while decrying the "nostalgia" of the southern past, the postsouthern directs attention away from the idealized best to the realized worst. The magnificent intensity of southern literature, of the *tableau sauvage* between desire and the reality principle, seems to have dissipated in favor of cartoonish reductions.

With few exceptions, this leaves the type of redneck grotesques drawn by Harry Crews and Larry Brown alone on the center stage of contemporary (post)southern fiction. In Crews's *A Feast of Snakes* (1973), the desperation of poor whites explodes: the father, Big Joe Mackey, kicks his pit bull to death after it has been beaten in a dogfight; the son, Joe Lon, unloads his shotgun into festival-goers at a rattlesnake roundup. All but the most desperate classes are absent. Crews's defenders would no doubt argue that Joe Lon is driven by a desperate passion and brooding horror not entirely different from any number of Faulkner characters; similarly, Larry Brown's champions might argue that the alcoholic underclass that populates his fiction embodies a stoic humor and endurance that Faulkner might have admired. But the major effect of this trend in contemporary southern fiction has been to redirect attention from the highways that all humanity travels to a few oddballs huddled in abandoned alleys. In such fiction, the postsouthern has come to stand for the ascendancy of—to cite McCarthy's memorable passage in *Suttree* (1977)—"thieves, derelicts, miscreants, pariahs, poltroons, spalpeens, curmudgeons, clotpolls, murderers, gamblers, bawds, whores, trulls, brigands, topers, tosspots, sots and archsots, lobcocks, smellsmocks, runagates, rakes, and other assorted and felonious debauchees" (457).

Of the living southern writers who might hope to escape the boundaries of local color to attain canonical stature, even McCarthy has focused upon the dregs of humanity; however, he elevates their stature through powerful rhetoric so that they appear as harbingers of an apocalypse. Tellingly, McCarthy's horses are, like Hannah's, archetypally associated with immortality—wandering through abandoned temples, drifting through dreams, they often appear at moments in his fiction where a world of the dead confronts the world of the living. Yet even McCarthy's latest Texas border story, *No Country for Old Men* (2005), seems scaled back; it has neither graverobbing child-eaters nor necrophiliac serial killers nor marauding scalphunters. Here, the suggestion that the apocalypse is at hand comes mostly from the shocked local sheriffs who register their helplessness against the cross-border drug trade. Its cold-blooded killer Anton Chigurh, the text's offering as a "true and living prophet of destruction," seems paltry next to *Blood Meridian*'s Judge Holden. One of the sheriffs muses that the trouble with the contemporary generation is not just that criminals have descended to the point of selling drugs to schoolchildren, but that "[s]choolkids buy it" (194). But for McCarthy, narrating the miseries and minor triumphs of ordinary, impoverished postsouthern outcasts is inadequate; as such, each of his novels up to and including *No Country for Old Men* also muses upon the relationship between God and man. In the current crisis, one of the lawmen in *No Country for Old Men* claims, "nothin' short of the second coming of Christ can slow this train" (191, 157).

Like McCarthy's work, Hannah's fictions stage a contest between a desire for un-sentimentalized truth and an emotional longing for transcendence, for larger significance, which typically manifests itself in archetypal images and sacred language. Although Hannah has produced numerous short stories and novels where heroism and idealism were reflected in images from the mythology of the old South, his latest novel, *Yonder Stands Your Orphan* (2001), follows in the postsouthern direction. The central evil seems to be the malevolent narcissism of Man Mortimer, a sadistic procurer who produces child pornography that will be sold from under shop counters, but the entire surrounding culture creates a place for him. Mortimer's name suggests death by sea or by mother (98): significantly, either form of death is a reflection of the archetypal drowning in/of narcissism. Having narrated a shift from the archetypal horse via the tank to the fighter jet in his previous works, Hannah suggests a further decline in the myth of cavalier heroism in *Yonder*: Mortimer cruising in his yellow Lexus "pimp-mobile," the old misanthropist Sidney Farté cavorting with teenage girls on the back seat. Hannah makes the contrast between his earlier neo-cavalier southern protagonists and modern Man more evident when he explicitly compares Mortimer's Lincoln Navigator to the fighting vehicles of Desert Storm (62). Similarly, the cavalier's sword is replaced by the pimp's knife and sword collection, and the local area around Eagle Lake has gone over to "Cash for Your Title civilization and pawnshop villages" (117). Nearly all the other characters are aging failures. All told, it is a paltry plague and a tinpot anti-Christ that devours contemporary Mississippi in *Yonder Stands Your Orphan*. Both Good and Evil seem to have been debased, stripped of mythic grandeur.

And yet, although the horses are gone, questions of transcendence, heroism, religion and immortality still lurk in Hannah's texts—even in *Yonder Stands Your Orphan*. In an interview with Dan Williams published in 2001, Hannah identified the backwoods church as the "hero" of the novel, apparently because it is the only locus of idealism or even good will (Williams 262). Ultimately, the motley congregation, despite the foul chaos around them, continues to act hopefully and to maintain faith. Hence the possibility of redemption may yet persist, albeit only in small doses. Interestingly—and though it probably comes as a shock to most of his readers—Hannah has since written a preface to a new translation of the *New Testament's Book of Mark* in which he identifies without irony the heroic sufferings of Christ's apostles. It would seem that the demand for transcendence present in Hannah's early fiction has now found an outlet in his non-fiction. In "Christ in the Room," an essay published in 2005, Hannah insists that he is "still a hard-eyed realist," but that his antagonism to Christianity has dissolved due to a vision he had while critically ill in hospital (75). This may too cast a different light upon Reverend Egan's diatribe in *Yonder* against writers with no conception of Christ:

> Books are a very mortal sin. Books are not wrote by the Christly. I got no idea why a writer of a book should have respect. Or even the time of day, *unless he's a prophet* [italics mine]. It's a sign of our present-day hell. Books, think about it, the writer of a book does envy, sloth, gluttony, lust, larceny, greed, or what? Oh, vanity. He don't miss a single one of them. He is a Peeping Tom, an onanist, a busybody, and he's faking humility every one of God's minutes. (73)

Faulkner's writing throughout his career was consistently concerned with how a man might endure or even transcend everyday life, and with what might invest life with meaning. Ultimately, Hannah's engagement with archetypal immortality operates in a similar mode. It is inevitable that, now that the South's rural isolation has diminished and the scars of the Civil War have largely disappeared, the region's literature will track the new social reality of suburbia and find some new postsouthern identity. However, we are only at the threshold of a new dispensation in the South.

For now, if the mythical idea of archetypal immortality stubbornly persists in cultural memory, then it might yet be taken as a sign that the human longing for transcendence survives too. The shade of Faulkner's horse in Hannah's fiction indicates that, though the forefathers' mythic outlook has dimmed, it still haunts the postsouthern world.

Works Cited

Faulkner, William. *As I Lay Dying*. 1930. New York: Random House, 1964.

———. *Collected Stories of William Faulkner*. 1950. New York: Vintage, 1971.

———. *Flags in the Dust*. New York: Random House, 1973.

Flanagan, John T. "The Mythic Background of Faulkner's Horse." *North Carolina Folklore Journal* 13.2 (1965): 134–45.

Frazier, Charles. *Cold Mountain*. New York: Atlantic Monthly P, 1997.

Gray, Richard. *William Faulkner: A Critical Biography*. Cambridge: Blackwell, 1994.

Hamblin, Robert W. "Saying No to Death: Toward William Faulkner's Theory of Fiction." *A Cosmos of My Own: Faulkner and Yoknapatawpha, 1980*. Ed. Ann J. Abadie and Doreen Fowler. Jackson: UP of Mississippi, *1981*. 3–35.

Hannah, Barry. *Airships*. New York: Delta/Dell. 1979.

———. *Bats Out of Hell*. Boston: Houghton, 1993.

———. "Christ in the Room." *Oxford American* (winter 2005) 70–75.

———. *Power and Light*. Jackson, MS: Paleamon P, 1983.

———. *Ray*. New York: Knopf, 1980.

———. *Yonder Stands Your Orphan*. New York: Grove P, 2001.

Howell, John M. "Faulkner, Prufrock and Agammemnon: Horses, Hell and High Water." *Faulkner; the Unappeased Imagination: A Collection of Critical Essays*. Ed. Glenn O. Carey. Troy, NY: Whitson, 1980. 213–59.

Jung, Carl. *Four Archetypes: The Collected Works of C. G Jung*. Vol. 9. Bollingen Series. Princeton: Princeton UP, 1959.

———. *Modern Man in Search of a Soul*. New York: Harcourt, 1933.

Kreyling, Michael. "*The Fathers*: A Postsouthern Narrative Reading." *Southern Literature and Literary Theory*. Ed. Jefferson Humphries. Athens: U Georgia P, 1990. 186–205.

McHaney, Thomas L. "The Development of Faulkner's Idealism: Hands, Horses and Whores." *Faulkner and Idealism: Perspectives From Paris*. Ed. Michel Gresset and Patrick Samway, SJ. Jackson: UP of Mississippi, 1983. 71–85.

Noble, Donald R. "The Future of Southern Writing." *The History of Southern Literature*. Ed. Louis D. Rubin, Jr. Baton Rouge: Louisiana State UP, 1985. 578–88.

Rankin, Elizabeth D. "Chasing Spotted Horses: The Quest for Human Dignity in Faulkner's Snopes Trilogy." *Faulkner, the Unappeased Imagination: A Collection of Critical Essays*. Ed. Glenn O. Carey. Troy, NY: Whitson, 1980. 139–56.

Shepherd, Allen. "Firing Two Carbines, One in Each Hand." *Notes on Mississippi Writers* 21.1 (1989): 37–40.

Smith, Curtis D. *Jung's Quest for Wholeness: A Religious and Historical Perspective*. Albany: State U of New York P, 1990.

Tate, Allen. "Remarks on the Southern Religion." *In I'll Take My Stand: the South and the Agrarian Tradition*, by Twelve Southerners. 1930. Reprint, Baton Rouge, Louisiana State UP, 1977.

———. *The Fathers.* 1938. Baton Rouge: Louisiana State UP, 1977.

Weston, Ruth. "Debunking the Unitary Self and Story in the War Stories of Barry Hannah." *Southern Literary Journal* 27.2 (1995): 96–106.

———. "'The Whole Lying Opera Of It': Dreams, Lies and Confessions in the Fiction of Barry Hannah." *Mississippi Quarterly* 44.4 (1991): 411–38.

Neo-Confederate Narrative and Postsouthern Parody

Hannah and Faulkner

—*Martyn Bone*

According to Harold Bloom's renowned theory of literary influence, "latecomers" have forever fought futile Oedipal battles to overcome their poetic antecedents. As this "anxiety of influence" exacts its toll, so Bloom sees literary history as a (meta)narrative of decline from the English Renaissance via Romanticism to "further decline in its Modernist and post-Modernist heirs" (Bloom 10). Within the somewhat narrower confines of U.S. southern literary history, William Faulkner looms large as the local equivalent of Bloom's "Great Original." Some forty-five years ago, Flannery O'Connor famously figured Faulkner as "the Dixie Limited" bearing down upon the "mule and wagon" of every southern writer who followed him (O'Connor 45); more recently, southern literary critic Michael Kreyling has termed Faulkner "our 'Major Figure,' the Michelangelo around whose achievement a cultural identity can be organized" (*Inventing* xiv).

Barry Hannah has endured comparisons to Faulkner ever since he won the William Faulkner Award for his debut novel *Geronimo Rex* (1972). These comparisons increased after Hannah moved to Faulkner's hometown of Oxford in 1982 and settled there in 1984. Speaking at that year's "Faulkner and Yoknapatawpha" conference, Hannah pointedly distinguished between the writer he affectionately referred to as "Uncle Willy" and "the *name*

Faulkner ... the name used for everything to sell this and that for the Chamber of Commerce ... the local Snopes of lit and art and parasitic industries" ("Faulkner and the Small Man," 191–92). In interviews, including the one that concludes this book, Hannah has expressed his chagrin at "lazy" interviewers "asking me what it's like to be an heir to Faulkner, or what it's like writing in the shadow of Faulkner" (Williams 185). Nevertheless, "lazy" hacks, literary critics and general readers alike might be forgiven for thinking that in *Boomerang* (1991) Hannah anxiously envisions himself as an inadequate "post-Modern heir" to Faulkner. In a particularly memorable passage from this semi-autobiographical novel, Hannah writes: "All the generations of wonderful dead guys behind us. All the Confederate dead and the Union dead planted in the soil near us. All of Faulkner the great. Christ, there's barely room for the living down here" (*Boomerang* 137–38).

At least one leading southern literary critic has taken a somewhat Bloomian view of the relationship between Hannah and "Faulkner the great." In *The Southern Writer in the Postmodern World* (1991), Fred Hobson initially extols Hannah's status as "perhaps the boldest, zaniest, and most outrageous writer of the contemporary South" (Hobson 32). However, when Hobson considers Hannah's relationship to "the shadow of Faulkner" (9), a less positive and pejorative tone creeps in. Having suggested that Hannah has "cultivated" a Faulknerian public persona, Hobson proceeds to argue that in terms of "strictly literary influence ... Hannah does not seem to be a direct descendant of Faulkner" because he is "[l]acking the tragic sense, devoid of Faulkner's high seriousness and social consciousness" (34). This view of Hannah's (non-) relationship to Faulkner is congruent with Hobson's wider "concern" that the work of contemporary southern writers—not only Hannah but also Bobbie Ann Mason, Richard Ford and others—exhibits "a relative want of *power*" when compared to that of Faulkner, Robert Penn Warren and William Styron. Though Hobson pointedly emphasizes "the very healthy condition of contemporary southern fiction" and acknowledges that "I am perhaps looking for a particular *kind* of power" (10), his sense of attenuation among the "post-modern heirs" to Faulkner is Bloomian.

In a 1993 article entitled "Fee Fie Faux Faulkner," Michael Kreyling argued that "Hobson's theory of influence or continuity [in the southern literary tradition] leaves insufficient clearance for irony" ("Fee Fie" 4).

Building upon Linda Hutcheon's conception of postmodern parody as (among other things) a mode through which contemporary writers liberate themselves from the burden of literary history, Kreyling formulates a theory of "postsouthern" parody.¹ He identifies *Geronimo Rex* as a text that seems "actively postsouthern" (11) in its knowing reinterpretation of Faulkner's oeuvre, especially in the novel's parodic primal scene: Harry Monroe's killing of a peacock called Bayard. The significance of this name is that it stands "for the chivalric southern tradition of heroism and male character"—not least in Faulkner's work, where the "Sartoris clan named every other male child Bayard" (12).

In this essay, I want to extend Kreyling's invaluable exploration of postsouthern intertextuality in *Geronimo Rex* via an in-depth discussion of later works in which Hannah parodically revises Faulkner's representation of "the chivalric southern tradition of heroism and male character." "Dragged Fighting from His Tomb" (from *Airships*, 1978) and "That Was Close, Ma" (from *Bats Out of Hell*, 1995) can be read as rewrites of an early scene in Faulkner's *Flags in the Dust* (first published in expurgated from as *Sartoris* in 1929) featuring Confederate heroes "Carolina" Bayard Sartoris and General J. E. B. "Jeb" Stuart. I will also discuss Hannah's novel *Ray* (1980) because it acts as a thematic bridge between Hannah's representation of the Civil War in "Dragged Fighting from His Tomb" and the depiction of postmodern war in "That Was Close, Ma." Ultimately, I will try to show that these three texts exemplify not only Hannah's parodic take on the literary legacy of "Faulkner the great," but also his interrogation of the wider influence of (neo-) Confederate ideology. First, however, I will explore the "creation of Confederate nationalism" itself, together with the narrative invention of the Confederate "figural hero," in order to demonstrate how Faulkner confronted the continuing cultural power of Confederate nationalism in the twentieth-century South.

In *The Creation of Confederate Nationalism* (1988), historian Drew Gilpin Faust points out that, like other cultural nationalisms, Confederate nationalism was not a natural phenomenon but the product of "a necessary and self-conscious process" (Faust 5). Faust also emphasizes that "[t]he study of Confederate nationalism must abandon the notions of 'genuine' or 'spurious,' of 'myth' or 'reality'" (6). Faust thus helps us to understand that, as Confederate nationalist ideology was naturalized, it became difficult to distinguish between historical event and narrative representation. The *post*-Civil War production of images and texts portraying the Confederacy only furthered the conflation of "reality" with "myth," fact with fiction, and authentic antebellum artifacts with postbellum simulacra. Indeed, historian Charles Reagan Wilson has described the "myth of the Crusading Christian Confederates" as "a novelistic tale," "the Southern view of the past" in "story form" (Wilson 39). Elsewhere, literary critic Daniel Aaron has noted the fundamental irony that once "[t]he War destroyed it [the Confederacy] physically ... [t]he ideal of the Old South—order, beauty, freedom—remained." Conveniently detached from the defeated nation-state and eliding the C.S.A.'s commitment to maintaining racial slavery, this enduring "ideal" enticed southern authors from Thomas Nelson Page to the Nashville Agrarians into the creation of what Aaron calls "neo-Confederate" narrative (Aaron 293; see also 285–309 passim).

In *Baptized in Blood* (1980), Wilson shows how neo-Confederate nationalism, expressed through the "civil religion" of the Lost Cause, achieved narrative coherence via "a symbol system" centered upon "a pantheon of Southern heroes" (Wilson 24). In *Figures of the Hero in Southern Narrative* (1987), Michael Kreyling demonstrates that this "semiotic system" of "figural heroes" was mediated through fictional texts (*Figures* 29). Kreyling identifies William Gilmore Simms's leading role in the narrative creation of Confederate heroism: the man who wrote *The Life of the Chevalier Bayard* (1847) believed that a metonymic fictional warrior-hero "satisfies a people's needs and feelings just as the actual hero's gestures do" (35). Even more powerful, however, were those fictional narratives based upon (an idealized image of) "genuine" Confederate heroes; as Kreyling pointedly observes, "[t]he figural [Robert E.] Lee concerns most southern writers more than the actual" (3). In the case of General J. E. B. Stuart, the process of figural reinvention was especially rapid. On the day that Stuart died, the poet John R. Thompson wrote

And thus our Stuart at this moment seems
    To ride out of our dark and troubled story
Into the region of romance and dreams
    A realm of light and glory. (quoted in Thomas, 298)

Thompson's eulogy surmounted the historical reality of imminent political and military defeat ("our dark and troubled story") by situating a
semiotic "Stuart" in a transcendent textual state (a "region of romance and
dreams").

Come the late 1920s, when William Faulkner was writing Jeb Stuart
into *Flags in the Dust*, such figural heroism was being perpetuated in the
neo-Confederate narratives of the Nashville Agrarians. In 1928, Allen Tate
sent forth his biography *Stonewall Jackson: The Good Soldier* before trying
and failing to complete a study of Lee. In 1931, Andrew Lytle published
the hagiographic (and distinctly novelistic) *Bedford Forrest and His Critter
Company*. On a personal level, too, Faulkner faced the shadow of those
"wonderful dead guys behind us" in the military *and* literary figure of his
great-grandfather and namesake, William Falkner, a Confederate colonel
who subsequently published a moderately popular novel, *The White Rose
of Memphis* (1881). Faulkner's fiction furnishes numerous examples of
young southern men afflicted by a military-ancestral anxiety of influence.
In *Flags in the Dust*, World War I veteran John Sartoris can escape the
shadow of his Confederate warrior ancestors only through his own suicide. Yet, for all such biographical or fictional signs of anxiety, one can also
find key moments in Faulkner's work that articulate an ironical, skeptical
attitude towards Confederate nationalism and the concomitant myth of
military heroism. Hence, before turning to the representation of Jeb Stuart
in *Flags in the Dust*, it is worth considering how both Faulkner's great novel
Absalom, Absalom! (1936) and the comparatively obscure story "A Return"
(written in 1938 but first published in 1979) exhibit what one might call
a "proto-postsouthern" skepticism toward the narrative forms of (neo-)
Confederate nationalism.

Quite early in *Absalom, Absalom!*, Mr. Compson identifies contemporary southerners' anxiety-ridden perception of Confederate-era heroism:
"we see dimly people, the people in whose living blood and seed we ourselves
lay dormant and waiting, in this shadowy attenuation of time possessing
now heroic proportions." The various narrators of *Absalom, Absalom!* are
initially driven by a need to recover and recount this heroic Confederate
past. However, as Mr. Compson notes, "something is missing . . . nothing
happens" (80). With this breakdown of a knowable, readable, and narrat-
able southern history, Quentin Compson and Shreve McCannon instead

begin to invent their own account of the mysterious Sutpen family. At one level, this move may seem to prove the desperate, suicide-inducing depths of Quentin's southern anxiety of influence. However, Quentin and Shreve's "fictional" turn can also be read as Faulkner's acknowledgement that the ostensibly "historical" recovery and representation of the southern past is *always* mediated and even produced by narrative. From this perspective, Faulkner's readers can begin to see neo-Confederate nationalism generally as a collection of "novelistic tales" expressing a (white) "Southern view of the past" in "story form"—that is, much like *Absalom, Absalom!* itself. On these terms, we can also reconsider Faulkner as a proto-postsouthern writer. Brian McHale has posited that, with *Absalom, Absalom!*'s shift "from problems of *knowing* to problems of *modes of being*—from an epistemological dominant to an *ontological one*," Faulkner moves from modernism to postmodernism (McHale 10). Building on McHale's argument, one can say that Faulkner moves from southern modernist epistemology (what Richard Gray once termed "the literature of memory") to postsouthern ontology as *Absalom, Absalom!* emphasizes that "the Confederacy" is not an object or essence "prior to and beyond human thought and construction" (Kreyling *Inventing* 13). Faulkner's intensely self-reflexive text suggests that *both* Confederate nationalist narrative *and* (post)modern southern literature are inventions of, and interventions in, a meta-discourse of southern identity.

"A Return" specifically interrogates the pernicious influence of neo-Confederate myths of heroism. In this story, Gavin Blount is obsessed with the primal scene of his somewhat skewed Oedipal romance: local belle Lewis Randolph's rejection of his father, Gavin Blount Sr., on the eve of the Civil War. The man whom Lewis chose instead, Charles Gordon, was then killed in action and immortalized as a Confederate martyr. Moreover, Lewis herself became an icon of the Lost Cause by confronting the Yankees who invaded her home. Blount Jr. is obsessed with meeting and ultimately marrying Lewis (who is now ninety) in order to redeem his father's humiliation. Paradoxically though, Gavin also believes that, as an original and authentic Confederate heroine, the old woman is immune to "all the Post-postulations in existence" (570). On his own impossibly demanding (and self-defeating) terms, Gavin is right: mired in the melancholic belief that "I was born too late" (567), Gavin can never triumph, in the name of his father, over Charles Gordon's ghost. As a latecomer, all Gavin can do is "post-postulate" a pastiche of that original, mythical moment when Lewis threw a pan of boiling milk at her Yankee adversaries. Having provoked the old woman to throw a bowl of soup over him, the euphoric Gavin tries to take succor from the fact that, though Lewis chose Charles Gordon over his father in 1861, "*it was Gavin Blount she threw the soup plate at*" (574). However, by revealing the comic-tragic aspect of Blount's cultural anxiety of influence—"the sickness [of] a man still young yet who had firmly removed himself out of the living world in order to exist in a past and irrevocable time"—"A Return" suggests that neo-Confederate mythology has no positive use-value. The story implies that if young white men like Gavin Blount are going to live "according to a scale of values postulated by the uncaring dead" (567), the South would be better off without such mythology.

Both *Absalom, Absalom!* and "A Return," then, exhibit a healthy skepticism of Confederate narrative and its figural heroes. However, when Faulkner wrote about Jeb Stuart and Carolina Bayard Sartoris in *Flags in the Dust*, even he seems to have been seduced. Initially, as Aunt Jenny du Pre begins to tell the tale of Stuart and Sartoris, the omniscient narrator remains detached; indeed, this distance enables a sly commentary on the way Aunt Jenny's verbose anecdote feeds into the wider Confederate mythos:

> as she grew older the tale itself grew richer and richer . . . until
> what had been a hair-brained prank of two heedless and reckless
> boys wild with their own youth, was become a gallant and finely
> tragical focal-point to which the history of the race had been
> raised from out the old miasmic swamps of spiritual sloth by two
> angels valiantly and glamorously fallen and strayed, altering the
> course of human events and purging the souls of men (*Flags* 14).

However, as the narrative of Stuart and Bayard proceeds, the third-person voice takes over the role of more and more richly telling the tale. As we read about Sartoris and Stuart raiding the Union camp for coffee, and Bayard's death during a second foray for anchovies, the omniscient narrator takes control until the tale has been told; only when the scene closes does the narrative return to Jenny's voice "proud and still as banners in the dust"

(*Flags* 23). It is not Jenny's voice that raises Stuart and Bayard to John R. Thompson's "region of romance and dreams" by describing the two men conjoined in "the thunderous coordination of a single centaur"; it is not Jenny who transfigures Stuart's "tawny locks" into "gallant flames smoking with the wild and self-consuming splendor of his daring" (*Flags* 18). Though one must be careful not to conflate the omniscient narrator of *Flags* with Faulkner the "Author-God" (Barthes 170), biographer Emory Thomas is surely right when he cites Faulkner's text as a case-study in Stuart's transformation into "man as metaphor," figural hero rather than flesh and blood: "For Faulkner ... Stuart stands for gallantry, dash, and romance. He is a symbol—a metaphor instead of a man" (Thomas 2). All told, this famous scene from *Flags in the Dust* reveals the failure or absence of that ironical attitude toward neo-Confederate narrative and figural heroism that Faulkner would develop in *Absalom, Absalom!* and "A Return."

In contrast, Barry Hannah's Jeb Stuart stories consistently and insistently interrogate the figural hero, the man *as* metaphor. In a 1991 article, Kenneth Seib usefully assessed the three Stuart stories in *Airships* as "a coherent commentary on the romanticized South and the mythicizing of historical figures like Stuart" (Seib 50). I want to reconsider one of those stories, "Dragged Fighting from His Tomb," with more specific, intertextual reference to *Flags in the Dust* and from the theoretical perspective of postsouthern parody.

In "Dragged Fighting from His Tomb," the reader immediately gets a perspective on Jeb Stuart's cavalry that diverges from the image of gallivanting, saber-wielding gallants presented in *Flags in the Dust*. As the narrator, Captain John Howard, relates, Stuart's flamboyant "sabers out" style comes up against the technological reality of modern warfare: at Two Roads Junction, Pennsylvania, a Union force armed with repeater rifles routs the Confederates (*Airships* 48). In *Flags in the Dust*, Jeb Stuart shows the utmost courtesy to the captured Union major because "[n]o gentleman would do less" (*Flags* 21). This Faulknerian fantasy of pre-modern chivalric deference stands in stark contrast to the actions of Hannah's Howard: in the aftermath of the battle at Two Roads Junction, and upon being awakened by an unarmed Union veteran, the wounded Howard whips out his pistol and roughly demands "the most exquisite truths you know." When the old Union soldier states that he believes in the Holy Trinity and "[t]o be American and free," Howard harshly interposes that "I asked for the truths, not beliefs" (51). There is a notable dramatic irony here: at this point, Howard does not acknowledge that *he* has uncritically assumed the essential "truth" of the Confederate cause that he is fighting for. Instead of interrogating the "beliefs" informing Confederate ideology, Howard spouts platitudes about southern freedom from supposed northern interference. And yet the aggressively defensive tone of Howard's dialogue with the old Union soldier suggests that the captain is uneasily aware of, even while trying to repress, the centrality of slavery to the Confederate cause. Howard himself invokes and then (protesting too much) overlooks the class divide between southern slaveowners with a vested economic interest in military success and secession, and non-slaveowning Confederate soldiers like himself:

"Tell me," I said, "do you hate me because I hold niggers in bondage? Because I do not hold niggers in bondage. I can't afford it. You know what I'm fighting for? I asked you a question."

"What're you fighting for?"

"For the North to keep off."

"But you're here in Pennsylvania, boy. You attacked *us.*" (53)

Flags in the Dust renders Stuart as a cavalier operating in "the spirit of pure fun"; the omniscient narrator remarks that "neither Jeb Stuart nor Bayard Sartoris, as their actions clearly showed, had any political convictions involved at all" (15). Faulkner's novel thus elides the political, economic and moral issue of slavery in order to foreground the figural heroic romance. By contrast, Hannah depicts a soldier who sublimates his anxieties about the "truth" that slavery is the cornerstone of the Confederate cause into an insufficiently critical "belief" in southern ideology about a War of Northern Aggression.

Hannah's darkly comic parody of Faulkner continues when the old northern soldier flees back towards the Union depot crying "secesh!" (54), prompting Howard to undertake a one-man mission that recalls Carolina Bayard's similarly single-handed ambuscade into the Union camp in *Flags in the Dust*. However, whereas Faulkner's Bayard reaches the breakfast table of the Union commissary tent only to be shot "in the back with a derringer" by a secluded cook (*Flags* 22), Hannah's Howard rampages through the Union depot staff house before beginning a squalid shooting spree. Howard kills at least five Union soldiers with their own repeater rifles before commanding his horse to run "back and forth over the Yank" who tries to shoot him in the back (much as the cook shot Carolina Bayard). After all that, Howard still demands that the old Union soldier—who is now cowering in the staff house with a prostitute—say "*something wise!*" The veteran wearily replies that "There is no wisdom, Johnny Reb. . . . There's only tomorrow if you're lucky. Don't kill us. Let us have tomorrow" (57). In *Flags in the Dust*, the captured Union major's taunts that "General Stuart did not capture our anchovies," and that chivalric gallantry is "an anachronism, like anchovies" (21), merely serve to inspire Bayard's final "fun"-filled foray. In "Dragged Fighting from His Tomb," the captive Yankee plays a notably different role: by pointing out that "you're here in Pennsylvania," and by speaking humbly against gratuitous murder in the name of the Confederate cause, the old Union soldier is the catalyst for Captain Howard's awakening into moral consciousness.

Having spared the old Union soldier and the prostitute, Howard returns to base. Inspired by his exchange with the Union soldier, Howard begins to question his commander's methods; moreover, the narrative suggests that Howard's earlier brutal behavior was inspired by Stuart's inhumane tactics and actions. Howard challenges Stuart directly: "You shit. What are we doing killing people in Pennsylvania?" Stuart responds phlegmatically that the Confederates are simply "[s]howing them that we can, Captain Howard!" (58). In contrast to Faulkner's Stuart, engaged in anachronistic but always chivalric derring-do for "sheer fun," Hannah's Stuart is a pioneer exponent of modern total war. Repelled by this ruthlessness, Howard pointedly reminds Stuart of what he said when Howard's horse, Black Answer, was killed: "Use your weeping on people, not on animals" (58). Again, Hannah may be making a subtle intertextual allusion to *Flags in the Dust*. In Faulkner's novel, Stuart offers to escort the captured Union major to the nearest horse-picket, where the Confederates will capture a mount for their prisoner. The major declines, noting wryly that "majors can be replaced much easier than horses" (*Flags* 19). Yet still Stuart insists, his gentlemanly courtesy prompting the incredulous major to ask: "Will General Stuart, cavalry leader and General Lee's eyes, jeopardize his safety and that of his men and his cause in order to provide for the temporary comfort of a minor prisoner of his sword?" (*Flags* 21). Here, Faulkner's Stuart appears as a man so chivalrous he will put his opponent's comfort above any concern for his own life, the military value of horses, and even the Confederate cause itself. By contrast, Hannah's Stuart fails even to practice what he once preached to Howard—no longer even claiming to privilege the lives of people above animals, Stuart now sees human flesh as cannon-fodder, as expendable as horse meat.

Howard's disgust at Stuart's methods becomes so pronounced that he deserts the Confederate army, joins the Union side, fights with Ulysses Grant, and ultimately avenges his misplaced faith in Stuart and the "truth" of the Confederate cause: "I shot him [Stuart] right in the brow, so that not another thought would pass about me or about himself or about the South, before death." Howard acknowledges that "I was killing a man with wife and children" (58), but goes ahead and shoots Stuart in the belief that his war crimes outweigh his status as loving *pater familias*. Of course, Captain John Howard did not really kill General Jeb Stuart, who was struck down by an unknown bullet at Yellow Tavern. But "Dragged Fighting from His Tomb" exemplifies what Ruth Weston has referred to as Hannah's tropic use of "the lie" to expose "defective myths about male prowess . . . in war" (Weston 3). For Hannah's fictional "lie" about Jeb Stuart's death makes a wider point. Howard is an alternative hero who displaces Stuart from center stage—as Hannah observed in a 1983 interview, "I was more concerned with Howard than Stuart. Stuart is just a foil who flames around" (Vanarsdall 330)—and confronts "truths" about slavery and the brutality of war that were previously obscured by his uncritical "belief" in the Confederate cause. Through the figure and first-person narrative of Howard, Hannah's short story exposes the cultural-historical "lie" of a neo-Confederate (meta)narrative that absolves its figural military heroes of association with the defense of slavery by elevating them into "a region of romance." Moreover, through a postsouthern parodic rewriting of *Flags in the Dust*, Hannah gives the lie to Faulkner's uncharacteristic collusion in that romance.

In *Ray*, the eponymous narrator's experiences in Vietnam and his fragmented textual attempt to comprehend them dramatize the dehumanized, technological brutality of what cultural theorist Chris Hables Gray has called "postmodern war." More than that, though, Hannah interrogates the enduring myth of Confederate chivalry by conflating Ray's Vietnam memories with his hallucinatory visions of fighting for the South under Jeb Stuart's command. Notwithstanding romantic portrayals of gallant southern gentlemen-warriors, the Civil War has often been defined as the first "modern war"; in *Ray*, Hannah suggests the grim continuities between the actions of both the Union *and* the Confederate forces on the domestic battlefields of the Civil War, and the postmodern technological warfare practiced by the U.S. Army in Vietnam. Hannah also once again interrogates and parodies (albeit more loosely than in "Dragged Fighting from His Tomb") *Flags in the Dust*'s representation of Confederate chivalry. In contrast to the apolitical gallantry of Faulkner's Carolina Bayard, Hannah's Ray echoes Captain Howard by musing upon the meaning of the Confederate cause: "Your hat's rotting off. It's hot. You're not sure about your horse. Or the cause. All you know is that you are here" (*Ray* 96). On the battlefield, chivalric heroism gives way to the brutal methods of modern warfare: it is not Stuart's cavalry but John Pelham's artillery which decimates a rookie Federal outfit. In the apocalyptic aftermath of the artillery attack, a dying Union soldier looks at Ray and asks: "Are you Jeb Stuart?" (40). The grim irony is that the soldier expresses near-religious awe of this mythic figural hero even as the slaughter of his comrades heralds a new era of destruction that condemns the cavalry warfare for which Stuart was famed to the dustbin of history.[2] Indeed, in stark contrast to the hard-hearted Stuart of "Dragged Fighting from His Tomb," in *Ray* the general seems profoundly disturbed by the death and destruction that Pelham's artillery has wreaked: Ray remarks that Stuart "went out in the forest and wept" (41) for the Union dead.

Of course, Ray Forrest is not really "here" on the battlefield with Stuart at all, and his post-Vietnam trauma is such that he hardly knows where he is: "Oh, help me! I am losing myself in two centuries and two wars" (45). Here we have another example of Hannah's strategic use of the fictional "lie." Though Ray is, at best, confused about fighting with Jeb Stuart's cavalry, his narrative yet rings true by suggesting the grim historical continuities between the two wars. Ray himself makes this connection most explicitly when he recounts another Civil War battle in which "[e]verybody was killed" except "[o]ne Union private [who] lived to tell the story. If warriors had known this story, we would have taken the war to the gooks with more dignity" (66). Chris Hables Gray notes how alternative forms of knowledge and narration, including war veterans' own "stories, poems [and] memoirs," challenge the military "metarules" that seek to order the chaos of death and destruction that occurs during wartime (*Postmodern War* 161, 96). In *Ray*, the eponymous anti-hero's fragmented, confused, and perhaps even schizophrenic veteran's narrative serves to challenge both the metarules of war and the southern metanarrative of military heroism. Contrary to the warrior myths fostered by neo-Confederatism, neither "dignity" nor chivalry characterized Ray's contribution to the American war effort in Vietnam. It is not the saber-wielding Stuart but the anonymous artillerist Pelham who foreshadows Ray's role as "a living cog in the (post)modern war machine" (*Postmodern War* 90), a cyborg soldier[3] abstracted from the firefights and carpet bombing in which, as the pilot of an F-4 fighter plane, he (barely) participates: "Then the buttons when he got into the middle of the scope. It's so easy to kill. Saw him make the bright, white flower" (64). Ultimately, Ray is not like Gavin Blount, anxiously trying to recover some *epistemological*, historical sense of heroism through the "post-postulation" of a moment more mythical than real. Rather, Ray's *ontological*, "fictional" invention of a whole other self—a Confederate soldier under Jeb Stuart's command—constitutes an (albeit confused) attempt to get beyond the cultural "lies" that inform both neo-Confederate mythology and the metarules of postmodern warfare.

Postmodern war is also central to "That Was Close, Ma," a story that further can be read as Hannah's most recent postsouthern parody of *Flags in the Dust*. Though the conflict featured in "That Was Close, Ma" is not specifically identified or located, there are notable echoes of the first U.S. war in Iraq. Certainly, the way that the "war" (*Bats Out of Hell* 347)—the ironical quotation marks are the narrator's, a young American soldier who is writing home to his mother—is fought entirely through technological mediation evokes the U.S. Army's approach throughout 1991's Operation Desert Storm against Saddam Hussein. When the narrator recalls witnessing enemy "minions, scuttling distraught" from their "[k]nocked over anthill" as "a big one of ours comes in" (345), the scene grimly approximates (censored) film of Iraqi soldiers "like ghostly sheep flushed from a pen" by Apache helicopter raids, "cut down by attackers they could not see ... blown to bits by bursts of 30mm exploding cannon shells" (Gray *Postmodern War* 36).

Like his fellow postmodern warrior Ray Forrest, the (unnamed) narrator of "That Was Close, Ma" seems at times to "live in two centuries." At one point, he also conflates the Confederate South with the Wild West: "Oh Vicksburg, Vicksburg! I am, personally, the Fall of the West" (345). However, and again like Ray, the narrator recognizes that the cultural fiction of the Confederate warrior (like that of the Western gunslinger) distracts him from the dehumanizing reality of postmodern warfare: "For isn't it a given that culture drags you flat away from wherever you are ... ? For instance, I am not the Fall of the West nor is this remotely Vicksburg" (348).[4] He observes his Commander's ridiculous appearance, "wear[ing] twin bone-handled Uzis at his hips as if face-to-face combat with the enemy was imminent" (346). This updated, Rambo-like performance of military heroism seems even more absurd given that, in actuality, the Commander has little to do. As in *Ray*, the romantic image of a Jeb Stuart figure leading his cavalry into battle is replaced by the postmodern heirs to John Pelham: the "third stringers" and "scrubs" (345), including the narrator himself, who man the missile-launchers and peek through periscopes at an enemy line that is more than forty miles away.

Yet in the midst of this postmodern war, the scrub-narrator launches a daring one-man mission that both parodies Carolina Bayard's single-handed quest in *Flags in the Dust* and contrasts with Captain Howard's initial, brutal rampage through the Union camp in "Dragged Fighting from His Tomb." Whereas Faulkner's Sartoris went after the elusive anchovies, Hannah's scrub steps forth into "no-man's land" without "even a pistol" to capture a root-plant called ceruba. Unsurprisingly, he is bombarded by the enemy's "antipersonnel" weaponry, but exposing his body to this barrage instills the narrator with a delusional sense of heroism: "I was flattered. I felt enormous" (356). The enemy troops are so stunned by this apparently suicidal adventurer that they stop shooting and simply stare. As the narrator raises the ceruba above his head, "they began cheering" (357) at his sheer bravado.

At first glance, the narrator's heroism seems similar to that of Carolina Bayard in *Flags in the Dust*—indeed, by awing the enemy into silence, he may even appear to outdo Faulkner's Confederate chevalier. However, there is a telling difference between the two characters, and the two texts. In *Flags*, Bayard's solo raid was based on little more than a "spirit of pure fun" and the defense of pre-modern myths of chivalry. Hannah's scrub goes on his quest for ceruba in order to impress Naomi Lee, a prisoner of war with whom he has fallen in love. He believes not at all in the U.S. military cause, even observing that "[i]t's well known that the other side is more passionate and impetuous than we are. 'Real' men with a religion and something to prove" (347). Nor does the narrator have any faith in military heroism, whether for fun *or* chivalry. He asserts that: "The war has never concerned me, as war, so I should be the last trusted voice about whatever gallantry is ascribed to anybody." And yet, when he gathers "the roots for Naomi Lee" (357), the scrub attains a level of "gallantry" that goes beyond Stuart's gentlemanly attention to the captured Union major, or his own Commander's lecherous interest in Naomi. Indeed, the narrator's romantic love for Naomi transcends the ideological opposition between the Americans and the "heathen" and "savage" (353) enemy. By overleaping the banal horror of postmodern war, the scrub becomes one more of Hannah's "postmodern romantics" (see Weston).

If the narrator's sudden "gallantry" still seems too much like that of some contemporary Carolina Bayard, there yet remains a final parodic and apocalyptic twist in this postsouthern tale. Whereas Faulkner's Bayard goes once more unto the breach at the merest suggestion that General Stuart's gallantry is outmoded, Hannah's scrub commits murderous treachery against his military superior. Enraged by the Commander's designs on Naomi, the narrator (ab)uses his "third string" knowledge of the American war machine to destroy his rival: "I ... doubled the image on the Commander's bunker. Thirty minutes later they hit him with at least three huge ones direct" (359). Like "Dragged Fighting from His Tomb," "That Was Close, Ma" ends with treason against Commander and Cause. And with it, Barry Hannah concludes another successful salvo in his career-long assault on neo-Confederate mythology and (Faulknerian) figural heroism.

Notes

1. For Linda Hutcheon's theory of postmodern parody, see *A Poetics of Postmodernism* (New York: Routledge, 1988), especially Chapters 2 and 8.

2. In 1983, interviewer R. D. Vanarsdall observed that "[t]he Civil War was the last war that really used cavalry"; Hannah responded by noting that the turn to trench warfare generated a "mechanized" form of battle that replaced the "glory" of cavalry warfare. However, Hannah was also careful to qualify that "all that glory . . . was pompous and phony" anyway. He noted too that Stuart "failed gravely at Gettysburg. . . . He was up there riding for glory," adding wryly "[t]hat's the kind of asshole soldier I would be, I fear" (Vanarsdall 330).

3. On the postmodern cyborg soldier, see Chris Hables Gray, *Postmodern War*, 195–211.

4. For more on the links between the South and the West in Hannah's fiction, see the next two essays in this volume by Mark Graybill and Melanie Benson respectively.

Works Cited

Aaron, Daniel. *The Unwritten War: American Writers and the Civil War*. New York: Knopf, 1973.

Barthes, Roland. "The Death of the Author." In *Modern Criticism and Theory: A Reader*. Edited by David Lodge. London: Longman, 1988. 167–72.

Bloom, Harold. *The Anxiety of Influence: A Theory of Poetry*. London: Oxford UP, 1973.

Faulkner, William. *Flags in the Dust*. New York: Vintage, 1973.

———. *Absalom, Absalom!*. 1936. New York: Vintage International, 1986.

———. "A Return." In *Uncollected Stories of William Faulkner*. Edited by Joseph Blotner. New York: Vintage, 1981. 547–74.

Faust, Drew Gilpin. *The Creation of Confederate Nationalism*. Baton Rouge: Louisiana State UP, 1988.

Gray, Chris Hables. *Postmodern War: The Politics of Conflict*. London: Routledge, 1997.

Gray, Richard. *The Literature of Memory: Modern Writers of the American South*. London: Edward Arnold, 1977.

Hannah, Barry. "Dragged Fighting from His Tomb." In *Airships*. New York: Alfred Knopf, 1978. 49–60.

———. *Ray*. 1980. New York: Penguin, 1981.

———. "Faulkner and the Small Man." In *Faulkner and Humor: Faulkner and Yoknapatawpha, 1984*. Edited by Doreen Fowler and Ann J. Abadie. Jackson: UP of Mississippi, 1986. 191–94.

———. *Boomerang/Never Die*. Jackson: UP of Mississippi, 1994.

———. "That Was Close, Ma." In *Bats Out of Hell*. 1993. New York: Grove P, 1994. 343–60.

Hobson, Fred. *The Southern Writer in the Postmodern World*. Athens: U of Georgia P, 1991.

Kreyling, Michael. *Figures of the Hero in Southern Narrative*. Baton Rouge: Louisiana State UP, 1987.

———. "Fee Fie Faux Faulkner: Parody and Postmodernism in Southern Literature." *Southern Review* 29.1 (winter 1993): 1–15.

————. *Inventing Southern Literature.* Jackson: UP of Mississippi, 1998.

McHale, Brian. *Postmodernist Fiction.* New York: Methuen, 1987.

O'Connor, Flannery. "Some Aspects of the Grotesque in Southern Fiction." In *Mystery and Manners: Occasional Prose.* Edited by Sally and Robert Fitzgerald. New York: Farrar, Strauss and Giroux, 1969. 36–59.

Seib, Kenneth. "'Sabers, Gentlemen, Sabers': The J. E. B. Stuart Stories of Barry Hannah." *Mississippi Quarterly* 45.1 (winter 1991–1992): 41–52.

Thomas, Emory. *Bold Dragoon: The Life of J. E. B. Stuart.* New York: Harper and Row, 1986.

Vanarsdall, R. D. "The Spirits Will Run Through: An Interview with Barry Hannah." *Southern Review* 19.2 (spring 1983): 317–41.

Weston, Ruth. *Barry Hannah: Postmodern Romantic.* Baton Rouge: Louisiana State UP, 1998.

Williams, Daniel E. "Interview with Barry Hannah, October 13, 2005." Included in this volume. 183–90.

Wilson, Charles Reagan. *Baptized in Blood: The Religion of the Lost Cause.* Athens: U of Georgia P, 1980.

Accountability, Community, and Redemption in *Hey Jack!* and *Boomerang*

—Matthew Shipe

Introducing the 1993 reissue of Barry Hannah's *Boomerang* (1989), Rick Bass praised the work, a fusion of autobiography and novel, as "the sweetest of [Hannah's] books, one of the sweetest books ever written" (vii). While Bass's comment conveys the spirit of *Boomerang*, it applies equally to Hannah's previous novel, *Hey Jack!* (1987). Written at the midpoint of Hannah's career, these novels have attracted relatively little critical attention beyond their original notices and Mark Charney's chapter in his critical volume on Hannah. Charney argues that the texts' formal and thematic similarities provide a convincing basis for their being read in tandem. Like *Ray* (1980), both novels are made up of a series of brief vignettes; this formal fragmentation reflects the chaos and violence that the respective narrators, Homer in *Hey Jack!* and Barry in *Boomerang*, perceive in both themselves and their communities. In addition to these formal similarities, both novels hinge on the killing of an adult child: Jack's daughter, Alice, in *Hey Jack!* and Yelverston's unnamed son in *Boomerang*. Both deaths are senseless and epitomize the random violence that afflicts the respective communities. Alice is killed by rock star Ronnie Foot, with whom she is having an affair, when (in an act reminiscent of William S. Burroughs's infamous killing of his wife) Foot attempts to shoot a bottle off her head; at his trial, Foot describes the act as "more capital boredom than capital crime" (*Hey Jack!* 131). Yelverston's son's death

MATTHEW SHIPE   { 103 }

appears just as random; he is killed, and his new wife severely wounded, by dope pirates "running free" on the Tombigbee waterway (*Boomerang* 60).

Although these meaningless killings link the two texts, Hannah's focus shifts as he moves from community in *Hey Jack!* to individual relationships in *Boomerang*. "My eyes get bigger than ever over the situation of this town and my passing through it," Homer declares in the opening pages of *Hey Jack!*, signaling the preoccupation with community that will unite the vignettes that constitute the narrative (2). Despite the destructive forces (embodied by Ronnie Foot) that threaten the small southern town in which the novel is set, the narrative locates in Jack's endurance, his ability to move onward after the death of his daughter, hope for a community plagued by violence. In contrast to *Hey Jack!*'s emphasis on community, *Boomerang* remains a largely personal affair, a shifting mixture of autobiography and fiction that chronicles Hannah's own struggle to forge a respectable identity in the face of the violence he has witnessed and created.[1] The redemption that Hannah imagines for both himself and his community is especially evident in the act of mercy at the novel's conclusion: Yelverston's decision not only to forgive his son's killers but also to house them and involve them in the upbringing of his newborn son. Yelverston's act of mercy contrasts with Jack's inability to forgive Foot for Alice's death, and vividly illustrates the transition from endurance to forgiveness that Hannah maps over the course of the two novels. The conclusion of *Boomerang* marks the culmination of an affirmative, progressive movement towards communal and individual redemption that began in *Hey Jack!*

More broadly, Yelverston's act of forgiveness counters the bleakness that had surfaced in Hannah's fiction during the first half of the 1980s. From *Ray* to *Captain Maximus* (1985), a growing sense of despair is apparent in Hannah's work. Discussing this period of Hannah's career, Fred Hobson observes that "[t]here is little redemption, then, anywhere in *Ray*, nor in Hannah's later, even more bizarre work, *The Tennis Handsome*" (39). In a passage characteristic of the despair that afflicts him, Ray Forrest declares that "I am infected with every disease I ever tried to cure. I am a vicious nightmare of illnesses" (*Ray* 51).[2] "I am looking at the swelling hordes," Ray proclaims toward the novel's conclusion. "I know too many goddamned people, too many wretched Americans at this point. Between the hours of healing, I dream of dropping the ace on much home real estate in hopes that many citizens will get trapped inside in the wide hand-shake of phosphorus" (100–101). The sense of hopelessness escalates in *The Tennis Handsome* (1983), a work that depicts contemporary existence as an absurdly comic and violent misadventure that offers little meaning or redemption. The only redemption available to Baby Levaster, Jimmy Word, and Bobby Smith is that vicariously experienced via French Edward's bra-vura performances on the tennis court. But this glimpse of grace is thor-oughly overshadowed by the onslaught of horrific incidents that humiliates all of these characters. French Edward himself nearly drowns and loses part of his mind; later, he survives a lightning strike but becomes addicted to electrical charges. Word survives a stroke, a suicide attempt, and a mauling by dogs only to die of a heart attack, his body dumped in the Mississippi River and devoured by a "mad alligator below Natchez" (133). Levaster is shot, presumably dead, by French Edward's wife. Last but not least, Smith's aunt and lover is nearly raped by a walrus. Yet the despair is most pro-nounced in *Captain Maximus*, in which the brevity of the stories (only the aborted screenplay "Power and Light" is longer than fourteen pages) seems to underscore the depressed mood of the collection. "I was among dwarves over in Alabama at the school, where almost everybody dies early. There is a poison in Tuscaloosa that draws souls toward the low middle. Hardly anyone has honest work," Ned Maximus, the narrator of "Ride, Fly, Penetrate, Loiter," rails in a moment typical of the bitterness at the center of these stories (*Captain Maximus* 36). "I haven't had a 'good time' in a long time," the pilot John explains just before his plane crashes in "Even Greenland." "There's something between me and a good time since, I don't know, since I was twenty-eight or like that. I've seen a lot, but you know I haven't quite *seen* it. Like somebody's seen it already. It wasn't fresh. There were eyes that had used it up some" (32). John's comments exemplify the sense of exhaustion that pervades the collection, in stark contrast to the lust for life evident in Hannah's earlier fiction.

Read alongside these immediately preceding books, *Hey Jack!* and *Boomerang* constitute an affirmative turn in Hannah's career; they reveal an optimism that is conspicuous by its absence from *The Tennis Handsome* and *Captain Maximus*. As opposed to the anguish that afflicts Ray Forrest, Baby Levaster, and the various male protagonists in *Captain Maximus*, Homer and Barry appear renewed with optimism and at peace with them-selves and their loved ones. At fifty-six, Homer is rejuvenated by a new romance: "In love, in love, in love. A mule can climb a tree if it's in love. A man like me can look himself in the mirror and say, I'm all right, everything is beloved, I'm no stranger to anywhere any more" (*Hey Jack!* 59). Reflecting on the trajectory of his tempestuous life, Barry in *Boomerang* is similarly optimistic, thanking his "nephews and nieces" and other relatives who have "cheered me through the hopeless and stunned times" (68). Compounding the renewed sense of optimism, both *Hey Jack!* and *Boomerang* profess a belief in cosmic accountability that counters the nihilism of *The Tennis Handsome* and *Captain Maximus*. This emphasis on accountability is especially apparent in the metaphorical significance accorded to the (substitute) golf ball at the end of *Hey Jack!* and to the boomerang in the novel of that name. Commenting on the significance of the boomerang, Richard Gray suggests that "it is an image that neatly captures both the errant mobility and the sense of a specific history, revolt, and return, at work" in both *Boomerang* and Hannah's fiction in general (398). More than this, though, Hannah discovers in the elliptical flight of a boomerang a useful metaphor for the accountability that he believes governs the universe:

> There is a day for everybody who ever practiced cruelty. The boomerang, if you throw it well, as I did yesterday, almost comes back into your palm.
> Every good deed and every good word sails out into the hedges and over the grass and comes to sit in your front yard. Only the creeps forget a good deed. (34)

This faith in a kind of cosmic comeuppance for those whose "cruelty" constitutes a failure to hold themselves to account for their own actions does not seem to offer any immediate protection from the violence which remains as ubiquitous in *Hey Jack!* and *Boomerang* as it was in *Ray* or *The Tennis Handsome*. Still, the meaning that Barry attaches to the boomerang encourages him to act ethically. As Barry throws the boomerang again at the end of the novel, its flight reassures him that, despite the chaotic appearance of the universe, moral behavior (not least his own) does indeed have value and meaning:

> I threw the boomerang and this one acted amazingly. It took off seventy yards or so and then came back higher and much lazier. It was spinning in this beach grayness and taking its time,

extremely patient to come back, hovering out there and seeming
to inch toward us directly back to my hand.

> I held my hand out as stunned as I was. It came in so easy
> and catchable I closed my fist (140).

Boomerang's emphasis on accountability through the symbolism of
the boomerang's flight is foreshadowed in *Hey Jack!* by the closing image
of Jack rolling up Ronnie Foot's suicide note and chipping it as if it were
a golf ball. As Charney observes, Homer's fragmented narrative endeavors
"to discover a purpose and logic to a world that denies him meaning" (92).
Charney further suggests that "Alice's death is ultimately as inevitable as
the murders that occur at the Chosin Reservoir [a Korean war battle in
which Homer participated]—both episodes of violence reflect a nihilistic
universe whose inhabitants seek meaning through relationships with others" (92). Indeed, Homer worries that attempting to forge meaning in an
infinite universe leads only to insanity: "My universe is growing smaller.
Nobody has a prayer if it's getting any bigger. Thinking of infinite largeness
is what drives people nuts, I say. I stand uncorrected. All you need is a roof,
a prayer, and some pussy" (68). Accordingly, Homer discovers meaning
largely in the relationships that he forms with members of his community;
however, a belief in accountability also emerges toward the conclusion of
his narrative. Having initially dismissed his murder of Alice as deriving
from "capital boredom," Foot belatedly takes responsibility for his actions
by killing himself; this act goes some way to redeeming the rock star and
providing Jack with the justice that he seeks for his daughter's death. Yet
accountability is most vividly symbolized not by Foot's suicide but by the
final image of Jack hitting Foot's suicide note like a golf ball:

> "They gave me and you a certain hell, Homer," [Jack] said to me.
> "They made us know everything."
>
> He balled up the piece of notebook paper [Foot's suicide
> note] and chipped it up high in the wind, so high it came back to
> us and landed behind.
>
> "No mercy," he said. (132–33)

This conclusion could be seen to provide further evidence of the "nihilistic universe" identified by Charney; in such a reading, the reverse flight

path of the suicide note cum golf ball would be a final, cruel "cosmic joke" perpetrated on Jack. Alternatively, however, the circular flight of the "golf ball" follows Foot's suicide in emphasizing that there is some measure of accountability within the universe. Such an interpretation of the "ball's" flight seems especially germane when considered in intertextual relation to the trajectory of the boomerang in Hannah's subsequent novel.[3] For while the boomerang is emblematic of the optimism that Hannah more fully embraces in *Boomerang* (the toy's elliptical flight persuading Barry to act more ethically), Jack's final "golf shot" signals a similar sense of return that points toward an underlying moral order: the shot's reverse flight path offers reassurance that actions do indeed have consequences. In many regards, the conclusion of *Hey Jack!* gestures toward an Old Testament version of justice, of an "eye for an eye." However, this conception of justice ultimately provides little comfort or closure to either Jack or Homer. From this perspective, Jack's final shot suggests that, although justice has been served with Foot's suicide, such violent retribution will not absolve Jack's pain, and that he will never entirely overcome his grief for his daughter.

Despite the emphasis on accountability in both *Hey Jack!* and *Boomerang*, violence is no less prevalent in either novel than in Hannah's earlier fiction. "In modern life there is no sheriff and no police and we all know it," Homer observes in *Hey Jack!*. "If you are in jeopardy with your feelings, there is no one at all. The police come around to laugh about the fire" (47). Of the two novels, *Hey Jack!* accords more with Hannah's previous treatment of violence; for example, the death of the professor crushed by his own car recalls the outlandish violence that permeates *The Tennis Handsome*. The violence in *Boomerang* is less grotesque, more recognizable and, as such, all the more brutal. Typical of the ordinary but shocking forms of death which punctuate *Boomerang* is the depiction of David Holman's heart attack on a golf course at the age of thirty-seven—a mundane death that nevertheless makes Holman's wife a widow and leaves his young son without a father. In a 1996 interview, Hannah observed that "I began seeing that much of our best writing was in history and biography—I think because reality has caught up with imagination, as Philip Roth suggested in the sixties. The novel no longer stuns us. You're never shocked. I saw on CBS news the other day the first thing I've actually been shocked by recently. Men driving stakes through their stomachs on videotape. I couldn't sleep"

(Lilley and Oberkirch 29–30). Extended to Hannah's own fiction, such remarks suggest a belief that the outrageous violence which characterizes *Hey Jack!* and, especially, *The Tennis Handsome* has lost its power to shock. This would also explain why the violence in *Boomerang* does not *strive* to shock; in contrast to Aunt Beth's near-rape by a walrus in *The Tennis Handsome*, incidents such as the murder of Yelverston's son grimly reflect a culture of violence that renders more overtly outrageous fiction impotent—and which violence is, ultimately, all the more shocking for it.

While *Hey Jack!* and *Boomerang* are united by a shared sense of optimism, Hannah's focus shifts over the course of the two novels. Written following Hannah's move to Oxford, Mississippi, in 1983 after a period of three years largely spent outside the South, *Hey Jack!* exhibits Hannah's renewed appreciation for (southern) community. In 1996, Hannah explained that:

> Probably that [the idea of community] became more important to me when I finally found a town—Oxford. I really think pals are heaven, as I say in my dedication to the Howorths [in *High Lonesome*, published in 1996]. There is something bracing about it. I have lost my folks. You gather pals and girl and boy friends and that's your civilization. It is a small marriage: you have your own language, your own values. I like the different points of view in a community. I like the little fights—the fights over trees, over grass. It is something I personally need. (Lilley and Oberkirch 24)

In *Hey Jack!*, Homer embraces the university town, apparently modeled after Oxford, that he has made his home: "I have settled here because of the university library and the distinguished bookstore, and also the old gentlemen who sit on the chairs around the square to reminisce," Homer declares in the novel's opening paragraphs. "These old men have not been treated well in other fictions by the authors in other states in other times. But you cannot ignore their wisdom and you cannot ignore the fact that it takes a certain strength to sit out in such a hot shade in the summers and watch the cars and young scoundrels" (2). By attempting to depict accurately the "old men [who] have not been treated well in other fictions," Homer combats the negative and patronizing image of the South often projected in popular culture. However, Homer also indicts the South's often-romanticized view of its own history, as when he exclaims that "Christ, the South has been pickled in the juice of its own image" (20). Homer here identifies a version of what Richard Gray calls that "particular kind of commodification that turns the South itself—or, to be more exact, an idea or image of the South—into a product, a function of the marketplace" (356). This process of commodification and simulation is again evident when Homer takes a trip to Nashville and laments the demise of the Grand Ole Opry into a tourist attraction, a "plastic ripoff costing $12 per ticket and a parking lot the size of a major university" (104).

Hobson has described the South that emerges in Hannah's fiction as "a world of Lear jets, fast cars, easy sex and drugs, high-tech rockabilly, new-style misogyny, and general social and cultural fragmentation—a postmodern South in which place, community, traditional family, and even class play little part" (36). In many regards, Hobson's description accurately characterizes *Hey Jack!*'s treatment of the region, as when Homer observes caustically that "[y]ou get a place like Nashville that tries to mass-produce heart and soul, and what's really there is a sad nineteen-year-old working the Waffle Hut counter, looking out at no prospect at all" (105). Indeed, cultural homogenization has not only overcome large cities like Nashville; it also threatens the small town where Homer lives. "The town had grown very much [since the 1950s]," Homer tell us at the start of his narrative:

> There were some tax advantages and good schools for white
> people who worked in the nearby city, and the town was spread
> out in subdivisions around the old little village with brick streets,
> the college, the great Baptist church. Some of the homes south of
> town were worth upwards of $300,000, he'd [the exiled dentist]
> heard. He didn't know. What was sure was that the old town was
> grown and gone, and there was nowhere else to escape to. (15)

Nevertheless, Homer's depiction of the contemporary South does not negate the value of place and region, as Hobson suggests. Nor does Hannah's revitalized interest in community result, in *Hey Jack!*, in a sentimentalized view of the South. Indeed, the text at times appears to relish parodying the South's (and southern literature's) glorious past, as when Foot masturbates over the grave of William Faulkner, "making hunching motions on it, never giving up the night until he came, with a shout" (122). Ultimately, though, Homer values his community and its history. Considering Hannah's relationship to and representation of the southern past, Matthew Guinn points out that while Hannah "subjects the very act of looking backward to irreverent scrutiny . . . he also demonstrates that the past is viable for an artistic vision beyond mythoclasm or emigration—that the mature southern artist of the postmodern era need not leave the South behind" (178).[4] Hannah's complex response to the Southern past is suggested in Homer's reaction to a trip to the Civil War battlefield at Shiloh. "Went humbly into the souvenir and history place, saw the movie with the startling lecture about the numbers killed," Homer writes. "Nothing really registered that much with me; I did not care if this was the first 'modern battle.' I will not bleed any more with the solemn historians, making their living by their accountants' blood and their thin armchair poetry about the 'horrible misunderstanding'" (102). While Homer here claims that the battlefield does not affect him, he soon admits to "feeling for the old dead sad Confederates and Yankees" and wonders "how many of them had anything like a Porsche ride and a bit of mouth from the little woman" (103). While such a response is certainly irreverent (recalling Foot's defiling of Faulkner's grave), Homer's sympathy for the Confederate *and* Yankee dead indicates an unwillingness to disregard the specter of the (southern) past.

Even though Homer's relationship with the South's past remains conflicted, his specific connection to the local community of the university town is more straightforward, more quotidian: "When I reached the lights of our little town, I was sorely missing my wife," Homer muses after a trip to Pensacola. "My old man was a traveling salesman, and now I felt especially akin to him. Never understood it before. The town seemed to throb with improbable and deep life, beyond its tiny geometry" (93). Even though he resembles many of Hannah's earlier protagonists in his fascination with war and problematic relationships with women, Homer differs from them in the explicit concern he demonstrates for his community. As Ruth Weston has pointed out, Homer is "named for the ancient Greek quintessential teller of tales" (31); he privileges the stories of others over his own, deflecting attention away from himself throughout his narrative. "I lose myself in the stories of our friends in the town," Homer writes. "I go out and stand around in their stories. Don't get too close to me, husbands, wives, and lovers. Nothing is sacred, I tell everything" (64). Homer's preoccupation with others differentiates him from his predecessor Ray Forrest, whose tendency to refer to himself in the third person signals not only that he is mentally unstable but also that he remains narcissistically self-centered throughout his narrative. Whereas Ray's narrative remains largely directed inward, Homer's relative sanity allows him to move beyond himself and imagine the situation of those he encounters in the town. "You will find me changing voices as I slip into the—let us say—*mode* of the closer participant," Homer informs the reader at the beginning of his narrative. Unlike *Ray*, however, the shifting "voices" of *Hey Jack!* do not signify the narrator's own mental instability: "Otherwise I am sane, except for once in my life, and do not speak in tongues or hear voices as they do in certain churches" (1–2).

Throughout *Hey Jack!*, Homer largely focuses on men who exist on the periphery of the community—troubled characters such as the hypochondriac professor crushed to death by his own car; the dentist scared out of town because he is unable to come to terms with his homosexuality; and the frustrated painter and Korean War veteran, Wally Cooper, who writes death threats to the town's artists. Of the veteran, Homer says: "Rather helplessly, I have affection for him. In another way, I found a kind of mirth and even necessity in Wally Cooper's death threats. Had he called me I'd have been flattered" (50). By recounting the despair that unites these men, Homer arbitrates between them and the community; he restores their role within a community that has rejected them. Given his own experience in Korea and his brief ("once in my life") descent into madness—"I had a whiff of one [book] one afternoon that was exactly the aroma of Chosin. How could it be? Then I went nuts. But only for a month" (26)—Homer is perfectly suited to the role of mediating between these tortured men and the community. He is able to sympathize with not only the Korean War veteran, but also the hypochondriac professor and the dentist. Indeed, Homer calls attention to the way that the community's identity has been constructed through or against people and acts that it designates abnormal and harmful. In *The Narrative Forms of Southern Community* (1999), Scott Romine debunks the assumption that communities cohere around a "commonly held view of reality" (1); Romine explains that a social group "lacking a commonly held view of reality, coheres by means of norms, codes,

and manners that produce a simulated, or at least symbolically consti-
tuted, social reality" (3). Moreover, "community is enabled by practices of
avoidance, deferral, and evasion; in a certain sense, as [Allen] Tate implies,
community relies not on what is there so much as what is, by tacit agree-
ment, not there" (3). The "community" of the university town in *Hey Jack!*
bears out Romine's argument: it coheres and is enabled through the ostra-
cism of people who, like Wally Cooper and the dentist, it deems deviant.
While the violence of Ronnie Foot is accepted (until he kills Alice) because
of his celebrity, the town refuses to condone the relatively harmless acts
of men like Cooper, forcing them to live on the fringes of the community.
By acknowledging and narrating men like Cooper, Homer posits a new
understanding of community that challenges the town to recognize the
violence within its borders and to embrace those men it has banished to
its margins.

Near the end of *Boomerang*, Barry declares: "Cut it down, babies. Cut it
down all around the world. Quit shooting. Quit it, quit it, gallant Mississippians. Take time to write everybody a love note that you love. Take take
take time to examine your own wife's anatomy and her clean clothes for
you and take care of your children" (146). Throughout his narrative, Barry
writes specifically of his friends and family and refers to his children and
current wife by name. Because of this, it is tempting to read *Boomerang* as
Hannah's attempt at autobiography. To read *Boomerang* solely as an autobiography, however, would be to miss the novel's larger concern with individual relationships, a concern that Hannah largely explores through the
fictional dimension of the book featuring Yelverston. Indeed, in many
regards, Yelverston's role proves to be more vital than Barry's since his
decision to forgive the men who brutally murdered his son becomes the
narrative's defining act:

> Why should the niggers and the Texan still live in Parchman?
> They were all on death row now but Yelverston decided to
> change that. He decided to get them out of jail and own them.
> He no longer feared his own death. Death was nothing, death
> was the least of his worries. His son was dead but here was he
> with his handsome head of gray hair and his Pall Malls, five a

day, and his habit of having five drinks a day, even though he had developed an ulcer. He realized he was an old fart and he and his wife had listened to old fart music coming down to Key West. . . . He wanted to own one of the killers. He wanted to work him and train him until he was a close friend. (123–24)

In deciding to "own" the men who killed his son, Yelverston forgoes violent revenge and comes to emphasize the necessity of forgiveness and of rehabilitation. "Barry, I had millions at one time," Coretta Haim, one of the killers, confesses after Yelverston has secured his release from death row, "but I was nothing" (147). Haim, once a flashy drug dealer, is now a "humble-looking man in a good brown suit" (146) who, as an indication of his rehabilitation, donates five thousand dollars to the Humane Society (149). It is this belief in rehabilitation—whether it is Haim's renunciation of his violent past or Barry's struggle to forego his self-destructive behavior—that propels *Boomerang*'s optimism.

Taken together, *Hey Jack!* and *Boomerang* signal a move away from the despair that characterized *The Tennis Handsome* and *Captain Maximus*. Yet while Homer and Barry express a positive outlook, neither achieves a complete sense of peace. They both flirt with violence and struggle to restrain the self-destructive impulses that consumed so many of Hannah's previous male protagonists. After a brief sexual encounter with Alice, a tryst that he fails to confess to either his wife or Jack, Homer castigates himself for his destructive behavior and his unwillingness to confess his indiscretion: "What an inadvertent lecher I was, what a dog; I could not bear my transparency and my red lying face. I stood up in the air of the house, then went out standing in the air of the town. Good oxygen fled from me with a sort of hideous laughter, it seemed; I could not breathe the kind air I used to breathe. I felt to be a new alien to my town, and my sin ran around my legs like a dog dyed red" (75). In *Boomerang*, Barry is not above celebrating his continuing capacity for offensive behavior: "I have no conscience, I guess. After the hideous Sundays I've had in our godless clime with all these males on the pulpit screaming and talking, I must rescue our women. There's only one way to do it, ladies: make a big pot roast with onions, carrots, and potatoes in it and then get naked except for your high-heeled shoes, if you've got any legs and fanny left" (44–45). Still, despite these lapses,

Homer and Barry strive to accept the peace that domesticity offers and struggle with the moral boundaries of marriage. They both move beyond the restlessness evident in the conclusion of "Ride, Fly, Penetrate, Loiter" when Ned Maximus rejects the domestic comfort offered by his girlfriend and children and plunges back into the promise of violence on the open road. Barry asserts that "[m]arriage is a long-scale idea and you just can't live that close without having a fight" (*Boomerang* 119); similarly, Homer takes brief trips to the Mississippi Gulf Coast and Los Angles to escape the constraints of marriage: "Behind me was an alarmed wife, but I could not help it, I had to be here, waking up in pain and staring at the brown water of the Mississippi Gulf" (*Hey Jack!* 90–91). In both *Hey Jack!* and *Boomerang*, marriage underpins the narrators' struggle to abstain from violence that they still find compelling. "Shoot, shoot, shoot, is what I say," Barry exclaims early in *Boomerang*, suggesting the continued temptation that violence poses for him (15). However, Barry largely limits his own violence to shooting the heads off snakes. Homer's narrative more clearly suggests the damaging effects that violence generates. At one point, Homer is moved to avenge Jack's accidental shooting by Ronnie Foot's grandfather, Gramps (a crazed man who spends his days firing at chickens from his window in the mansion). But having opened fire on the Foot mansion, Homer "drove out of the place, feeling much the coward, seeing that old man [Gramps] run out naked toward my car. He was the first out. I fled. Oh, children, I fled. Such uttermost the coward, the peacenik, the fiend has been offered and I run. I only suggested there should be a reply. Even at my age, I have no more control than a shy midget" (82). The moment is significant in Hannah's oeuvre; unlike earlier Hannah protagonists, Homer's guilt suggests that he has come to understand that such violent acts are misguided and ultimately self-destructive: "My lover came to me and knelt down, asking what she could do to console me. I felt I was in deep trouble, for having fired the shot and seeing the old man come out running naked toward me. . . . There must have been something hideous in my eyes" (82–83).

In their attempt to abstain from violent behavior, Homer and Barry strive to emulate older men: Jack (seventy-eight) and Yelverston (sixty-two) respectively. Despite having experienced terrible violence, Jack and Yelverston have now abjured it themselves. "He has been a man of action," Homer writes admiringly of Jack, a former sheriff in Kentucky, "and now he is quite at peace as a shopkeeper, always polite but never groveling, as you find in the false little country restaurants hereabouts" (*Hey Jack!* 20). Demonstrating a similar respect for his role model, Barry describes Yelverston as "a man before he was a man. He was early at everything. He was a good ballplayer but he was never too good" (*Boomerang* 51). Both Jack and Yelverston embody Hannah's conception, at this turning point in his career, of the "uncle" figure as a new model of positive masculinity. Strictly speaking, Jack is a friend rather than relative of Homer, and while Yelverston is explicitly introduced as an uncle, his fictional status is foregrounded: "When I was fifteen, I already thought about a great uncle whose name would be something like Yelverston" (33). Barry subsequently states that "[a] dad cannot win against the great uncles" before introducing the fictional Yelverston into his own ostensibly autobiographical narrative: "When I finally met him at Syd and Harry's and his son had been killed, and he was sixty-two and I was forty-six, I thought, All right, uncle, tell me everything and I will be your nephew, learning in the new distance" (33). The key point, however, is that in both books the "uncle" figure takes on an almost mythical dimension as an ethical mentor to the narrator. Homer tells us that

> Jack is a better man than I. He never needs a drink and barely even smokes. . . . I was fifty before I considered myself older than anything. As for Jack's age, he must be twenty years older than I, but there is a pleasant accord between himself and the passing times that almost belies age altogether. He will take a drink, mind you. You will recall I mentioned he never needed one, and there is the vast difference. You can bring your own liquor into the coffee shop. He neither encourages nor resents it. But you can detect a little sadness in his eyes behind the wireless spectacles when somebody gets obviously lushed (*Hey Jack!* 18–19).

As *Hey Jack!* progresses, Homer's conception of Jack as an uncle becomes clearer; at one point, he juxtaposes a memory of a "country trip" with Jack alongside a recollection of his Uncle Bill, an uncle by marriage, with whom he had once shared a close relationship (64). Homer recalls that "I had real Dexedrine when I went back to college and memorized entire books of chemistry and algebra, but this was better, out in the sticks under a ten o'clock moon with Uncle Bill, who was ready to go down in the swamps, but he liked me. His brother had burned up four days ago but he was ready for the panther or me, and I was doubled over with hospitality. I even loved my wife" (67). While Homer never overtly compares the two men, the implication is clear: he sees in Jack the same generosity of spirit that he had witnessed in his Uncle Bill (eighty years old when Homer spent time with him).

Even though Jack's standing as an uncle remains more oblique than Yelverston's, both men serve as moral mentors to their respective narrators, their reserve replacing the violence that previously inspired Hannah's protagonists. Barry's appeal for guidance from Yelverston ("All right, uncle, tell me everything and I will be your nephew. . . . One of us has got to be wise" [33]) might have been spoken by Homer to Jack: both narrators strive to match their respective "uncles'" sense of wisdom and peace as they, too, enter later life. This rejection of violence stands in stark contrast to Hannah's earlier fiction, particularly *Geronimo Rex* (1972), in which violence is conceived as an essential component of maturity, as when Harry Monroe discovers in the Apache warrior's brazenness a compelling role model:

> What I especially liked about Geronimo then was that he had cheated, lied, stolen, mutinied, usurped, killed, burned, raped, pillaged, razed, trapped, ripped, mashed, bowshot, stomped, herded, exploded, cut, stoned, revenged, prevenged, avenged, and was his own man; that he had earned his name from the Mexicans after a battle in which he slipped up close enough to shoot their senior officer with an arrow; that the name Geronimo translated as "one who belches" or "one who yawns" or both at the same time; that he had six wives all told; that his whole rage centered around the murder of his first wife and three children by the Mexicans; that he rode with the wind back and forth across the Rio Grande and the Arizona border and left behind him the exasperated armies of the moonlight. I thought I would like to go into that line of work. I would like to leave behind me a gnashing horde of bastards. And I did have on my action boots. (231–32)[5]

In contrast to the reckless capacity for destruction that Harry celebrates in Geronimo, Homer and Barry admire the reserve that Jack and Yelverston demonstrate after the deaths of their children. Charney argues that Homer's perception of Jack as a "man of peace" is "biased and untrue" and that nonviolence "is impossible for either Jack or Homer as long as the Ronnie Foots of the world infest communities and place the immediate needs of the self before the needs of the town" (92). Charney's reading is too pessimistic, however: it does not give due consideration to Jack's ability to resist his violent impulses toward Foot.[6] Moreover, it is important to recognize that Homer admires Jack most of all for his ability to endure his daughter's death: "He had never looked so old and handsome before," Homer observes. "The wind kept at him. His hands seemed full of liver spots. His eyes dimmed. He was barely carrying his weight. I thought he was going to fall. But he didn't" (132). For a writer known for his manic sentences, Hannah's prose here is remarkably sparse, reminiscent of Hemingway, the formal economy underscoring the capacity to continue onward that Hannah celebrates in men such as Jack and Yelverston.

Yet there is, ultimately, a notable difference between Jack and Yelverston. Rick Bass observes of Yelverston that he represents "all the characteristics our species is capable of on our best days: sterling loyalty, a masculine muscularity and feminine sensitivity, an almost Christlike amount of forgiveness" (vii). *Boomerang* is finally not only a tale of endurance, but also one of forgiveness. Yelverston's "Christlike" ability to embrace and rehabilitate his son's killers contrasts with Jack's inability at the end of *Hey Jack!* to pardon Ronnie Foot for giving him "a certain hell." The shift from endurance to forgiveness between the two novels is significant: although Homer locates hope for both himself and his community in Jack's capacity to endure the murder of his daughter, Yelverston's exhibition of the rejuvenating power of forgiveness extends the hopefulness generated by Jack's perseverance in *Hey Jack!*. *Boomerang* moves toward its conclusion in almost fairy-tale fashion with the men who murdered Yelverston's son moving into his Memphis mansion and helping Yelverston raise his newborn son. Through Yelverston's act of mercy, Hannah imagines a redemption that is capable of transforming and saving both the individual and the (southern) community. Having said that, Hannah never loses sight of the shock, pain, and grief that can invade one's life with little warning: at the very end of the narrative, Barry learns from Haim that Yelverston's wife, Ruth, is dying from cancer. Still, despite raising the prospect that Yelverston is facing further devastating personal loss, *Boomerang* closes by celebrating his capacity for endurance and forgiveness: "Throughout the hate and the temporary madnesses, and the envies and the lack of regard and the calamities that have occurred and all the deaths that have happened as given to us by the mad U.S.A. and the mad god, Yelverston has kept on" (143). "It's a lifetime deal," Yelverston declares in the last line of *Boomerang*, a final reminder that redemption, for both Hannah's protagonists and their communities, is never fully secured: it is contingent and must be continually earned (150).[7]

Notes

1. *Boomerang*'s mixture of autobiography and fiction recalls a number of works by a major contemporary American writer who has declared his admiration for Hannah: Philip Roth. Much like Roth's characters "Philip" in *Deception* (1990) and "Philip Roth" in *Operation Shylock* (1993), *Boomerang*'s protagonist "Barry" blurs traditional generic definitions. While much more might be said about such formal and generic issues, in this essay I will refer to *Boomerang* as a novel.

2. This is not to say that this passage is completely representative of Ray's mental state throughout the novel. Rather, his outlook on life fluctuates wildly throughout, from the pessimism of the aforementioned passage to the triumphalism of the novel's concluding lines. Even then, there is no sense that the conclusion to the narrative marks a permanent "victory" for Ray.

3. This optimistic reading of Jack's final shot as a metaphor for moral accountability is bolstered further if we consider the value that Homer continually places upon the game of golf throughout *Hey Jack!* Echoing Bobby Smith's advocacy of French Edward's tennis skills over warfare in *The Tennis Handsome*, Homer depicts golf as an alternative to violence, as when he celebrates Jack's golfing siege on the Foot mansion as a "masterful" expression of passion that averts violence (113).

4. Guinn employs the term "mythoclasm" to refer to the ways in which contemporary southern writers "use postmodern techniques to undermine to undermine, attack, and parody the traditional themes, motifs, and cultural fixtures of southern writing" (xii). "Emigration" alludes to the tendency of writers such as Cormac McCarthy and Richard Ford (also discussed by Guinn in *After Southern Modernism*) to turn the focus of their more recent fiction away from the South to other regions of the United States.

5. Likewise, Ray Forrest celebrates violence, particularly the violence of war, in a manner reminiscent of Harry Monroe: "Sabers up! Get your horses in line! They have as many as we do and it will be a stiff one. Hit them, hit them! Give them such a sting as they will never forget. Ready? *Avant!* Avant, avant, avant! Kill them!" (51–52). Ray even engages in vigilante justice by attacking a college student who assaulted a bum in a public park: "I bashed the fuck out of his [the student's] ribs with it [the club which he had used to attack the bum] and his grandmother screamed" (65).

6. It is true, however, that Jack comes very close to giving into his desire for revenge against Ronnie Foot: "[Jack] was taking out his pistol and showing it behind the counter. It was

a long-barreled .38. . . . Jack was unhinged. I talked him back. I counseled him. His eyes were bright and he was sorely depressed. He kept handing the gun from this hand to that, he stood up suddenly, he sat down, deflated by his audaciousness, having served somebody coffee with the weapon in the other hand" (57–58).

7. I do not mean to claim that *Hey Jack!* and *Boomerang* mark a conclusively optimistic or peace-loving turn to Hannah's career; after all, his next novel *Never Die* (1991) remains his most violent work. In many regards, *Never Die* operates as *Boomerang's* antithesis: the outrageous violence and the absence of any redemptive characters counters the goodness embodied by Yelverston. That said, *Never Die* does not render *Boomerang's* optimism redundant: while *Boomerang* celebrates the potential goodness in contemporary society, *Never Die* centers on how history has transfigured the violence of the past into something heroic and romantic.

Works Cited

Bass, Rick. Introduction. *Boomerang* and *Never Die,* by Barry Hannah. Jackson: UP of Mississippi, 1993. v–xi.

Charney, Mark J. *Barry Hannah.* New York: Twayne, 1992.

Gray, Richard. *Southern Aberrations: Writers of the American South and the Problems of Regionalism.* Baton Rouge: Louisiana State UP, 2000.

Guinn, Matthew. *After Southern Modernism: Fiction of the Contemporary South.* Jackson: UP of Mississippi, 2000.

Hannah, Barry. *Boomerang.* Boston: Houghton Mifflin/Seymour Lawrence, 1989.

———. *Captain Maximus.* New York: Alfred A. Knopf, 1985.

———. *Geronimo Rex.* 1972. New York: Grove P, 1998.

———. *Hey Jack!.* 1987. New York: Penguin, 1988.

———. *Ray.* 1980. New York: Grove P, 1994.

———. *The Tennis Handsome.* 1983. Baton Rouge: Louisiana State UP, 1995.

Hobson, Fred. *The Southern Writer in the Postmodern World.* Athens: U of Georgia P, 1991.

Lilley, James D. and Brian Oberkirch. "An Interview with Barry Hannah." *Mississippi Review* 25.3 (1997): 19–43.

Romine, Scott. *The Narrative Forms of Southern Community.* Baton Rouge: Louisiana State UP, 1999.

Weston, Ruth. *Barry Hannah: Postmodern Romantic.* Baton Rouge: Louisiana State UP, 1998.

"Peeping Toms on History"

Never Die *as Postmodern Western*

—*Mark S. Graybill*

In his thoughtful essay, "Home by Way of California: The Southerner as the Last European," Lewis P. Simpson explores what seem to him basic differences between the mind of the South and its western "other." The latter, contends Simpson, has corollaries in the artistic vision of northeasterners—Henry David Thoreau, James Fenimore Cooper, and the "father" of the popular western, Owen Wister—who create fictions in which a hero transcends history amid the pristine, naturally democratic vistas of the American landscape. In contrast, the former extends a tragic European outlook that sees the individual as a creature trapped, the hapless victim of history. Simpson's paradigm has been very influential in southern studies, and one can indeed see how the tragic ethos he identifies informs to grand effect the body of southern writing produced during the fabled Renaissance, a literature acutely concerned with the past in the present (to paraphrase Allen Tate's famous formulation) and the doomed yet heroic efforts to cope with or survive history, rather than escape from it—an outlook reflected in William Faulkner's famous proclamation in his 1950 Nobel Prize speech that humanity will not merely "endure," but "prevail" (120).

Yet this South-versus-West theory tells only part of the story, for the West has, since the early nineteenth century, occupied a special place in the southern imagination. Historian Richard Slotkin notes in particular how southerners have "mythologiz[ed] ... the Frontier ... as a new Garden of Eden"; he locates this mythos in a Jeffersonian agrarianism in which the "frontier ... promises complete felicity, the satisfaction of all demands and the reconciliation of all contradictions" (69–70). No less a canonical southern text than Mark Twain's *Adventures of Huckleberry Finn* (1884)—identified by both Tate and Louis D. Rubin as the first modern southern novel—bears out this agrarian vision, as Simpson himself tacitly admits. Huck's account shows that life is "satisfying" only when marked by a pastoral plenitude beyond the artificial and hypocritical constraints of southern (read eastern) culture, a realization that ultimately impels him to "light out for the Territory" of the western frontier (Clemens 229). Twain's story may lack the gunplay of the novels that were already beginning to gain popularity in the 1880s, but in its fusion of the southern pastoral and the unadulterated frontier romance, it is in many ways the prototypical "western." Its influence continues as contemporary southern fictionists, including Charles Portis, Richard Ford, Ishmael Reed, and Cormac McCarthy, stake out territory west of the Mississippi. The popularity of McCarthy's *Border Trilogy* confirms most decisively how alluring the West remains for southern writers and readers alike.

Such recent authors, however, offer a more complicated version of the western than does Twain. Whereas the modern (or proto-modern) *Huckleberry Finn* helped establish the cultural authority of a mythologized West, its successors have done much to question that authority. In this respect, they might be called "postmodern." The western's role as a totalizing construction that organizes history into a coherent, "satisfying" set of patterns that essentialize American identity marks it as an example of what Jean-François Lyotard calls "metanarrative."[1] For Lyotard and other noted theorists, postmodern art exhibits a thoroughgoing "incredulity toward metanarratives" (Lyotard xxiv) and usually strives to undermine these over-arching "stories" from within. Linda Hutcheon has shown that postmodern novels about the West, in particular, exhibit a "contradictory attraction/repulsion to structure and patterns" that uses and abuses the western as a genre, ultimately destabilizing the historical, political, and personal fantasies it tries to fulfill (133). One of the most well-known novels by a southerner to do this is McCarthy's prelude to the *Border Trilogy*, *Blood Meridian* (1985).

McCarthy's fascinating account of exploitation and violence parodies *Huckleberry Finn* and later westerns. *Blood Meridian*'s protagonist, minimalistically named "the kid," lights out for the territory emptied of Huck's moral sensibilities, lacking even the modifier that gives western heroes such as Billy the Kid, the Sundance Kid, and the Cisco Kid their uniqueness. If, as John Cawelti says, the western landscape traditionally "suggest[s] the epic courage and regenerative power of the hero" (40), there is no such symbiotic relationship between character and land in *Blood Meridian*. Absent also are the civilizing forces typically found in westerns: wife, schoolmarm, reverend, and sheriff. Moreover, Robert Jarrett has shown how the novel turns inside out the tendency of the "Golden Age western . . . to divide territorial antagonists into allegorical groups of 'good' white and 'bad' black hats (or white and red skin)" (70). As the novel unfolds, it alternately celebrates, condemns, and ignores the violence typical of westerns. The plot "fail[s] to constitute a pattern, to unveil a mystery or to serve any comprehensible purpose" (Shaviro 147), thus calling into question at every turn the ability of any paradigm to explain either history or the novel itself.

Representative of the entire book is the brilliant, brutal Judge Holden, a philosopher who holds forth continuously on the idea of order in the West and in the world at large. Holden stresses order's singular sovereignty as well as its utter provisionality. His presence not only problematizes "the West" as we have come to know it, but reminds us continually "that there are all kinds of orders and systems in our world"—Christianity, pastoralism, capitalism, manifest destiny—"and that we create them all," a realization that radically "condition[s] their truth value" (Hutcheon 43). Praised by commentators such as John Emil Sepich for its scrupulous attention to historical detail, *Blood Meridian* nevertheless makes it very difficult to find meaning in the past, or to locate in it the essential authority of myth. Holden's sinister dance near the novel's close, after he has likely murdered the kid in an outhouse, might be a metaphor for the entire novel, a performance that sweeps the reader along with a perverse, carnivalistic energy: "He dances in light and in shadow and he is a great favorite. He never sleeps, the judge. He is dancing, dancing. He says that he will never die" (335). Is Holden good or evil? Is he, in his ultra-rationalism, a product of the Enlightenment, or does his desire for elemental violence make him pre-modern, a throwback to the days of ancient ritual and myth? Was the western frontier fundamentally moral (as countless versions have asked us to believe), immoral, or amoral? *Blood Meridian* proffers the "true" West insofar as it reflects how chaotic a dance history is, and how limited yet intoxicating human attempts to render it harmoniously are. In its insistence on the raw, overwhelming power of history, the novel bears out Simpson's notion of a southern world view; in its recognition that the coherent patterns we impose on the past are both inevitable and illusory, it strikes me as postmodern.

Barry Hannah's *Never Die* (1991) has not, unfortunately, enjoyed the attention generated by *Blood Meridian*, with which it shares some notable features. Hannah has called *Blood Meridian* his "favorite" McCarthy novel,[2] and his admiration is evident in several ways in *Never Die*. The most obvious sign is Hannah's title, almost certainly a direct reference to the repeated phrase in Judge Holden's concluding performance. *Never Die* engages in many of the same subversive pleasures as *Blood Meridian* and exhibits a similar mixture of violence and humor. History and language both take on the quality of a mad dance. As in McCarthy's novel, an important movement in *Never Die*'s dance is the subversion of metanarratives such as pastoralism, Christianity, industrial capitalism, and the heroic ethos of the "large-hearted" West. Hannah offers a cast of expatriate southerners, each of whom, having gone west to shape a destiny in the wake of the Civil War, must watch his or her designs fall apart. Those of us familiar with the popular western also watch our expectations of the genre disintegrate. As in *Blood Meridian*, a sense of instability obtains as the story unfolds, and in the end we are left without most of the comforts the western typically offers. Hannah denies us even the grandiosity of high tragedy; violence never delivers catharsis. One of the book's points is that the sequence of natural events, in all its otherness, continues apace, regardless of our attempts to slow it. But if history will "never die," neither will the human desire to contain it in narrative.

For all it has in common with *Blood Meridian*, though, *Never Die* is a much zanier novel whose parody leads more frequently to peals of laughter than to uncomfortable smiles or snickers. Whereas McCarthy draws upon certain elements of the conventional western and abandons others, Hannah offers up a parodic smorgasbord of characters and scenarios in order, as Hutcheon might say, "to challenge [them] and yet to use them, even to milk them for all they are worth" (133). All the recognizable constituents are there: the small outpost of a town, a place "even the map seem[s] barely interested in" (92); the sheriff charged to keep order; the legendary gunfighter; the schoolmarm and the good-hearted saloon whore; the "civil servants," including a doctor and judge; the villain and his entourage; and the requisite showdown between "good guy" and "bad guy." Yet this is all off-center, sometimes radically so. The obligatory action usually does not yield the expected results. The characters, who go by names like Fingo, Edwin Smoot, Kyle Nitburg, and Luther Nix, have a cartoonish quality not unlike what one finds in Thomas Pynchon's fiction. There are no white hats-versus-black hats tableaux; this is a lawless country in which everyone is just as much "bad guy" as "good guy"—including the hero manquè, Fernando—and violent farce, not morality, reigns. As one reviewer approvingly put it, with its skewed take on western conventions of characterization and plot, *Never Die* reads "like pure burlesque scored for ukulele" (Coates 3). However, not all reviewers agreed on the merits of Hannah's approach. Janet Kaye complained that the requisite violence of the western "is unsettling" in this novel "but for all the wrong reasons. The perpetrators are presented as if they were the Marx Brothers doing a combination western parody and slasher film." The real problem, as Kaye saw it, is that the "characters in this novel are undeveloped, and Mr. Hannah's fine, wry insight is wasted when applied to caricatures." She concluded by asking, "when, as in *Never Die*, bad things happen to bad caricatures, who is to care?" (18).

As the 1990s drew to a close, a few voices in academe began to challenge overly simplistic reviews of *Never Die* such as Kaye's. Ruth D. Weston considered the novel briefly but sensitively in *Barry Hannah: Postmodern Romantic* (1998), and Robert Brinkmeyer devoted part of a chapter to *Never Die* in *Remapping Southern Literature: Contemporary Writers and the West* (2000). Weston's book was valuable for its focus on Hannah's use of certain postmodern techniques, while Brinkmeyer's study was instrumental in situating *Never Die* among fictions that illustrate a "diminishment of place" in southern letters by turning away from the south toward the west. However, neither Weston nor Brinkmeyer developed a detailed reading of the novel as a postmodern western. There has, though, been at least one thorough and compelling article published on the way western conventions are appropriated by postmodern writers more generally. While Theo

D'haen's "Popular Genre Conventions in Postmodern Fiction: The Case of the Western" appeared several years before *Never Die*, many of its points prove useful in understanding Hannah's postmodern western and help to correct further overly reductive readings like Kaye's.[3] D'haen suggests that though popular forms like the western are anti-modernist in that they challenge "'high art' ... as the last metanarrative, the last bastion of the humanist world view" espoused by New Critics T. S. Eliot and F. R. Leavis (163), they nevertheless seek to create a kind of literary and moral "consensus" in society (164), a project that Lyotard would see as basically modernist. Citing Cawelti, D'haen explains how "formula stories," of which the western is a prime example, "serve their audience's needs of escape and relaxation" by "project[ing] 'collective fantasies shared by large groups of people.'" Hence, they "help to maintain a culture's ongoing consensus about the nature of reality and morality" (Cawelti, qtd in D'haen 164). But one important difference between formula stories and "serious" literature, argues D'haen, is that "the formula's frame of reference ... is primarily 'generic' [rather than] 'mimetic,'" a distinction that "tallies rather well with the Postmodernist idea of the world itself as story," as a network of fictional codes. Postmodern writers including E. L. Doctorow, Richard Brautigan, and Louis Ferron (all of whom D'haen discusses in some detail) exploit popular genres by

> turn[ing] the blatant codedness of these formulas upon itself in order to express their distrust/disbelief in all metanarratives: they play havoc with the formulaic conventions to upset, rather than uphold, the very idea that there could be such a thing as a tenable metanarrative, and to reveal literature's complicity in ideology building (165–66).

While postmodernists employ the various codes upon which the western relies—D'haen mentions just a few, including the conflict between hero and villain, which ends with the former reestablishing order through violence over the admonitions of "an eastern schoolmarm or a heart-of-gold saloon lady or whore madam"—they subvert those codes "to reveal the projective character of these principles by first invoking them, and then negating the conventions evoking them" (166). This is very much Hannah's tactic in *Never Die*.

Consider, for example, the novel's "hero," Fernando Muré. At first, he appears to be precisely what his Spanish-sounding name suggests: a kind of *caballero* who walks the streets in a "fedora [with] his long tan Mexican cigarettes" (5). Fernando is a "mediocre gambler" who nevertheless wins "a fortune" in money and respect when he demonstrates his prowess with a gun after a poker game gone bad. Confronted by "three angry men" with guns,

> Fernando sensed what was happening [and] threw over the table, got behind it and received fire. With his left hand around his groin he ducked his head and fired through the table itself, took out the other pistol and did the same. When the smoke cleared, the table was shredded, but he had not suffered a scratch. All three of his adversaries lay dead. (4)

After this, Fernando's legend grows. Later we learn that around town "it was rumored that [he] could not only see behind his back but around corners" (87). This is all pretty standard fare for a western. But almost as soon as Hannah establishes Fernando as a mythical (and typical) desperado, he begins to subvert the role. We are told, for example, that the rival gamblers bore "shotguns loaded for doves" (4), a small detail that diminishes their ominousness and Fernando's heroics. The more we learn about this legendary gunslinger, the more quirky and less imposing he seems.

For one thing, he is not a Mexican but an idle, terminally bored New Orleans native with a lisp, a university education, and a severe case of melancholia. In talking about Fernando, Hannah admits he had in mind the stereotypical faded southern aristocrat, a product of a "sad" cultural "incest you see in the delta of Mississippi where big old boys are really just kind of mama's boys wandering around in the right clothes" with "nothing to assert" (interview). One can see Fernando as a parodic, middle-aged Quentin Compson, brooding and hypersensitive. The narrator assures us that he was not always so emotional and ineffectual. We are told how as a young man Fernando "could scheme, plunge through, grapple, pitch" with the best (23). But as Hannah says, Fernando "knows that he is not a hero" (interview). The character himself claims as much, lamenting the way he has been mythologized: "I didn't want to be this much Fernando. You know, you start with little things, they grow, pretty soon there's something grown beside you looks like you" (104). Even the recounted escapades of his early years, when he was a "bad guy," evoke laughter, not fear or respect. Out one night on the range, a rattler "just came up and bit him on the mouth, and since then, the despised lisp." On another occasion, he robbed a train carrying mail and then sobbed "over the letters to loved ones he had deflected" (23). In the present, the town's women secretly wish for him to "assault them like a shovel of passion pushed in the grave of their lusts," but his sadness is "turning [him] androgynous" (7). Fernando is an alcoholic whose greatest talent might be his ability to make his testicles—comically named Juan and Manuel—dance.

As in the westerns that D'haen discusses, in *Never Die* "the reader is made to reflect on the difference between [this character] and the typical western hero" (D'haen 168). This is especially true when Fernando faces his primary nemesis, Edwin Smoot, who himself does not conform to the conventional image of a western villain. A dwarf likely imported by Hannah from the arguably postmodern TV western *The Wild, Wild West*, the "low man" Smoot lays Fernando low early in the narrative, not through cunning or physical prowess, but by bashing one of his kneecaps with a baseball bat as Fernando stumbles drunkenly through town. Later, as Fernando lies passed out in the office of Doc Fingo—a homosexual who is in love with Fernando and gives his patient a morphine addiction that will plague him throughout the novel—Smoot returns with the bat and cracks his other knee.

Fernando is, of course, outraged at being defeated by a "mere nub of a villain" (21), but he is powerless to avenge himself through most of the book. Instead of finding Smoot, he tries to burn the entire town of Nitburg. In a more conventional western, this might be an act of heroism, a purification ritual meant to cleanse the corrupt town run by Smoot's boss, Judge Kyle Nitburg, the man who gives the order to wound Fernando. In this novel, however, it is anti-climactic and anti-cathartic, a mere accident of history. The blaze gets out of hand, and Fernando realizes that he is not a shaper of history, but a bit player. Commenting on such "climactic" scenes, Hannah wryly points out: "Nothing's been accomplished. You've burnt down half of a town. It doesn't prove anything. . . . Burning up the edifices looks good in the movies, but it doesn't prove a damn thing, you know? You're just knocking down shit, like teenagers" (interview). When Fernando and

Smoot do eventually have a showdown, it is another parodic scene both laconic and comic. There is none of the anticipated "gunplay"—which should not be surprising, since the judge warns earlier that there never was "much . . . play. People shot each other, from the back at close range, preferably" (48)—and Smoot actually demands that Fernando kill him. When Fernando "raise[s] the gun without much determination," Smoot says he wants the deed done with a knife, and his adversary, who admits "I ain't never been a knife man . . . and I ain't got the strength," begins to walk away. Then comes one of the funny yet disturbing exchanges at which Hannah is so adept:

> —I'll shoot you where you stand, nigger! cried Smoot.
> Fernando looked around again.
> —Smoot, I'm not a nigger.
> —In my world you are! You ain't never known my world!
> This ain't over! I'll shoot you where you stand! (*143*)

With that, Fernando grudgingly fires on and kills Smoot, winning the "duel" without a trace of the usual drama.

Hannah's subversion of the hero and villain figures might be enough by itself to thwart the reader's expectations and expose the fissures in the mythology that westerns rely upon for their cultural authority. But Hannah takes similar liberties with most of the other character types as well. The local preacher, McCorkindale, is plagued by lust and proliferating body hair. The powerful Judge Nitburg, who seems at first reminiscent of McCarthy's Holden, turns out to be an ambivalent, lonely soul "so exquisitely friendless" that "some afternoons . . . he roll[s] over and over in a hot tub of water trying to suck himself" (30). The women characters are even less conventional. They occupy the traditional positions in this society, but do not behave in the traditional ways. Stella, the tubercular "slut" who serves as Fernando's love interest (6), is not really convincing as the typically kind, sexless village whore, though she is passive enough. But with Tall Jane—a "tall and strong lesbian prostitute" who procures opium for Nermer, the town hermit (124)—Hannah thoroughly subverts the stereotypical image of the western saloon madam. When Nitburg erupts into flames and gunfire, it is she, not Fernando, who steps out into the street in "her high heels" and performs the role of gunslinger, cutting down two men and then dancing on their lifeless bodies—because "they killed two of [her] domino partners" (125).

While women traditionally bring a measure of civility, even domesticity, to the western, *Never Die* never offers "a clean, god fearing, gentle and loving Eastern schoolmarm" like Molly Wood in Wister's 1902 novel, *The Virginian* (D'haen 168). Nandina Nitburg is the closest we get. Though a schoolteacher who occasionally memorizes a Psalm, Nandina does not play the devoted girlfriend to Fernando; she plays the field, flirting with and seducing men in Nitburg as she mines for financial prospects. Nandina's initial appearance in the novel confirms that while she may share Molly Wood's profession, she shares none of her domesticity and moral rectitude: we see Nandina kissing her own father down to the "teeth," attracted to him "just an elf's step beyond common practice . . . because of the judge's late rapid wealth" (13). Like Tall Jane, Nandina can take care of herself, as she demonstrates when the aptly named Randy Black solicits sexual favors from her in the desert. After Randy gets "down on his knees" expecting that Nandina will "commit something with [him]," she spits on him and rides away (77). She does so because Randy cannot offer her what she really wants: to own "an automobile"—that symbol of power and freedom coveted by many in the book—and ride along with "the wind in [her] hair, the cock of a gun or whatever you call it in [her] hand, the thrashing putrid smoke around [her]" (21). In the popular western, it is very rare, of course, for a woman—particularly a schoolmarm—to dream of being "a member of some riding gang" so she can "rain unprovoked violence on something, someone!" (20).

Nandina's fantasy never comes to fruition, nor do the dreams of the other characters in *Never Die*—and if the members of this motley group have one thing in common, it is that they dream. Yet, among their fantasies there is, as one character says about Fernando, not "one dream that'd square with the earth" (94). This is one of the more serious aspects of a novel filled with madcap humor: human dreams—whether in the form of a grand "design," a waking fantasy, a reverie during sleep, a vision induced by alcohol or morphine, or a novel—do not "square with the earth"; that is, with the inscrutable processes of nature, history, the real. If the traditional western novel fulfills our own fantasies about how the region was "won," *Never Die* disturbs those fantasies by drawing our attention to their ideological underpinnings. If the classic western provides us a window on history as we want to see it, Hannah's postmodern version makes us aware of our looking, our readerly voyeurism, and shifts our focus to the window's frame.

Nitburg, the town in which the action of the novel occurs, is itself the apparently realized dream of Judge Kyle Nitburg, a southerner and self-made man who, like Huckleberry Finn and Faulkner's Thomas Sutpen before him, lights out for the territory. He seems motivated both by a desire to escape history and a need to take advantage of and shape it. His journey begins in the wake of the Civil War, which pitted "brother against brother" or, in his case, "child against mother" (89): upon learning as a twelve-year-old in New Orleans that his mother is a spy for the Confederacy, Nitburg promptly turns her in to the Union, collects his one-hundred-dollar reward, and watches her "hanged on a railroad bridge" (1). "He was in the main sweep of an awesome history," the narrator says, "and he could not help it" (89). But Nitburg tries to carve his niche in history by taking the money, heading west, and building his own modest empire. He marries, then sells his wife to a Comanche tribe "for four thousand dollars in real gold" (2). Soon after, the west Texas hamlet of Dolores Springs becomes Nitburg, a town the judge manages through violence and the distribution of drugs.

Kyle Nitburg reminds one of Faulkner's Flem Snopes, a southerner for whom the old ways have no value and capitalism seems the only authority. "This is who settled the West," says Hannah. "It was not done by well-meaning spirits; it was done by rather vicious capitalism" (interview). Although Hannah betrays a certain sympathy (both in the novel and in his comments about it) for the ingenuity and drive of the judge and his kind, he seems most interested in exposing the economic and social ideology that motivated settlement of the West—an ideology ignored or disguised in most westerns. Hutcheon observes that postmodernists use the western "not, as some have claimed, [as] a form of 'Temporal Escape,'" but as "a coming to terms with the existing traditions of earlier historical and literary articulations of Americanness" (133). The point seems quite appropriate vis-à-vis *Never Die*. The novel, in a fashion similar to Doctorow's 1960 novel *Welcome to Hard Times* (and one of its intertexts, Stephen Crane's "The Blue Hotel" [1899]), "underline[s] ... the power of money, greed, and force on the western frontier: through intertextuality, it is suggested that some noble myths have capitalistic exploitation at their core" (Hutcheon 133–34). As

Hannah interrogates narrative constructions of "Americanness," he simultaneously questions representations of the old South by giving us a glimpse of Snopesism before the letter.

Capitalism, for all the power it affords Kyle Nitburg, does not secure for him a place above or outside history. As a metanarrative, it is just as provisional as those it has supplanted. The judge, grown older, senses that his town is on the brink of destruction, and tries to convince himself of its—and his—sovereignty. Reflecting on the corruption and violence that have brought him control—and perhaps on the irony that violence will presently destroy his dream—Nitburg asks Smoot: "Yet Nitburg is, is it not?" (99). But the West is not a script waiting for him to write it. History rolls on, according to its own unknown narrative momentum, as the town of Nitburg burns outside the bathroom window where the judge has spent afternoons masturbating. Although the town does recover from the fire, as does the judge, the glory, such as it was, dissipates. Though he "still ha[s] a great deal of money" afterward, "he [can] not think of one thing to buy" (150): capitalism has failed him.

Part of the irony in Nitburg's fall is that it is made possible by the technological innovation ushered in by industrial capitalism: a Winton Flyer automobile, owned by Navy Remington, Nitburg's foe, and a World War I biplane both play roles in the destruction of the town. By introducing these symptoms of modernization, Hannah again breaks the rules of the classic western, for, as Jane Tompkins notes, the genre "requires a technologically primitive environment" in which characters can prove themselves man-to-man (34). No one in the novel is comfortable with these new machines, though some of them recognize the possibilities for freedom and power that they offer. Smoot, for instance, fantasizes about stealing the automobile and kidnapping Remington's pet monkey:

> He dreamed of the picture, the things, the revulsion of the town, the rambling buckboard, the smoke of South Texas dust, himself ramming through it in the long steely automobile, beyond it all, circling it, the monkey in goggles sitting next to him. He would mount two steel barrels of gasoline in the back seat so he would never run out of fuel. He could drive to Brazil and meet that monkey's relatives if he wanted to. (38–39)

Nandina, too, dreams of the car. For her it represents wealth, power, freedom, and an erotic pleasure of the kind J. G. Ballard associates with automobiles in his controversial novel, *Crash* (1973). The Winton Flyer (already described in decidedly phallic terms in Smoot's daydream) becomes most blatantly a sex object during Nandina's surreptitious visit to Remington's garage, where she samples some of the oil left in the car's parking place:

> She knelt and put her fingers in the oil, right down to the clay.
> Then she put a finger in her mouth. This was a first for her. So
> this was what made the New World run. There was something
> awfully familiar about the taste, something from way back there
> in the swamps, the gas, the rotten roots, the scaly alive things
> heaving mud around. She put her finger in again and sucked the
> oil off. Actually, she thought, this tastes better than men. (46)

Tellingly, Nandina later dies in the Winton Flyer. Though she envisions the automobile as her deliverance into a brave new world, Hannah knows differently. This is nothing new, he seems to say; where there were horses and guns before, there are now cars and airplanes mounted with guns. The "New World" should not be exalted any more than the old, the era of the "damned, woolly west," as one character calls it (148). Thoughout *Never Die*, Hannah deconstructs both the myth of the wild West and the industrial/technological metanarrative that supposedly succeeds it.

Hannah also targets two older symbolic orders which complement each other but are equally illusory: Christianity and the pastoral. True to the form of his other novels, Hannah is particularly hard on Christianity. As in Zane Grey's *Riders of the Purple Sage* (1912), the resident schoolmarm in *Never Die* reads from that most pastoral of Psalms, the twenty-third. But whereas Grey's Jane Withersteen subscribes to it faithfully, Nandina dismisses it as nothing more than "a tidy dream" (17). In this respect, Hannah's western does something that Jane Tompkins argues many westerns do: it "asserts ... that Jane Withersteen's goodness and mercy, the 23rd Psalm, and the whole Judeo-Christian tradition it represents won't work when the chips are down" (34). Yet it does so in a way that inverts Grey's text, because it is not the gunfighter but the school teacher, the "good Christian woman," who demonstrates the untenability of Christian pastoralism. Others in the novel mock the idea that the West could be a new Eden, a Christian paradise for southerners on the run from the nightmare of history. Ironically, the Reverend McCorkindale is one of the most vociferous. His warning to his oblivious congregation—"The Lord giveth and the Lord taketh away. Rotten Indian-giver, eh? There is no mercy. Things can turn on you like a stomped snake" (57)—echoes, with comic difference, the eulogy that John Wayne's character, Thomas Dunson, delivers over the body of a man he has killed in *Red River* (1948).[4] When McCorkindale does try to play the role of traditional pastor, suggesting that Fernando sing the hymn "I Walk in the Garden Alone," Fernando quips, "That's for them that can walk. I can hardly tumble toward the outhouse" (36).

As unviable as Christianity and the pastoral may be, visions of Eden seem to permeate other characters' dreams of what the West should be, just as Richard Slotkin suggests it did for many southerners in the nineteenth century. The hermit, Nermer, continuously reads Psalm 23, convinced it is "the only verse a man need[s], really" (28). Sheriff Neb Lewton has strange dreams in which "he curses God," but in which "something still calls him from a cool garden in his memory" (5). And then there is Navy Remington, the eccentric sea captain and veteran of the Confederacy, a gentleman who remembers fighting for "the Old Cause," whose "life ha[s] been heavy with honor and duty" (82). More than any of his fellow expatriates, he seems to believe he can transplant the dispossessed garden of the South to the open, virginal spaces of the West. Though he has purchased a piece of the industrialized world in the Winton Flyer, Remington's style of life might be best described as agrarian. He has established a little pastoral island, a sheep ranch with a garden forty miles east of Nitburg (3). He has also taken up writing as a gentlemanly avocation, evidenced by his manuscript, *The History of My Life and Times by Capt. A. Navy Remington* (41). But, unknown to Remington, his pastoral design is being sabotaged by Smoot, who breaks into his house and "poison[s] his garden every solstice." As Smoot thinks about how he has duped Remington, an image of the former sea captain emerges that is both humorous and pathetic: "Navy Remington might have been a big man on the sea, but he was a fool moving his garden from place to place in a sublime watered meadow. Probably looking up at the sky toward God and asking what the deuce were these last two years, Papa? Smoot smiled, but not very much" (40). The humor and pathos of this scenario spring, oddly enough, from the same realization. Remington's predicament parallels that of all the characters: he journeys west with a dream, a design, only to see his desires mysteriously, inexplicably thwarted.

Readers who find special pleasure in classic representations of the West—that is, representations that emphasize its mythical qualities—likely have similarly frustrated expectations as they make their journey through *Never Die*. As they see less than heroic fates befall Hannah's collection of weirdo outcasts, they sense the dissolution of the West as they have always known and loved it, not because they identify with the characters, but, paradoxically, because they do not. The novel has the effect of making us aware of our own readerly desires, our own need to have the history of the West (intermingled, in various ways, with the history of the South and of all the United States) assume a particular shape and order. It achieves this effect by manipulating generic conventions, of course, but it also employs other self-reflexive strategies to focus our attention on the processes by which myths and fantasies are made.

Some of those strategies are blatant, some subtle. Fernando talks rather overtly about how "real" people and events are inevitably subsumed into narrative: "Comes to a point where you ain't nothing but a couple of stories blowing around like a weed" (83). The stories get started by assorted chroniclers—poets, photographers, newspaper men—and then become their own essence, their own reality. Hannah consistently mocks the human appetite for myth on which they thrive. He parodies, for instance, the inflated rhetoric of myth with L. P. Sheheen's account of the final confrontation between Fernando and Smoot. A man supposedly obsessed with "facts," Sheheen's version is rife with clichés characteristic of the dime novel, the cowboy movie, and the television western: "The sun was dark and hot. But their guns were long. . . . How it begun was not wrote out well for Fernando. . . . The last to fall was the low man Smoot. . . . We will be here at the same time tomorrow, my children" (144–47). This parodic scop's oration is devastatingly funny largely because the "children" to whom Sheheen speaks are actually hogs. But at times, Hannah abandons knee-slapping humor in favor of something more subtle. In the novel's opening, the narrator mentions that Kyle Nitburg had been photographed next to his mother's dangling corpse after betraying her: "An early cameraman got it perfectly in black and white. He was a student of Matthew Brady, the great Civil War photographer" (2). Though it seems an insignificant detail, it hints at the way history has been "captured" on film, framed for easy viewing. The mention of Brady—a kind of legend in his own right who purportedly "staged" some of his pictures to get the best effect—might also remind us to what degree historical representations are always illusory, inherently fictitious.

As D'haen observes, postmodern novels usually foreground the "projective character" of representations, especially when society has afforded them, for whatever reason, some special authority. Perhaps *Never Die* does this most effectively by employing a theme beloved by postmodern authors from Nabokov and Pynchon to Julio Cortázar and John Fowles: voyeurism. Of course, the story depicts for the reader sexual scenes usually absent in westerns—the judge diddling himself, Remington "ravishing" Nandina, Stella watching Fernando's testicles dance—but Hannah is interested in more than sexual appetite. He is concerned with the more intense, perhaps connected, desire to see the past made into myth, to see history "screwed" with.

Near the end of *Never Die*, the eastern newspaper man Philip Hine, introduced earlier as a "kindly verisimilitudinist" (128), expresses most clearly Hannah's conception of reader-as-voyeur and history-as-fantasy. Hine, whose occupation supposedly depends on objectivity, "freely admit[s]" to being "a voyeur ... [a] peeping Tom." When his listeners puzzle at this statement, he tries to illustrate with an example: what if, he proposes, "an average sidewalk-walking woman ... came in here right in your face, took off her clothes, I mean jaybird naked and just stood there with her things hanging out." His audience members all agree: "Well. Not really so good." "But see," says Hine, "a woman at night across the way through gauze curtains, lighted from behind, doing the same thing with, say, just a little grace, just a little—here we are—slowness. ... Time and distance. Distance from the woman. The time it would take to get her. The whole thing becomes something else entirely. And who is to say not more real" (151). Though Nermer and McCorkindale do not understand, Hannah undoubtedly hopes the reader does. We are all somewhat like Hine, Hannah suggests; we who read the novels and histories and watch the films and documentaries about the West are all "peeping Toms on history" (interview).

The western genre has provided a window on the past, replete with gossamer drapery to give it the right effect. As the poststructuralist psychoanalyst Jacques Lacan might say, the western has satisfied its readers' desires to see "the object as absence." The voyeur relies on time and distance, and on a mediating structure—which, in the case of the novel, means language—to place between him and the fantasy object. But Lacan explains that voyeurism is always an act of projection, a passive externalization of desire: "What the voyeur is looking for and finds is merely a shadow, a shadow behind the curtain. There he will phantasize any magic of presence, the most graceful of girls, for example, even if on the other side there is only a hairy athlete" (182). Traditional representations of western history, which have often been taken for "truth," facilitate this projective process; put simply, they show us what we want to see. Such is the goal of Hine and other chroniclers of the West. He says as much on the last page of the book, speaking of how the mythical status of Fernando and the others will continue to grow: "Every day, more light from behind, more softness, more gauze. It's time we held the dance of history. You're all heroes, and folks will miss your kind. History won't let you hate yourselves anymore" (152).

Never Die consistently frustrates its readers' voyeuristic designs and desires, presenting the outlines of characters and events we expect to see in a western, only to pull aside the gauze and reveal misfits, caricatures, and parodies. It resists the temptation to reduce in a realistic narrative the irreducible "sweep of an awesome history" (89). It never takes itself too seriously, never allows readers to think for very long that this might be the "real" West; as the author himself admits, the book is "false history" whose territory is not the actual West, but "Hannah's West" (interview). A delightful exercise in postmodern humor, *Never Die* counters Hine's choreographed but seemingly fluid dance of history with the banal and ridiculous, the dance of Fernando's testicles.

Hannah's only published novel of the 1990s also recognizes that the fantasy of the mythical West will go on unabated, even in an era when books and films are contesting in their various ways that myth.[5] Ironically, the western's "gleam," as Hannah has called it, will continue partly because works such as *Never Die* and *Blood Meridian* perpetuate it even while parodying it.

As David Cowart writes, no matter how derisive parody is, inasmuch as it "imitates" in some measure its target or "host" text, it "revitalizes as it subverts." In this regard, "even as the truth quotient of the host diminishes, even as its pretensions to absolute insight dissipate, the host benefits from the attachment of its postmodern guest" (Cowart 39). This is a phenomenon of which Hannah, who speaks lovingly of westerns as his generation's opera, seems quite aware—so much so that he concludes his subversive western with a moment of pastiche, a sly nod to the pastoral fantasy that the West once seemed to offer: the aging, unheroic Fernando, saddled with a "paunch" and a "face . . . slack and grotesque," sits fishing, "the river lap[s] green and merry in the cove under the willows" (152). The myth, Hannah seems to acknowledge, will never die. But at least we can laugh at it.

Notes

1. My conflation of myth and metanarrative here might seem counterintuitive, but, as Lyotard makes clear, they are two sides of the same epistemological coin: both "legitimate social and political institutions and practices, forms of legislation, ethics, modes of thought, and symbolics." The only difference is that metanarratives "ground this legitimacy not in an original 'founding' act," as myths do, "but in a future to be brought about, that is, in an Idea to realize" (Lyotard 50). As I show, *Never Die* confronts both myth and metanarrative through its "serious play."
2. From an interview with Barry Hannah conducted by the author on 27 July 1997 in Oxford, Mississippi. Subsequent quotations are noted parenthetically as "interview."
3. Hannah himself seems ambivalent about being called a postmodern writer (just as he has seemed, at times, to harbor mixed emotions about being called a southern writer). While he notes that he has never taken "anti-narrative" as a technique or "the fragmentation of existence . . . as a theme," he clearly admires McCarthy at least partly because "his novels are postmodern" (interview). Elsewhere, Hannah has expressed admiration for fictionists such as Donald Barthelme, Samuel Beckett, and Kurt Vonnegut, all of whom critics often consider postmodern.
4. Dunson says: "We brought nothing into this world, and it's certain we can carry nothing out. The Lord gave and the Lord hath taken away. Blessed be the name of the Lord. Amen."
5. *Never Die* bespeaks a familiarity with a number of these films, including Sam Peckinpah's *The Wild Bunch* (1969), which features a gang of aging "heroes" in confrontation with a world increasingly run by machines, and Robert Altman's *McCabe and Mrs. Miller* (1971), which, as Hannah noted during our 1997 interview, treats the often ignored role of drug abuse in the "wild West." The year following *Never Die*'s publication saw the release of Clint Eastwood's *Unforgiven* (1992), a film that, among other things, reminds us of the role that writers like Hine have played in creating a mythologized but enduring view of the West.

Works Cited

Brinkmeyer, Robert H. *Remapping Southern Literature: Contemporary Writers and the West.*
    Athens, GA: U of Georgia P, 2000.
Cawelti, John G. *The Six-Gun Mystique.* Bowling Green, OH: Bowling Green U
    Popular P, n.d.
Clemens, Samual Langhorne [Mark Twain]. *Adventures of Huckleberry Finn.* New York:
    Norton, 1977.
Coates, Joseph. "Barry Hannah's Wild West Gunman Seeks a Place Where a Boy Can
    Roam." Rev. of *Never Die.* By Barry Hannah. *Chicago Tribune* 26 May 1991: 3.
Cowart, David. *Literary Symbiosis: The Reconfigured Text in Twentieth-Century Writing.*
    Athens: U of Georgia P, 1993.
D'haen, Theo. "Popular Genre Conventions in Postmodern Fiction: The Case of the
    Western." *Exploring Postmodernism.* Eds. Matei Calinescu and Douwe Fokkema.
    Amsterdam: John Benjamins, 1988. 161–74.
Faulkner, William. *Essays, Speeches, and Public Letters.* Ed. James B. Meriweather. New York:
    Random House, 1966.
Hannah, Barry. *Never Die.* Boston: Houghton Mifflin/Seymour Lawrence, 1991.
———. Personal interview. 27 July 1997.
Hutcheon, Linda. *A Poetics of Postmodernism.* New York: Routledge, 1988.
Jarrett, Robert L. *Cormac McCarthy.* New York: Twayne, 1997.
Kaye, Janet. "Is Nitburg Burning?" Rev. of *Never Die.* By Barry Hannah. *The New York
    Times Book Review* 7 July 1991: 18.
Lacan, Jacques. *The Four Fundamental Concepts of Psycho-Analysis.* Trans. Alan Sheridan.
    New York: Norton, 1981.
Lyotard, Jean-François. *The Postmodern Condition.* Trans. Geoff Benington and Brian
    Massumi. Minneapolis: U of Minnesota P, 1984.
———. *The Postmodern Explained.* Eds. Julian Pefanis and Morgan Thomas. Trans. Don
    Barry et al. Minneapolis: U of Minneapolis P, 1992.
McCarthy, Cormac. *Blood Meridian; or, The Evening Redness in the West.* New York: Vintage
    International, 1985.
Sepich, John Emil. "The Dance of History in Cormac McCarthy's *Blood Meridian.*"
    Southern Literary Journal 24.1 (1991): 16–31.
Shaviro, Steven. " 'The Very Life of the Darkness': A Reading of *Blood Meridian.*"
    Perspectives on Cormac McCarthy. Eds. Edwin T. Arnold and Dianne C. Luce. Jackson:
    UP of Mississippi, 1993. 145–56.
Simpson, Lewis P. "Home by Way of California: The Southerner as the Last European."
    Southern Literature in Transition. Eds. Philip Castille and William Osborne. Memphis:
    Memphis State UP, 1983. 55–70.
Slotkin, Richard. *The Fatal Environment.* New York: Harper Perennial, 1985.
Tompkins, Jane. *West of Everything.* New York: Oxford UP, 1992.
Wayne, John, perf. *Red River.* Screenplay by Borden Chase and Charles Schnee. Dir.
    Howard Hawkes. MGM, 1948.
Weston, Ruth D. *Barry Hannah: Postmodern Romantic.* Baton Rouge: Louisiana State UP,
    1998.

Southern and Western Native Americans in Barry Hannah's Fiction

—*Melanie R. Benson*

> But it's the cowboys and Indians, on a much fiercer level, that make you admit things to yourself. . . . That kind of grotesque need to maim that you don't acknowledge as a part of yourself. You may deny it, and you don't do it of course, but it helps to notice that's a part of you.
> —Barry Hannah, Interview with James D. Lilley and
>   Brian Oberkirch

> To understand the South and southerners, we need to understand southern representations of Indians.
> —Joel Martin, "'My Grandmother Was a Cherokee Princess'"

In the spring 2005 special issue of *South Central Review* entitled "Rethinking Southern Literary Studies," Patricia Yaeger investigates a litany of ghosts haunting southern literature as shattered reminders of its imperfectly repressed racial trauma. We must pay attention to these tropes, she suggests, "lest we forget, in this halfway house beyond segregation, that we are still recreating, in our lives and stories, the conditions of racial haunting" (107). Yaeger locates this "return of the dispossessed" primarily in African American fiction (95, 101, 104). In her contribution to the same special issue, Sarah Ford agrees that southern studies itself is "haunted by ghosts from the past," but notes that the spirits we consider nowadays tend to be ex-slaves rather than Confederate heroes (23). Both Yaeger and Ford endorse the promising trends in southern studies that provide overdue attention to the African American southern experience; nonetheless, both critics fail to address a less visible but no less troubling category of southern dispossession: the dispossession of American Indian southerners. For all that the "new southern studies" has begun to listen to and address the haunting ghost stories of African American slaves, the work of channeling the South's first inhabitants and most repressed ghosts has hardly begun.

Leslie Fiedler begins his classic work *The Return of the Vanishing American* (1968) with the observation that "all of us seem men possessed" by the soul of the Indian, and remarks that "[a]n astonishing number of novelists have begun to write fiction in which the Indian character, whom only yesterday we were comfortably bidding farewell ... has disconcertingly reappeared" (13).[1] Fiedler's focus—in keeping with that of most Native American scholarship—is primarily on the West: he explains that while southern literature revolves around white confrontations with the stereotypical "nigger," the "heart of the Western is ... the encounter with the Indian" (17–19, 21). Numerous critics have recapitulated Fiedler's paradigms; only a few have transgressed these scholarly boundaries to interrogate the South's disturbingly repressed Indian encounters. Yet, as Mick and Ben Gidley suggest in a recent essay, "[t]he eradication of Indian tribes in the Southeast was probably more wholesale than in any other culture area" (167). As devastating as this phase of Removal was to southeastern tribes in the 1830s, it seems to have been largely forgotten. The idea of a southeastern Indian is now virtually obsolete, emblematic only of "an entire vanished way of life" (Peterson 4). This history has attracted only scant attention in the work of Gidley and Gidley, Eric Gary Anderson, Annette Trefzer, Michael Green, Theda Perdue, and Joel Martin. Yet even many of these well-intentioned scholars adopt the "eradication" hypothesis. The fact is that many Indians *do* remain in the South, either having resisted Removal or returned in later decades. The real problem is that they remain unseen, unnoticed: Tom Mould observes that despite the Mississippi Choctaw's remarkable cultural and political revitalization, one might today "visit Mississippi and ... have no idea there is a major American Indian community here. Live in Mississippi and the Choctaw could escape you as well" (xxii–iii). How do we explain these evasions, particularly at what is arguably (new) southern studies' most progressive moment? And how, in this critical vacuum, do we begin to account for the parade of apparently extinct Indians resurfacing in the writings of present-day southerners?

On the one hand, Indian ghosts confirm the impotence of "savagery" in the wake of "civilization" and "progress"; on the other hand, they announce a nation's nagging ambivalence about its ruthless origins. As Reneé Bergland notes, while Indian ghosts often possess Americans with supernatural guilt, they can also be transformed into useful ideological material by whites, as "nationalist narratives continue to be hungry for resistant ones" (4). In his survey of Indian representations throughout southern history, Joel Martin observes the compulsion to erase actual Indians yet to preserve their memory in a plethora of place names; these residues paradoxically make southern *white* civilization "seem as if it had been there forever" (138). Words like Tuscaloosa and Tallahatchee memorialize and negate Indian precedence in one convenient package; however, actual, surviving southeastern Indians are more difficult to suppress. Indian resurfacings in southern literature are particularly troubling because they indicate not just an attempt to cover over the region's messy colonial beginnings, but also a disturbing desire to erase the Indian traces that still exist.

Despite Barry Hannah's numerous representations of Native American histories and figures, particularly in works like *Geronimo Rex* (1972) *Ray* (1980), and *Never Die* (1991), not a single scholar has attempted to explore their significance to Hannah's crisis-ridden contemporary South. The gap is puzzling, given that Hannah's first, highly-acclaimed novel is named after the infamous Apache warrior Geronimo, and that several of his subsequent novels play upon western settings and motifs. I want to suggest that Hannah's representations of Native Americans must be understood in a somewhat reactionary tradition of southern self-interest. Situating Hannah in this context may seem antithetical to recent critical work by Michael Kreyling, Martyn Bone, Matthew Guinn and others which places him in a *post*southern context. To be sure, while Hannah publicly "adores" the South, he certainly does not glorify or romanticize it (Trucks 227); instead, he depicts a region still battling the demons of its historical transgressions, imprisoned, like the protagonist of *Ray*, "in so many centuries. Everybody is still alive" (41). Besieged by memories of both the Civil War and the conflict in Vietnam, Ray Forrest's fragile mental state demonstrates that not only the South but the entire country remains haunted by the specter of imperialism. Guinn traces *Ray*'s even bleaker connections between the war in Vietnam and the De Soto expedition that "discovered" the Mississippi River and inaugurated the displacement and slaughter of the southeastern Indians. But Hannah's representation of unquiet *Indian* histories and spirits is more telling and troubling than Guinn allows because Hannah does not seem to acknowledge them as victims of the South's own nightmarish origins. Rather, his Indian characters fall into two general categories: first, the romantic, violent, vengeful, and (crucially) western figures who serve as allies of white southerners; and second, a much sparer collection of "actual" southeastern Indians who are depicted as diseased, artificial, greedy, and in need of eradication. The former group figure as elegiac ghosts serving a nationalist agenda through which a still-shaken (white) South can inspire and re-empower itself; the latter are *made* into ghosts, denied existence and respect, another "race" altogether. In a specifically southern twist on what Bergland describes as the remembering/forgetting ambivalence of Indian hauntings, Hannah's work eerily evinces the South's "unsuccessful repression" (Bergland 5) of its own dead *and* living Indians.

Alan Trachtenberg and Philip Deloria have suggested that whites tend to "play Indian" in order to "naturalize" themselves as authentic, original Americans.[2] Such strategies proved particularly useful during the South's secession, Martin reports, as Indian personas offered models of "warlike patriotism and rebellious nationalism, the glorification of a lost cause" (140). But in order to serve a southern agenda, these Indians must not be southern themselves. Several of Hannah's characters "play Indian" by acting violently through Indian proxies who are, significantly, *not* southeastern. In both *Geronimo Rex* and *Never Die*, Hannah instead creates decontextualized western Natives who invigorate his southern white male characters without the risk of regional association or conflict. As romantic icons of loss and resistance, western Indians are figures with whom the southerner can identify—albeit ambivalently.

In the 1997 interview with James Lilley from which this essay's epigraph is taken, Hannah claims that the western genre's prototypical "cowboys and Indians" motif strikes at the heart of humanity's "grotesque need to maim"; this suppressed "part of yourself," generally kept in check by social controls, can be explored in imaginative settings and fictions. Hannah's theory raises a question, however: which "part" of the cowboy/Indian dyad supplies or symbolizes the naturally wicked urge, the grotesque tendencies that must be restrained in and by civilization? Hannah's answer to this question is as ambivalent in interviews as it is throughout his fiction, where cowboys and Indians appear equally culpable for their violent actions. Commenting on a history of the French and Indian War in a more recent interview with Dan Williams, Hannah admits that "I don't ever know how hostility starts, or who's to blame. . . . Indians, like all white men, have been variously cruel and enormously generous and kind. . . . Why were there massacres, and who really started the massacres?" (266). Such comments effectively elide the displacement and genocidal destruction of Indians by Euro-Americans. In Hannah's fiction, however, the conflation of southern cowboys and western Native American warriors permits Hannah to align southern dispossession with Indian Removal; moreover, by relocating the entire drama to remote western settings, Hannah's fiction symbolically redeems the South. Such narrative acts represent at best a kind of wishful amnesia; more disturbingly, they participate discursively in a southern history of repressing, dispossessing, and appropriating Native American experience. [3]

Joel Martin explains that Indian invisibility in the South has much to do with white southerners' animosity toward the stubborn few who remained after the Removal of the 1830s. Federal aid, beginning with the Choctaw Land Acquisition Program in 1920, seemed to many white southerners like "unnatural, even scandalous special treatment from the federal government" (Martin 144).[4] Despite these regional struggles, generations of Mississippi Choctaws have been steadily rebuilding tribal solvency for nearly a century; in 1971, just one year before the publication of *Geronimo Rex*, the Choctaw acquired an 80-acre industrial park that would eventually house several manufacturing and retail plants and make them one of the largest employers in the state. Barry Hannah does draw our attention to the Mississippi Choctaw in *Geronimo Rex*—but what he depicts is decidedly not a vibrant, resurgent community. Instead, the Choctaws come across as an "unnatural" and repulsive group who *still* receive special treatment from the federal government in the form of free medical attention. *Geronimo Rex*'s protagonist Harry Monroe is entering the University of Mississippi medical center for an anatomy class when he runs into a number of local Choctaws waiting on the lawn. The same Indians had already "tried to collar" him the previous weekend. He ignored them then; this time, though, he pays attention:

> The women wore dresses that looked like the flag of some
> crackpot nation. I'd seen two Choctaw women come in at the
> last minute to deliver. When they had their legs in the straddles,
> you could see the dye rings on their thighs which came off the
> dresses. Their vaginas were fossileums of old blood. Their babies
> came up in a rotten exhumation; then the baby was there, head
> full of hair, wanting to live like a son of a gun. It almost belied
> the germ theory of disease. The mothers did not cry out for
> Jesus like the Negro women. They bawled in shorter shrieks, but
> higher, as if in direct, private accusation against some little male
> toad of a god. It made my blood crawl. (281)

These Indian women sustain a "crackpot nation," the dye from their home-made "flag"-like dresses rubbing off symbolically onto their thighs—clearly, their proprietary claims within the South will not be taken seriously or sustained. Moreover, as "fossileums of old blood," their vaginas deliver only "rotten exhumations," rendering their attempts at reproduction a form of necromancy to revive an already extinct race. Still, the babies keep coming, "wanting to live like a son of a gun," negating all that Harry has learned in medical school about what should happen to diseased or decaying things. Harry's use of terms like "flag," "crackpot nation," and "disease" indicate his fear that these grotesquely fertile Indians threaten to contaminate the clean (white) American nation-state that houses and supports them. Moreover, he cannot fit them into the standardized social order of the South, which became increasingly and ideologically biracial after the Civil War: the Choctaws' outsider status is confirmed when Harry tries but fails to compare them to "Negro women." The Choctaws' alien matrilineal and pagan culture also poses a dual threat to southern patriarchy and Christianity: the women's "shrieks" against some specifically "*male* toad of a god" (italics mine) make Harry's "blood crawl." Harry ultimately maintains his composure, and his privileged status as a white male, by quite literally reinscribing the Choctaws' supposedly obsequious dependency on the U.S.

government. When a "squaw" hands Harry some Bureau of Indian Affairs medical aid forms so that he can authorize treatment of a sick Indian who appears to have eaten "roadkill," Harry signs them. As a mere student of medicine, he has no authority to do so; nonetheless, he tells us, "I took out my pen"—a euphemistic yet distinctly phallic gesture—and signs the forms "*Harriman Monroe, M.D.*" (282). In this performative act, Harry's superiority is confirmed, as is the Choctaws' reliance on the authority he fraudulently represents.

This brief and otherwise forgettable scene is one of only a handful in Hannah's corpus featuring "actual" southeastern Indians, and thus it is disturbingly resonant. The Indians who more regularly frequent Hannah's fiction are displaced both geographically and temporally from the contemporary South. "Having hated and 'removed' most literal Indians," Martin contends, "southerners fell in love with figurative ones" (136). Even before he meets and dismisses the all-too-real and corporeal Choctaw, Harry Monroe has adopted the legendary Apache warrior Geronimo as his braver, wilder, more violent alter ego. Initially, he chooses books about Geronimo from the college library shelf simply because of their similar names: "I realized that *my* last name [Monroe] could be found mixed up in it" (160). The coincidence is merely fortuitous: "I didn't know why I had [the books]," Harry admits, except that "it was like being related to some mad bore in town whom you would have to visit sooner or later" (161). Indeed, this notion of "being related" to an Indian has a literal as well as figurative dimension—a dimension that Harry will have to acknowledge "sooner or later." Earlier in the novel, Harry remembers being told that he resembles an "Indian long-distance runner," with a stereotypically "Asian cut of face no one in the family can account for" (43). We can infer from this hint that Harry may perhaps have some suppressed Native ancestry besides his own classically white southern lineage—"French-Irishmen with memories of the Middle Ages" (43). This possibility resurfaces when Harry hears another western Indian, "Navajo Ben," lambasting American excess on a radio show broadcast out of Phoenix, Arizona: "that faraway Indian voice was unsettling to me; there was a torment in it that cut too far into me. . . . I was ready to go with him" (135). The "testimony of bruises" offered by resentful western Indians like Geronimo and Navajo Ben cuts Harry to the very core of his identity (135). These stirring figures also motivate him to action: "I was ready to go." However, rather than acknowledging his familial or regional relationship to Indian ancestors, Harry "goes" on flights of fantasy and romance that take him imaginatively out of the South.

Western Indians represent drama and romance, which southerners often invoke in order to "affix the romance of the 'frontier' to their region's narrative" and to participate symbolically in a "wild past" (Martin 140). Harry desires this wildness, though his motives are ostensibly adolescent: "What I especially liked about Geronimo," he enumerates, "was that he had cheated, lied, stolen, mutinied, usurped, killed, burned, raped, pillaged, razed, trapped, ripped, mashed, bowshot, stomped, herded, exploded, cut, stoned, revenged, prevenged, avenged" (231). In Harry's exhaustive catalogue of Geronimo's crimes, we see the Indian repeating the atrocities that whites committed against Natives across the continent. However, Harry mitigates the culpability of the original offenders: men like Geronimo didn't just "revenge," they also "*pre*venged" and "*a*venged"—who knows, Harry seems to ask, who fired the first shot? Disturbingly, this key moment in the novel approximates the author's own ambivalence (in the interviews with Lilley and Oberkirch and with Williams) about who is truly responsible for the violence of colonial contact. In the midst of such confusion, adolescent fantasies about violence become viable metaphors for social action. The idea of freewheeling aggression indeed excites Harry, who begins tying a scarf around his neck and pocketing a pistol; he feels suddenly "drunk with freedom to do *anything*" (161).

Playing the Indian paradoxically empowers Harry to act like a southerner. Yet despite dressing up like his Indian hero, Harry is repeatedly mistaken for a cowboy: "'Ah no,'" he protests to his roommate Bobby Dove Fleece, "'I'm an Indian, not a cowboy'" (166). While Harry sounds like he might simply be explaining his Halloween costume, as we have seen, hints about his exotic heritage suggest that his "true" identity may well *be* that of a part-Indian in a land of southern cowboys. However, the sharp-witted Fleece rejects the notion that one can be or play Indian in a contemporary South that is configured in primarily biracial terms:

"You talk like you want to *discover* a country, is the hopeless thing," said Fleece, in the new tone of an impartial observer.
"You've been reading about that Indian. But, although it's true

you look like Hernando DeKotex with the swamp boots, you
ought to know that Mississippi has already been discovered,
and that . . . it's enough of a rectangle of poor woe without
you putting on that costume and pistol roaming around out of
some *pageant* of gunslinging. They could use you in the United
Daughters of the Confederacy as a salute-shooter at the cemetery
in their birthday of the Civil War service. . . ." (180)

Despite Harry's Geronimo outfit, Fleece casts Harry as "Hernando
DeKotex," a pastiche of the Spanish conquistadors led by Hernando DeSoto
who first colonized Mississippi and its Indian tribes. Fleece effectively
emasculates Harry too: the reference to the United Daughters of the Confederacy conjures a specifically southern tradition of conquest and com-
memoration, but in sentimental, female terms. Furthermore, the allusion
to menstruation (Kotex) both emphasizes the emasculating wound of
the Confederacy's military loss and explains Harry's appropriation of
Geronimo as an antidote to this white southern history of humiliation and
feminization. Nevertheless, wounded by small-town rumors that he is
a homosexual—rumors which are compounded by a series of botched
attempts to relate to women—Harry keeps using Geronimo to assert his
masculine virility. It seems to pay off when a new girlfriend delightedly
dubs Harry her "Indian prince" (196) and "*Apache Valentine*" (202); in a
later erotic encounter, Harry imagines that Geronimo is urging him to
"[p]ush on in" (272). Thus sexual conquest is equated with colonial adventure; performing such acts in metaphorical Indian-face, Harry reveals his
desire to "discover" not just women but (as Fleece points out) the honor of
his native South.

Yet both Harry and Fleece himself continue to engage in their own
personal "pageant[s] of gunslinging" (not to mention sexual conquest)
throughout the novel. In such situations, Native American figures continue
to emerge as complex containers of both historical defeat and contemporary revenge. Hannah's characters do not yearn for a literal resurrection of
the antebellum South, but they do in many ways testify to its alteration. As
Michael Spikes has observed, there are but "few references" to the Civil War
in *Geronimo Rex* (411); the allusions Hannah does include are revealing,[5]
though, particularly in what they suggest about his interest in Indians.

Hannah once explained in an interview that the Civil War remained simply and powerfully emotive for southerners: "You don't have to be that bright," he told John Griffin Jones in 1980, "to be full of history. . . . It's kind of your heritage. . . . So you don't have to go to the library and read about it" (Jones 148). In keeping with Hannah's own sentiments, Harry and Fleece leave their college campus behind and drive to the Vicksburg battlefield, where Harry professes he "didn't know beans" about the battle itself but still finds himself moved and "irked" by it (217). "Jesus mercy, I was sad," he remembers; "the strange *silence*, then, is what got me—as if you walked in a dream of refracted defeat. The horror was, I could think of nothing to say. I couldn't even think of what to think" (218). Harry's remarks suggest that this contemporary southerner does not mythologize the glories of battles past; rather, he suffers the endlessly "refracted defeat" in a gloom he can neither articulate nor intellectualize. The Indian surfaces as an uncanny tool to dispel this shadow of "defeat." When Harry leaves Vicksburg and returns to Hedermansever, "afflicted with a nervous gloom," his dreams turn instead to "old Geronimo, peering out miserably from a cage in the zoo of American history" (221). Geronimo, the heroic Native rebel held captive as an "exhibit" at the World's Fair, dehumanized, and humiliated by the American government, stands in here for the Confederate dead. Textually, "America" (that is, the North) becomes responsible for the doom of both white southerners and Indians, and in the process the South is absolved of any responsibility for corralling and destroying its own Native Americans.[6]

Geronimo Rex also suggests that the South's material recovery from "defeat" requires the region to embrace a morally questionable national faith in progress and the way to wealth—forces which, historically, have shown little mercy to those southerners or Native Americans who resist or simply get in the way. Western expansion has promised growth and opportunity for Americans generally, but southerners have been more ambivalent. On one hand, as Martin notes, the invocation of western motifs reinforces the South's connection to "American History with a capital H" (142). On the other hand, as Robert Brinkmeyer argues in *Remapping Southern Literature: Contemporary Southern Writers and the West* (2000), novelists including Hannah have critiqued rather than celebrated the myth of the western wilderness as a landscape of opportunity—as, in Wallace Stegner's famous

definition, the nation's "geography of hope." Contemporary southern writers, Brinkmeyer demonstrates, cannot help but view westward movement
pessimistically from "a perspective grounded in the Southern experience
of poverty and defeat that stands diametrically opposed to the American
legend of unlimited progress and success" (31). Brinkmeyer finds that postmodern southern writers like Hannah, James Dickey, Clyde Edgerton, and
Cormac McCarthy blur the line between native and pioneer, aligning the
southerner historically with Native American exploitation while redeeming the white southerner-turned-cowboy textually. I would suggest that the
problem here is one of sympathies: ultimately, in works by self-interested
southern whites, the cowboy wins these imaginary, ambivalent contests,
helped along by association with a Native whom he ultimately discards.

Hannah's postmodern western *Never Die* moves beyond Harry
Monroe's cowboy-and-Indian entanglement with Geronimo in the South
and out to the western frontier itself. Yet despite its carnivalesque cast of
outlaws and its west Texas setting, *Never Die* alerts us to its barely repressed
southern dimensions in the opening line by situating the story's origins
"[b]ack during the Civil War" (1). *Never Die*'s central villain, Kyle Nitburg,
is a New Orleans native who discovered that his mother was spying for the
Confederacy and promptly sold her to the Union army for "one hundred
real dollars" (1); we are told that he watched coldly, "smiling," as the Union
soldiers hung her from a railroad bridge (2). Nitburg then "moved west to
escape the infamy" and married a well-to-do Texan lady, whom he soon
sold to a Comanche chief named Bad Cloud for "four thousand dollars in
real gold" (2). Finally, Nitburg became a lawyer in a town called Dolores
Springs that was soon renamed after the man who "continued to cheat, lie
and steal [until] ... pretty soon the town and much land around it was
his" (3). In just three pages, Hannah depicts Nitburg as a thoroughly corrupt contemporary conquistador. But what is revealing about the wicked
Nitburg is how indistinguishable he appears from his enemies. First, the
Union army not only purchases Nitburg's mother but also kills her on
a railroad bridge that symbolizes the invasion of "progress" associated with
the North; second, the Comanches buy Nitburg's wife into "slavery" (2).
Ultimately, the opening pages of *Never Die* imply that the sins of the
Confederate slaveholder are indistinguishable from those of the Union
profiteer; similarly, there is little to separate the wrongdoing of the white

man from that of the Indian, a moral equivalence made clearer by placing a Comanche chief in the figurative role of plantation master.[7]

It can be argued that Hannah's postmodern parody of the western genre vividly showcases such ambivalence; as Mark S. Graybill notes elsewhere in this volume, there are in *Never Die* "no white-hats-versus-black-hats tableaux; this is a lawless country in which everyone is just as much 'bad guy' as 'good guy' " (124). But while Graybill helps us to understand Hannah's critique of the "vicious capitalism" (Graybill 130) that fueled westward expansion, his argument overlooks what such nakedly economic motives meant for the Indians implicated in every phase of American settlement. If we read *Never Die* in the context of Indian genocide (which critics focusing on Hannah's parodic subversion of southern and western myths have consistently failed to do), Hannah's depictions of cruelty to Natives seem rather more disturbing. One central character, Fernando Muré, habitually plunders nearby Indian reservations (18); another, the hermit Nermer, once "shot an Apache child in a wide desert" simply "for getting in his way" (53). Yet however egregiously these Indians are mistreated, *Never Die* invariably muddies the issue of culpability. The narrative emphasizes that these Comanches and Apaches are "vicious" (89) and that they retaliate: an Indian appears suddenly at the end of the novel to avenge the slain Apache child, representing "a vision of despair and vengeance . . . else the man made no sense" (134–35). In other words, an Indian represents nothing intelligible *but* despair and vengeance. Furthermore, the Indian's revenge is fruitless and uncivilized, as "nobody hired [him] . . . he came for mean fun" (146). It is such moments as these that begin to set *Never Die*'s cowboys and Indians apart. Hannah depicts his southerners and Native Americans in similar conditions of loss and desperation, but recuperation—because it inevitably entails involvement in the national ethos of "vicious capitalism"—seems available only to the southerner. Ultimately, the spirit of the Indian only takes the white southerner so far.

Still, the displaced southerner's quest for accumulation necessarily involves stepping on the souls of the Natives who continue to compete for resources. Nitburg's lascivious daughter Nandina, a shallow woman who parades the frontier in the latest urban fashions, puts it baldly: "out West, you owned everything nobody wanted to possess" (77). The problem with this claim is that it does not just refer to skirts but also, implicitly, to the land formerly occupied by Plains and Southwestern tribes. Nandina elides these Indians, reducing them to "nobody," because they refused to "own" the land that they felt no one ought to "possess." To be sure, Hannah satirizes Nandina's perverse interpretation of "vicious capitalism" in action on the western frontier. In a memorable scene in Navy Remington's garage, she dips her fingers into a pool of motor oil and tastes it, thinking pleasantly "[s]o this is what made the New World run" (46). Nandina's imperial epiphany become more explicitly sexual when she returns her finger to the pool and "suck[s] the oil off," deciding "this tastes better than men" (46). Nandina's reaction seems to suggest that while the riches of the New World are powerfully tantalizing, they are also base and corrosive to "natural" human relationships and affairs.

The perverse sexiness of colonialism here recalls Harry Monroe's sexual conquests, which are stimulated by the idea of Geronimo; Nandina's lecherousness is also a suggestively Indian trait. Born to Nitburg's wife just before her sale to the Comanches, Nandina grows up to have long black hair and "widened raiding eyes. Dark-balled and hot like an Indian's" (46). The narrative hints strongly at the possibility that Nandina's father is not in fact Nitburg but an Italian man with whom Nandina's mother had a sexual encounter; indeed, this transgression amounted to "the final punch on her ticket to Indianland" (89). "Indianland" here signifies punishment, slavery, and exploitation, a sentence supposedly befitting Nandina's mother's adulterous behavior. The association between Nandina, her mother, and "Indianland" is also made when, immediately preceding the scene in Remington's garage, Nandina wishes fervently to commune with "Comanche stargazers . . . and my mother, too, calling out to me from the Indians" (46). Finally, for all that Nandina's black hair and "[d]ark-balled" eyes evince her father's Italian heritage, they also mark her as a symbolic Indian who exhibits the greedy desires that, as we have seen, southerners associated specifically with Native Americans. Like the Choctaw in *Geronimo Rex*, so too in *Never Die* both literal and symbolic Indians keep reproducing their greedy, "raiding," voracious spawn—the "rotten exhumations" of a race that refuses to die.

In other novels too, Hannah critiques the national character of "vicious capitalism" while depicting Native American figures who must compete, along with southerners, for their share of the nation's bounty.

In *Ray*, which is set in Tuscaloosa, Alabama, an Indian and an automobile appear juxtaposed again—but rather than thriving as they did for Nandina in the West, these southern iterations are in a state of advanced decay. In fact, the Indian is not even animate: it is a "wooden" statue seated in a station wagon rotting behind the home of Sister Hooch, a drug addict with whom the protagonist Ray Forrest is having an extramarital affair. Sexual excess and transgression are once more associated with consumerism; in the South, however, such impulses run aground. Not only is the car dead and the Indian inanimate, but Ray's lover Sister Hooch dies too. If, as Nandina suggests, motor oil "makes the New World run," it has bled dry in this particular southern scene. While Sister's grieving mother "raises a dreadful animal wail" of grief, "the wooden Indian in the station wagon never batted an eye" (59); the statue evinces neither human nor animal qualities, but simply sits "*rotting* off the fierce colors of its face" (49, emphasis added). The inverted syntax here, coupled with language recalling Harry's encounter with the Choctaw, suggests that the wooden Indian is actively effecting its own decay. Mr. Hooch further indicts the Indian in an elegy he composes for his dead daughter: "*Grief is/Looking at the wooden Indian where your little ones should be./I bought a new color teevee*" (90). Hooch's poem implies that it is Indians, not white southern girls, who are supposed to be dead; it also laments the fact that southerners, too, must try to dispel grief and pursue happiness through consumption—represented by the purchase of a new television set, rendered phonetically as "teevee" to conjure and replace the typical Indian habitation "teepee." The substitution reveals the degree to which the Indian's "home" has been overwritten and replaced, albeit by the heavily compromised world of consumer culture.

The Indian's eviction from this southern scene is telling. Repeatedly, Hannah depicts only southeastern Indians as diseased and decaying, while their western counterparts remain vividly alive and driven by stubborn rage and resistance. Geronimo does indeed invigorate Harry Monroe's exploits but, upon closer examination, Harry's conquests are based upon distinctly traditional definitions of white southern manhood as patriarchal, anti-material, and anti-modern. He is deeply imaginative, narcissistic, and misogynistic; he belittles others in order to aggrandize himself; his masculinity is occasionally dependent on African Americans deferring to him and calling him "man" (90); he repeatedly shoots things and people, and considers his pistol "the most manly thing" he could own (69); his feelings of sexual desire often turn violent, and occasionally he feels compelled to duel or "kill" for his beloved(s) (252); and he is concerned about money only when it might serve a romantic purpose, as in his desperate attempt to impress Ann Mick (52) or to sustain his spendthrift young wife Prissy.

Yet another automobile scene, this time in *Geronimo Rex*, both clarifies and complicates Geronimo's role as Harry's idol and model of anti-modern resistance. Having just stolen several books on Geronimo from the college library, Harry sneaks triumphantly out the bathroom window (231). The act itself is a response to the authority and control of the library, since the theft does not really gain him anything he might not have obtained by simply checking the books out. Nonetheless, inspired by the "thrill" of this petty larceny, Harry leaps out the window and strolls into the campus parking lot. There, he sees his music instructor Livace's car, a "DeSoto" which earlier in the narrative he described as a "weak old" vehicle that "stalled out on [Livace] perpetually" (198). Like the station wagon rotting in Hooch's backyard or the emasculated "DeKotex" himself, this allegorical vessel of conquest is rotten and decaying; Harry tells us that he "spat at it" (231). Harry's expectoration seems to trigger an energetic disgust for a number of other cars in the parking lot, but a closer reading reveals that he concentrates on those vehicles whose names are also associated with colonial exploration. His next target after the DeSoto is a "skyblue Cadillac. You pretentious whale, you Cadillac," he declares, just before jumping on the hood and repeatedly piercing it with his shoe heels (232). The Cadillac automobile is named after the French explorer Antoine Lamothe Cadillac. Cadillac "discovered" an American town, Detroit, that was already inhabited by Michilimackinac Indian tribes, and helped convert the city into what Milo Quaife has deemed "the foremost industrial center of the earth" (x); moreover, Cadillac served as Governor of Louisiana for a short time in the early eighteenth century. But the most powerful connection here is to Geronimo himself, who was famously forced to parade and be photographed in a brand new Cadillac convertible. In 1972—the same year *Geronimo Rex* was published—the "wandering cowboy poet" Michael Martin Murphey released his song "Geronimo's Cadillac" as a protest against this vivid example of the Apache warrior's exploitation.[8] Harry, who is himself a cowboy musician (he plays the trumpet with varying degrees of seriousness throughout the novel), performs his own protest, implicitly on Geronimo's behalf, by vandalizing the Cadillac in the campus parking lot.

But if Harry's actions under the guidance of Geronimo can be read as critiques of colonialism and industrial capitalism, the scene's symbolic meaning mutates when Harry attacks a third car. He leaps onto a "Lincoln" and begins "[d]oing the spurs" until it looks "diseased . . . caved in, speckled" (232). At one level, Harry's actions conjure the image of a cowboy bringing "disease" to the indigenous inhabitants of the West, leaving them "speckled" with new and deadly afflictions like measles, and "caved in" by physical and cultural depletion. But this car's namesake is no brash European explorer or western cowboy: it is Abraham Lincoln, the American president who ended slavery and left the (white) South permanently afflicted by its loss and perceived colonization. Thus, *Geronimo Rex* once again equates white southerners and Native Americans as victims of American aggression, and Harry Monroe and Geronimo converge suggestively in defense of their respective nations. Tellingly, the only car Harry doesn't attack is his own T-Bird, one of many American cars named after some iconographic element of Indian culture. Later in the novel, driving the T-Bird to Mother Rooney's boarding house, Harry senses the "ghost" of Geronimo in the vehicle with him, "wanting to be let out of the car" (302). But Harry implores Geronimo to stay and teach him the fine points of revenge, the semantic difference between "mean" and "petty" (302). In clinging so fiercely to his ally, Harry effectively traps Geronimo inside a powerful symbol of his historical destruction.

The "ghost" of Geronimo in the T-Bird (302) resembles both the historical Geronimo in the Cadillac and the wooden Indian in Hooch's station wagon. "I do not invite ghosts," Harry admits; "so far I've never needed them. But this was real" (302). The "ghost" of Geronimo in the T-Bird is paradoxically more "real" to Harry than the diseased bodies of the Mississippi Choctaw he also encounters; while the indigent Indians outside the hospital feed off the government (via Harry), Harry feeds off Geronimo like a "tick . . . waiting on the body of a true warm man" (303). Geronimo is "real" and a "true warm man" precisely because he is not alive. Geronimo stands for something heroic and "*not* petty" (303), yet Harry knows that he remains "petty" himself—perhaps a hint that, in the last instance, he recognizes the unbridgeable gulf between the imperially-minded white and the noble savage:

> I pronounced the name, *Ge Ron I Mo*. Two iambs, rising at the last with a sound which might be blown forever through some hole in a cliff in Arizona by the wind. A name which in itself made you want to cast off, even being landlocked, and kick off the past history that sucked you down. This wasn't petty, this Indian, Apache. I knew *that*. (302)

Just as he finds in "Geronimo" the letters of his last name, "Monroe," here he locates his "*I*" as well. His entanglement with Geronimo inspires him with eloquent but revealing imperial fantasies; the "landlocked" southerner dreams not just of "casting off" to some uncharted land (here, not an island but a western colony—Geronimo's Apache Arizona); he also yearns to "cast off" the burden of southern history. Harry's wistfulness here borders on despair, and we begin to sense the tragic fantasies of compensation that these western journeys might serve for the white southerner. Harry implies that he understands the terrible history "that sucked you down" as a southerner because the sound of Geronimo's very name reminds him of being "blown forever through some hole in a cliff in Arizona." However, Harry's white southern narcissism barely obscures the fact that this image is also a chilling metaphor for Indian Removal.

If Harry believes he understands his own history as a white southerner more poignantly through Geronimo, he still desires to "cast off" the ugliness of it—hence, his endorsement of romantic "ghosts" like Geronimo and his denial of the supposedly grotesque "real" Choctaw. Other Hannah characters seem determined to cleanse themselves and the South of reminders of colonial corruption. In *Ray*, the protagonist's friend Charlie De Soto (who claims to be descended from his namesake Hernando) manages a soap factory and is engaged in "antipollution" (11) efforts to cleanse the Black Warrior River that the factory's "nasty white soap" products have contaminated (25).[9] Recalling Harry in his Geronimo/DeKotex costume, Charlie De Soto dons a cheap headdress from K-Mart when he sets out to kill a man, Mr. Wently, who irks him (18). He accessorizes the look with both a "hatchet" (11, 15) and a "bow and arrow" (15). Charlie fails to execute his murder plot; Harry Monroe, however, does succeed in shooting someone at the end of *Geronimo Rex*: Peter Lepoyster, better known as "Whitfield Peter." Harry uses his cowboy pistol, but it is Geronimo who guides him: "'Now get him,' said a voice, loud. 'Don't let him get you. Don't lose your life to the man.' I knew the old corpse who was speaking to me. . . . His ghost, or whatever, rose and gasped from a corner of the living room: Geronimo. . . . 'Help me, Indian!' I shouted" (377). Whether "corpse," "ghost," or "whatever," Geronimo's role here is to legitimize the (redemptive) cause of the white southerner: the destruction of the racist Whitfield Peter, an embodiment of contemporary (1960s) white southern racism.

Harry Monroe is spurred on to violent exploits by his "mad relative" Geronimo, even though he looks more like a cowboy or "DeKotex." In a striking chiastic parallel, Charlie goes on his murderous crusade in Indian-face after reading the original De Soto's diary and finding himself "renewed" by "the adventurous perversity" of his Spanish ancestor (15). This intertextual chiasmus suggests the comprehensiveness with which white southerners have adopted both colonial and Indian antecedents to underwrite their idea of southern identity as a noble cause worth fighting for. But these constant returns to displaced indigenous antecedents in Hannah's work are both indicative and troubling. "At best," Gidley and Gidley suggest, white southerners' adoption of such Indians constitutes an attempt to embrace their "'almost ancestors'" (167)—attempts deeply compromised by the South's history of forcibly removing and repressing these forebears.

It is unclear whether Hannah intends to resurrect or memorialize the South's indigenous origins, but his novels make repeatedly and abundantly clear that "real" Indians no longer exist in the South that he writes about. The few that linger are bogus, diseased, or both; denying them life in his fiction, Hannah supports his characters' refusal to recognize these Indians as viable southerners. Instead, they appear as abominations, rivals, and mordant threats. In Hannah's short story "Ride, Fly, Penetrate, Loiter," which appears in his semi-autobiographical collection *Captain Maximus* (1985),[10] the protagonist Ned Maximus has his eye stabbed with his own filet knife by "a fake Indian named Billy Seven Fingers" whom he picks up hitchhiking "off the reservation in Neshoba County, Mississippi." Ned observes bitterly that the Indian is "white as me—whiter, really, because

I have some Spanish" (35). When Ned accuses Billy of "gouging the Feds with thirty-second-part maximum Indian blood," Billy promptly gouges Ned's eye with the stolen knife. Already looted and wounded by one Indian, Ned is confronted by the presence of another: Billy's "enormous sick real Indian friend" (35), who makes Ned's "[MG Midget] car seem like a toy" (36). These Mississippi Indians steal, defraud, maim, outsize, and even out-white the white southerner and his emphatically small possessions. Moreover, there is nothing remotely romantic or useful about these Natives: Ned spots a Dalmation dog and calls it "a miracle—it was truth and beauty like John Keats has in that poem. And I wanted a dog to redeem my life. . . . But [the Indians] wouldn't help me chase it. They were too sick" (36). No wonder, then, that those white southerners in Hannah's fiction who go in search of romance and redemption ultimately turn toward the opportunities and myths of the West, away from the sick and diseased remnants of a brutal southern past that never dies.

Notes

1. Works by Brian Dippie, Lucy Maddox, Walter Benn Michaels, and Renée Bergland variously explore the trope of the Vanishing American.
2. Colonial agitators famously conducted the Boston Tea Party in 1773 while disguised as Mohawks; during the same period, Maine's Liberty Settlers dressed as vicious "White Indians" to help intimidate wealthy speculators to lower land prices. For more on these and other examples, see Bernard Bailyn's *Ideological Origins of the American Revolution* (1992), Philip Deloria's *Playing Indian* (1998), Alan Trachtenberg's *Shades of Hiawatha* (2004), and Alan Taylor's *Liberty Men and Great Proprietors* (1990).
3. I am drawing here on Fredric Jameson's *The Political Unconscious: Narrative as a Socially Symbolic Act* (New York: Cornell UP, 1981), which advocates the "unmasking of cultural artifacts [like novels] as socially symbolic acts" with appreciable political significance, import, and influence (20). See also Lucy Maddox's *Removals: Nineteenth-Century American Literature and the Politics of Indian Affairs* (1991), in which Maddox argues that nineteenth-century U.S. writers inevitably participated discursively in the effects of Removal.
4. It is important here to note that the Indian Removal Act passed by the Jackson administration in 1830—effecting within a mere decade the migration of over 70,000 Indians from the Southeast's Five Civilized Tribes to lands west of the Mississippi—occurred prior to the Civil War and was instrumental in solidifying the South's cohesion: "the antebellum white South, devoted to slavery at all costs, was expanded, empowered, and consolidated by Indian Removal" (Martin 134).

5. For instance, the founder of Harry's Hedermansever College (modeled on Hannah's own alma mater, Mississippi College) is suggestively named "President Hannah," neé "Captain Hannah" of Civil War fame (125–26).
6. The South's role in racial slavery is also alluded to here. In fact, the image of Geronimo in a cage closely resembles a scene in Letter IX of Crevecoeur's *Letters from an American Farmer* (1978), in which John visits Charleston and witnesses the horrific treatment of a Negro slave, suspended in a cage and ravaged by birds and insects, left there to die "a living spectre" as punishment for killing an overseer (243–45).
7. It should be noted, however, that Hannah may be alluding to the little-known historical fact that some southeastern Indians, particularly mixedblood Cherokees, actually owned plantations and slaves in the antebellum South. See, for instance, Theda Perdue's *Slavery and the Evolution of Cherokee Society,* 1540–1866 (1979) and R. Halliburton's *Red Over Black: Black Slavery Among Cherokee Indians* (1977).
8. The song was a hit, and it resulted in Murphey's eventual adoption into the Lakota Nation by the Dull Knife family. "Geronimo's Cadillac" has since been recorded by other singers such as Hoyt Axton, Mary McCaslin, and Cher. See Murphey's official website: http://www.michaelmartinmurphey.com/bio.htm.
9. Deepening this allegory is the fact that De Soto died by the Mississippi River and was interred there. See Charles Hudson's exhaustive compilation of all records of De Soto's expedition in *Knights of Spain, Warriors of the Sun* (1997).
10. The blurb on the back cover of the first Penguin edition states, "In this bold collection Barry Hannah blends the events of his own life and the 'life' that literary notoriety has attributed to him."

Works Cited

Anderson, Eric Gary. "Native American Literature, Ecocriticism, and the South." *South to a New Place: Region, Literature, and Culture.* Eds. Suzanne W. Jones and Sharon Monteith. Baton Rouge: Louisiana State UP, 2002. 165–83.
Bailyn, Bernard. *The Ideological Origins of the American Revolution.* Cambridge: Belknap/Harvard UP, 1992.
Bergland, Renée. *The National Uncanny: Indian Ghosts and American Subjects.* Hanover: UP of New England, 2000.
Bone, Martyn. "Neo-Confederate Narrative and Postsouthern Parody: Hannah and Faulkner." Included in this volume. 85–101.
Brinkmeyer, Robert H., Jr. *Remapping Southern Literature: Contemporary Southern Writers and the West.* Athens: U of Georgia P, 2000.
Crevecoeur, J. Hector St. John de. *Letters from an American Farmer.* New York: Fox, Duffield and Co., 1904.
Deloria, Philip. *Playing Indian.* New Haven: Yale UP, 1998.
Dippie, Brian. *The Vanishing American: White Attitudes and U.S. Indian Policy.* Middletown: Wesleyan UP, 1982.
Fiedler, Leslie A. *The Return of the Vanishing American.* New York: Stein and Day, 1968.
Flans, Robyn. Michael Martin Murphey: Official Biography. July 2001. http://www.michaelmartinmurphey.com/bio.htm.

Ford, Sarah. "Listening to the Ghosts: The 'New Southern Studies': A Response to Michael
Kreyling." *South Central Review* 22.1 (spring 2005): 19–25.
Gidley, Mick and Ben Gidley. "The Native-American South." *A Companion to the Literature
and Culture of the American South.* Eds. Richard Gray and Owen Robinson. Malden:
Blackwell, 2004. 166–84.
Graybill, Mark S. "'Peeping Toms on History': *Never Die* as Postmodern Western." Included
in this volume. 120–38.
Guinn, Matthew. *After Southern Modernism: Fiction of the Contemporary South.* Jackson:
UP of Mississippi, 2000.
Halliburton, R. *Red Over Black: Black Slavery Among Cherokee Indians.* Westport:
Greenwood P, 1977.
Hannah, Barry. "Ride, Fly, Penetrate, Loiter." *Captain Maximus.* New York: Penguin, 1986.
35–43.
———. *Geronimo Rex.* New York: Penguin, 1972.
———. *Never Die.* Boston: Houghton Mifflin, 1991.
———. *Ray.* New York: Penguin, 1980.
Hudson, Charles. *Knights of Spain, Warriors of the Sun: Hernando de Soto and the South's
Ancient Chiefdoms.* Athens: U of Georgia P, 1997.
Jameson, Fredric. *The Political Unconscious: Narrative as a Socially Symbolic Act.* New York:
Cornell UP, 1981.
Jones, John Griffin, ed. Interview with Barry Hannah. *Mississippi Writers Talking.* Jackson:
UP of Mississippi, 1982. 131–66.
Kreyling, Michael. "Fee, Fie, Faux Faulkner: Parody and Postmodernism in Southern
Literature." *Southern Review* 29 (winter 1993): 1–15.
———. *Inventing Southern Literature.* Jackson: UP of Mississippi, 1998.
———. "Toward 'A New Southern Studies.'" *South Central Review* 22.1 (spring 2005): 4–18.
Lilley, James D. and Brian Oberkirch. "An Interview with Barry Hannah." *Mississippi
Review* 25.3 (1997): 19–43.
Maddox, Lucy. *Removals: Nineteenth Century American Literature and the Politics of Indian
Affairs.* New York: Oxford UP, 1991.
Martin, Joel W. "'My Grandmother Was a Cherokee Princess': Representations of Indians
in Southern History." *Dressing in Feathers: The Construction of the Indian in American
Popular Culture.* Ed. S. Elizabeth Bird. Boulder: Westview P, 1996. 129–47.
Michaels, Walter Benn. *Our America: Nativism, Modernism and Pluralism.* Durham: Duke
UP, 1995.
Mould, Tom. *Choctaw Prophecy: A Legacy of the Future.* Tuscaloosa: U of Alabama P, 2003.
Perdue, Theda. *Slavery and the Evolution of Cherokee Society, 1540–1866.* Knoxville: U of
Tennessee P, 1979.
Perdue, Theda and Michael D. Green, eds. *The Columbia Guide to American Indians of the
Southeast.* New York: Columbia UP, 2001.
Peterson, Jr., John H. "Setting the Stage: The Original Mississippians." *Ethnic Heritage in
Mississippi.* Ed. Barbara Carpenter. Jackson: Mississippi Humanities Council, 1992.
Quaife, Milo Milton. Ed. *The Western Country in the 17th Century: The Memoirs of Antoine
Lamothe Cadillac and Pierre Liette.* New York: Citadel P, 1962.
Stegner, Wallace. 1962. "Wilderness Letter." *The Sound of Mountain Water.* New York:
Penguin, 1997.
Taylor, Alan. *Liberty Men and Great Proprietors: The Revolutionary Settlement on the Maine
Frontier, 1760–1820.* Chapel Hill: U of North Carolina P, 1990.
Trachtenberg, Alan. *Shades of Hiawatha: Staging Indians, Making Americans, 1880–1930.*
New York: Farrar, Straus, and Giroux, 2004.

Trefzer, Annette. "Postcolonial Displacements in Faulkner's Indian Stories of the 1930s." *Faulkner in the Twenty-First Century.* Ed. Robert W. Hamblin and Ann J. Abadie. Jackson: UP of Mississippi, 2003. 68–88.

Williams, Daniel. Interview with Barry Hannah: February 6, 2001. *Mississippi Quarterly* 45.2 (spring 2001): 261–68.

Yaeger, Patricia. "Ghosts and Shattered Bodies, or What Does it Mean To Still Be Haunted by Southern Literature?" *South Central Review* 22.1 (spring 2005): 87–108.

Orphans All

Reality Homesickness in Yonder Stands Your Orphan

—Scott Romine

"We don't love each other as much as we used to. You can see the
uncertain looks, the calculations, the dismissals. People are not
even in the present moment. Everybody's been futurized. . . . And
who gets the highest pay? Actors. Paid to mimic life because there
is no life. You look at everybody and maybe they're a little sad,
some of 'em. They're all homesick for when they were real."
—Ulrich in *Yonder Stands Your Orphan* (46)

At the conclusion of *Never Die*, Barry Hannah's venture to the West and the western, Fernando Muré
rejects the idea that he will be rendered a hero in a
West shrouded in nostalgia: "Thing is, it was all wrong and I am a villain.
Except. I'm here studying up how I can make the next years fine ones, by my
little Stella. I mean to be something extraordinary and make a high mark
for good" (152). His physical disfigurement gives him, he says, "a whole lot
better chance" (152) by exiling him from the provinces of romantic ico-
nography. The opposition here between a crudely articulated humanism—
"making a high mark for good"—and an escape from representation is
typical of Hannah's later work, which characteristically posits a domain of
ethical action besieged by images, roles, scripts, codes, and themed spaces

that threaten to colonize and eradicate the real. As Ulrich suggests in the passage quoted above, the absence of love correlates to the ascendance of actors. This essay reads *Yonder Stands Your Orphan* as a culmination of Hannah's concern with pathological mimicry, as an epic bracketing of a clumsy, inarticulate humanism by representational systems that gravitate toward fantasy and abjection. A meditation on pornography understood strictly and as a wider set of practices through which desire is directed toward an imaginary object, Hannah's novel imagines a redemptive space in which common decency—in the final analysis, it is little more than that (and for reasons I shall explore, *can be* more than that)—might operate as social practice. Diagnosing homesickness for the real as cultural pathology, the novel recovers the real as an antidote—that is to say, a desire for reality on the part of numerous characters acts as both the symptom of and prescription for their collective nostalgia. The deeply paradoxical nature of this relation produces a series of utopian gestures, attempts to wed desire and reality that degenerate into patterns of decay, degradation, and brutal abjection. But against the novel's dominant momentum of monstrous utopias, abject fantasies, and the erosion of reality runs a countercurrent of redemption in a minor key, of the "small acts of kindness" that constitute "almost all of life that's beautiful" (94). The novel's ultimate concern, however, is not so much to delineate these acts as to imagine a space wherein they might be practiced. The regime of the simulacrum, of empty performance, and of deadening consumption necessitates for Hannah an *apocalyptic* humanism organized around the disparate topoi of animals, music (as a form of expression uncorrupted by representation), and Christian redemption (as a vague logic).

In attempting to analyze reality homesickness as a sociohistorically distinctive malady, I want to situate Eagle's Lake, Mississippi, the "home" toward which the novel's comic trajectory moves, in relation to the surrounding dystopic terrain of Big Marts, bad restaurants, tourist traps, and Vicksburg casinos, the last described by one character as "math become a monster" (229). This is the world of what Hannah calls "pawn shop culture" ("Interview" 263), where an economy built on despair subjects even the family to its implacable laws of supply and demand: "Were the laws not just a little too stiff, you'd probably have found used children there" (*Yonder* 281). This is the world of Man Mortimer, perhaps the most fully realized and socially specific antagonist in Hannah's oeuvre. In its close attention to the economy of what I call post-familial culture, *Yonder Stands Your Orphan* stands as Hannah's most explicitly diagnostic novel. In *Eros and Civilization* (1955), Herbert Marcuse called attention to the "decline of the social function of the family" in a capitalist society "under the rule of economic, political, and cultural monopolies" (87–88). For Marcuse, the Oedipal conflict had been supplanted by "extra-familial agents and agencies" (experts, mass media) as the primary site of socialization, a transition that eroded culture and its attendant reality principle (94). But where, for Marcuse, a new form of alienation emerged from the repressive efforts of a new class of agents—a shift in which, broadly speaking, Capitalists displace Fathers—Hannah's focus is on a post-Fordist regime of flexible accumulation in which economic and pseudo-social activity is organized around the ephemeral consumption of pleasure. For Hannah, the erosion of family correlates to alienation and the loss of reality. His "solution," however, is not to think in Marcusian terms toward some "non-repressive civilization" "beyond the reality principle," but to imagine what reality might be shared in a "*posthuman, postmodern*" age—to imagine, finally, what home might look like in a world of orphans.

Following his disquisition on reality homesickness to the other old men on Eagle Lake's pier, Ulrich poses a question: "Who isn't an orphan, I ask you?" The question is pregnant because it is rhetorical: orphanhood obtains resonance not merely in (literal) relation to the orphan's camp, but in the novel's broader interrogation of family as a missing scenario of social regulation, and hence as distinctively implicated in pathological mimicry. Family is what the homesick for the real do not have. In *A Southern Renaissance*, Richard King offers, by way of Freud and Otto Rank, the family romance as a paradigmatic culture myth by which the South compensated for its historical deprivations and traumas; the plantation myth, as King describes it, provides a cultural analogue for the child imaging his "real" parents to be of higher station than his biological parents. Hannah's debut novel *Geronimo Rex* (1972), in which filial and Oedipal anxieties generate Harry Monroe's anarchic revolt against paternalistic, bourgeois Ode Elann and initiate the *bildungsroman*'s requisite search for the "spiritual" father, is entirely legible through King's paradigm. *Yonder*

Stands Your Orphan is, by contrast, relatively unconcerned with filiation as an organizing script of identity and desire.[1] In Deleuzian terms, desire is deterritorialized, irrevocably severed from the space-bound socius and its organizing Oedipal drama, while orphanhood, registering at the outset the absence of family structure, functions as a default condition.[2] Put simply, the family romance is unavailable either as compensatory fantasy or as a mechanism of social regulation and coded, territorialized desire. This is not to say that family goes missing, but that its existence follows the logic of the degraded counterfeit: there are no real families in the novel, only ineffective and desperate attempts to fake them. In relating this shift to the novel's broader concern with economy, I rely on Deleuze and Guattari's account in *Anti-Oedipus* of how capitalism, after decoding and deterritorializing flows of desire, "institutes or restores all sorts of residual and artificial, imaginary, or symbolic territorialities, thereby attempting, as best it can, to recode, to rechannel persons who have been defined in terms of abstract quantities." "Everything," they write, "returns or recurs: States, nations, families" (34). Although, as I want to argue momentarily, Hannah depicts capitalism as more symptomatic than causal and agential—at least, his causal patterns are more ambiguous than Deleuze and Guattari's—a recursive movement to artificial territoriality and the family pervades the novel, and ultimately organizes itself around the figure of the home, which, in situating the family in space, acts as a central site toward which reality homesickness is directed. It is not only that Hannah's characters can't go home again, but that there is no home to go to.

Nowhere are the limitations of the simulated home more evident than at the orphan's camp. Established by Gene and Penny Ten Hoor to compensate for the death of their child, the orphan's camp reproduces and intensifies the pathologies of the world it attempts to transcend.[3] Initially, Gene and Penny are real estate developers who view the land around Eagle Lake as an abstract commodity and dream of an empire of condominiums (40). Following the death of their son, they "r[u]n out of words" and develop a fetishistic compulsion for the real, for "things you touch and hold and appraise" (244). In a mechanical attempt at verification, they begin nailing things to the wall: money (no longer abstract), fish (representative of the wetlands destroyed in their real estate ventures), and finally themselves. This excessive oscillation between the abstract and the real is replicated in the orphan's camp, where Gene and Penny "presume to emit rays of instruction" (214) for the orphans to whom, in turn, they "seemed unconnected . . . individually but joined to their collective oversoul" (53). They are parenting machines whose mechanical efforts to plug in to the reproduced family—"You are the child we lost, come back to us in many souls" (331), they tell the orphans—terminate in horror, a kind of familial variation on what Dr. Frankenstein does to the human body. Even their sexual relationship is mechanical, not "purely natural man-and-wife devotion but a sort of scheduled thing like a cup of coffee" (330). They defend moral abstraction with high-grade weaponry; guns in hand, "Gene and Penny were always talking about love and trust at the center of the universe and how vigilant we should be against the Old World" (329–30). Such vigilance ultimately requires dynamite that turns their peninsular camp into an island, thereby grounding their abstract project in a physical terrain separate from the "Old World" (277). In Gene and Penny, benevolence and malevolence are strangely conjoined: just as the couple's good intentions do nothing to prevent the sexual predations of Man Mortimer, neither do they prevent Gene and Penny from being identified as predators themselves by the orphans as the camp finally succumbs to own apocalyptic momentum (330). As the novel reiterates on several occasions, they are insane.

If orphanhood is, at the most fundamental level, the condition of lacking a home, and through it coded, territorialized desire and the concomitant production and regulation of social reality, then the orphans camp does little to ameliorate the condition. I should clarify here, since I am borrowing the terminology of *Anti-Oedipus,* that the condition cries out for amelioration; in *Yonder Stands Your Orphan,* schizophrenia is not tapped for its revolutionary potential, nor are any radical politics located in post-Oedipal flows of desire. Homesickness for the real is a sickness, plain and simple, whose etiology implicates larger patterns of production and consumption. Max Raymond, the novel's most acute diagnostician, describes the syndrome this way: "*Everything about the zombie is ravaged except his obsession. . . . Dead to every other touch. They simply imitate when there is movement or sound. They imitate the conversations around them to seem human to one another.* He had seen them in scores from the airports to the bandstands imitating one another, mimicking the next mimicker in no time, no space, no place, no history" (175–76). Gene and Penny are, in effect, zombie parents who attempt not only to reincarnate their dead child in the orphans but also to reterritorialize the home through the artificial space of the orphans camp. Their wish to "seem human" is, however, merely an extreme instance of a pervasive desire to verify one's existence through the coordinates of time, space, and social reality. Compromised by representation and corrupted by consumption, the real is subjected to a dual movement toward virtuality and abjection; bodies gravitate simultaneously toward disembodiment *and* decay. Abstraction and rot are complementary, not oppositional. The deregulation of reality is not pretty. As Mimi Suarez says, "I don't know anyone who's not decomposing. Even Max says people are hardly necessary anymore, and they have no acts. They tend to float away. It's frightening" (279). In his thematically dense sermon—a jeremiad, really—Egan says that

. . . we have fed on the blood of our own.
We are not even kind to our own retarded that so fill the Southland.
We go off to other states and make fun and literature
And Hollywood movies about them.
The Best Southern Art On-Screen is Stupid and Heartwarming.
But you do not know what is beyond the window of your own
    home. (148)

Commodifying the ubiquitous retarded of the Southland is not merely objectionable traffic in stereotype,[4] but a profoundly anti-social, parasitic, even vampiric, act: blood is being consumed. The "wretched spectators, heads just out of your mama's womb," are born into a world of empty consumption: "Buy me sumpin, Ma. Plug me in" (149). Plugging under this dispensation is, however, an exercise in missed connection, and while the post-Oedipal world of missing parents might promise gratification through consumption, its desirable objects evaporate into virtuality. Dispossessed of home at the moment of birth, the orphan falls easy prey to the predators who command the economy of false gratification.

Still, homesickness persists. Here, however, it is useful to discriminate between those who are homesick and those who are simply dead. The dead include the Episcopalians, "*postwar, postmodern, posthuman*," who sweep up the "*waste of the stores and the storerooms [that] find their place in each consumer heart to rot and reek*" (201); the zombie mimickers; the casino musicians who, "although mistaken for the living by their audiences, *were* actually dead. Ghouls howling for egress from their tombs" (37–38); the "weak and bored" casino patrons lured in by "dime store Legbas" (177);[5] the doctors who have abandoned Eagle Lake for new vacation spots "where they mimicked life as best they could with the new big money" (177); and the subscribers to *New Deal* magazine, "the organ for reformed country people who now hated nature. People who had lost farms. Settlers between town and country who wanted even less. The homes pictured were like mausoleums beside highways, no grass and not a stick of a tree in sight. Paved lawns" (125). The dead patronize the "bad restaurant," which "served food for the dead," and "would stay when only zombies prevailed" (175):

> The bad restaurant even had bad-food loungers and loiterers,
> hard to shake when they got a good imitation of you going. The
> restaurant with its RESTAURANT sign. Its mimicking of the din-
> ing life, yet no edible food, bad water and a weak tea to go with
> that. *Refill that beige for you, sir?* Every dish served in contempt
> for what used to be human. (176)

The homesick, by contrast, eat at "Near 'Nuff Food," which is "far supe-rior" to the bad restaurant and has "[a] theme" (218): "medieval chaos, and people dumped buckets of ribs on a tablecloth of butcher paper" (288). As Patricia Yaeger explains in *The Geography of Identity*, the consumption of themed space

> gratifies much more than a whimsical desire for homogenized,
> coherent space; it suggests a longing for incorporation, a long-
> ing to inhabit credible space. What does it take for space to be
> credible? In the absence of the support systems provided by com-
> munal life, costumes, props and crowded stage settings help, and
> thus a whirl of costume dramas and artificial backdrops have
> invaded our lives. (18–19)

Hence the superiority of Near 'Nuff Food to the bad restaurant: its simulation of place at least caters to a desire to inhabit credible space, a desire that preserves a residue of sociality. If the bad restaurant serves food for the dead, Near 'Nuff Food caters to the partially living, those desperate for incorporation into *something*.

Yonder Stands Your Orphan is an elaborate meditation on the production and consumption of space. Relatively unconcerned with the coded, space-bound territories associated with the Oedipal family, the novel directs its attention to artificial territorialities as they attempt either to reconstitute and simulate the family (the orphans camp) or to generate credible space—and hence a social grid or "communal life"—in the absence of family.[6] The production of the latter kind of space, of "home" without family, is predictably anxious and fragile, and we should clearly understand the insufficiency of Near 'Nuff Food and its staging of medieval chaos in confronting cultural pathology. But while the restaurant's "festive and harsh" theme makes it "a success," the most compelling theme is clearly reality itself, or rather its artificial production. Although we learn that farmed catfish is Mississippi's leading export, local consumption is dominated by the nostalgia industry. In a state populated by "men and women nostalgic by age eleven" (40), spaces coded as authentic are desirable, most conspicuously in the novel's prologue, where Leon Jr.'s roadhouse "harked back to the fifties" and thus becomes a "must-visit" (1, 2).

The nostalgia industry sells because it reproduces both dimensions—space and time—in which Hannah's characters find themselves dispossessed. (The redemptive potential of animals, as we shall see, depends on their unconsciously *inhabiting* those dimensions.) Because nostalgia is rigorously spatialized—that is, located in special places discontinuous with incoherent modernity—it offers an implicit alternative history, a located might-have-been. But because nostalgia is intrinsically narrative—a tale of history gone wrong—it attains a capacity to expand its spatial limits, ultimately broadening to reproduce the South as artificial territoriality. That Vicksburg is adjacent to Eagle's Lake is no accident, since Vicksburg serves, as the novel registers on three separate occasions, as the pivot on which the South's military fortunes turned in the Civil War, the local analogue of the classic Faulknerian scenario from *Intruder in the Dust* in which every "southern boy fourteen years old" can imagine ("not once, but whenever he wants it") Pickett's charge at Gettysburg and "think This time. Maybe this time" (125–26). Immediately before their mutual wounding, Man Mortimer and Frank Booth ponder a "clean head shot on Sherman or Grant":

> They agreed that one expert Navy SEAL sniper could have won
> the war that month. When slavery would have perished as an
> institution. It was common wisdom that the South would have
> given the slaves their freedom the instant they kicked the North's
> ass, but that the slaves would have chosen to remain. . . . The
> South was so good. Why was this never discussed? (62)

The parody here—all the more striking as a recognizable *white* southern discourse—connects the alternative history it describes and nostalgia for an imagined present, the virtual "good" South "never discussed" because of "all this correctness" (62). If, as Egan says, the South is vulnerable to faking in Hollywood movies, it is equally vulnerable to the grotesque historiography that here waxes rhapsodic over a bizarre Lost Cause terrain. Booth and Mortimer briefly inhabit this imaginary geography as fellow citizens; that they are stabbing one another moments later suggests its tenuous social efficacy, its susceptibility to (literal) puncture.[7] In his jeremiad, Egan exposes the charade: "We have spoken of the fall of Vicksburg as if it mattered" (149).[8]

Nostalgia ultimately cannot sustain credible space because it is a symptom of reality homesickness, not its antidote or cure. Crucially, nostalgia itself has run out of gas; like the dinosaur on Leon Jr.'s Sinclair sign ("God knows the actual gasoline it pumped nowadays" [3]), it seems part of an earlier era. And while the consumption of "authentic" space is less intrinsically pathological than the novel's more overt forms of degradation, it is ultimately complicit in them. This relation is established in the prologue when Leon Jr., the careful entrepreneur of local color (his "narratives increased the cost of the liquor nearly twofold" [1]), offers a new commodity: "Boys," he says, "it's 'Teenage Lesbian Comedown,'" starring "local talent, even though it was slick as Hollywood" (4, 3). One potential customer, Robbie, resists the roadhouse's emergent economy: "I don't know. This place had a purity to it. Lowdown but pure. I hate to see him join the common, I guess go modern, you might say" (5). But his

friend, Cecil, counter-argues that it is selfish to watch "all those poor color-
ful folks . . . and wis[h] they'd never change" (5), and then explains why he
has purchased the video:

> "Nostalgia, shit, me too. I got it every second. Nothing new looks
> worth a shit to me. New houses seem like goddamn rest stops.
> We're dirty old men, already, Robbie, face it. And even the dirt
> don't seem as tasty as it used to. Now the whiskey's talking, but I
> tell you. I'm willing to look at anything'll change my life before I
> blow this weary head off." (5)

The practice of nostalgia and the consumption of pornography thus stand
in rough symmetry as attempts at virtual gratification. But Leon's roadhouse, with its "old-time titty-girl calendar" from an era "when it was daring" (2), will no longer suffice; stronger measures are needed if suicide,
which always lurks as the most logical social practice, is to be deferred. The
nostalgia of Leon's roadhouse thus gravitates incrementally to "Teenage
Lesbian Comedown," where the presence of "local talent" reterritorial-
izes desire (and locality itself) in an ever more extreme and artificial way:
"What it did was open your eyes to the potential in this state" (3). The
video's auteur is, of course, Man Mortimer.

In his most extended meditation on pleasure and space, Man Mortimer
wanders a Vicksburg casino "casting in his head for a video":

> *It's a family dream here. What men and some women pay for,*
> *dreams nobody else talks about. You ain't got your odors, your*
> *armpits stink. Everything smells like a new car and roses. No birth*
> *control, no AIDS, no sad sermonette the next day, no apology, no*
> *forgiveness. Nobody gets hurt. You get nasty, but nobody needs to*
> *kill or rob for it. This is my country.* (67)

Crucially, Mortimer situates his video in relation to family ("a family dream") and space ("my country") while simultaneously suspending
whatever resistance they might offer against the pure gratification that
he wishes to generate for profit. The pleasure of his text depends on the

body being cited but censored (no armpits, conception, AIDS), on sexual relations being simulated (as acquiescence, since without female pleasure, "*it's all queered*" [68]) minus the friction involved in relationships themselves (no sermonettes, apologies, forgiveness). Bondage itself is mimicked with "light little chains": "Fairyland bondage, like" (67). In this linkage as in others ("family dream," "my country"), Mortimer yokes together with violence terms of the real and the virtual. His "dream" is essentially post-familial—"*It's about Onan, careless with his seed. It's against populating the grimy little flybit species . . .*" (68)—and his "country" is radically deterritorialized, consisting mainly of SUVs that combine the "aphrodisiacs of new-car smell and White Diamond mist" and evade the space-bound law, impotent to "touch him because his bordello was spread in myriad chambers throughout the suburbs and even underpasses" (10). That Mortimer nevertheless gestures toward the family and the state, toward an "absurd" "patriotism" (67), signals an especially acute case of reality homesickness. This is why, even as he plots his latest pornographic video, he must offer the Internet as, literally, a virtual scapegoat, an excessive simulacrum that produces "*a lonely murderous kind of nerd who wears a raincoat in his own den, stepping out into the ether thinking it's real, realer than Mom, who he's hammered to death because she wasn't some Power Ranger with tits who makes waffles every day*" (68). The Internet signals the utter abolition of the real, here dramatized as the murderous obliteration of the mother who has failed to gratify totally, a family romance gone bad under the pressures of virtuality. Mortimer is compelled to imagine the Internet this way because he does not want to go there lest he give up even his residual connection to the real.

But the artificial reproduction of desire, at which the Internet stands as a terminal limit, is Mortimer's home ground, even if he does employ local talent. His identity and the design it spawns originates in pornography: "A neighbor boy showed him a pornographic picture when he was fifteen, and the bone-deep thrill of seeing that woman in her happy pain had never left him, had never diminished. He looked for it behind every curtain of culture, of law" (50). If Mortimer's design is more incoherent than that of Faulkner's Thomas Sutpen's—in point of fact, he nearly stumbles into his calling—this moment acts as the equivalent of Sutpen's being turned away from the plantation house door. Where paternity and dynasty organize the grand trajectory of *Absalom, Absalom!*, orphanhood and deterritorialized desire orient the diffuse narrative economy of *Yonder Stands Your Orphan.* Unlike Sutpen, for whom narcissistic trauma generates a pathologically coherent identity articulated in the territoriality of Sutpen's Hundred, Mortimer knows himself to be a wandering counterfeit: he is a duplicate who wants to be an original, a simulacrum who wants to be real, an exile who wants to go home. And if, like Sutpen, his malignant genius obtains a certain magnitude, he is also a virtual Popeye—complete with voyeuristic tendencies (117, 287–88, 321–22)—who mechanically performs his desire with videotape instead of a corncob; a buffoonish devil who, like Walker Percy's Art Immelman, badly mimics the human: "he seemed to be doing some imitation of warmth, friendship, trust. Childish, stilted gestures, as if studied from some old book on stagecraft" (52); a neo-Babbitt whose inferiorities are momentarily assuaged by consumption: "He felt dirty and low-rent. He went out the back and almost immediately drove at break-neck speed into Vicksburg to purchase a pair of shoes. He wanted bright white ones. Perhaps a boot, a soft suede pair you could hold in your hands while you went off to sleep in any house and feel perfectly at home" (249). Mortimer is, however, never at home, least of all in his own houses, three "strange empty homes" (325) from which he "flees one . . . to the other, the next house always a getaway from the last" (52). Similarly, his desire for Dee Allison, who "moved him in all ways" because she "could be visited but never occupied" (57), lacks altogether the comforts of home. Mortimer is a concatenation of copies—first Fabian, then Conway Twitty, finally a decomposing "thing that was hardly anything but a big head with a mass of white hair" (336)—and is himself duplicated by a rival, Frank Booth, who through plastic surgery achieves "a Conway Twitty face fresher than Mortimer's own" (308).

Mortimer's status as pure replica has its compensations, however, since it attunes him to the virtual logic from which he extracts a healthy profit. A simulated man, he is a real entrepreneur: "Men and women in this nation were changing, and he intended to charge them for it" (49). His SUVs are an elegant testimony to his command of themed space and (literally) deterritorialized desire. He capitalizes on the availability of flexible labor, offering "no retirement plan, no health insurance" to the women he employs as prostitutes because "[w]hat you did was just make money and watch out" (109). There are costs—ruined lives ("only twelve, maybe thir-teen")—all the more gruesome because his female workers eagerly desire a "step up" from their territorial fate "settl[ing] down . . . in some goddamn trailer home" with "puffed-up little dicks" who want the women "to breed more like them" (19). The deep logic of Mortimer's economic virtuosity suggests the evacuation of social reality performed by the economy he com-mands, a process replicated in Mortimer's peculiar relation to the family romance. If Freud's scenario turns on the child's replacement of actual par-ents with imagined parents as an imaginative script of social deprivation giving way to social ascent, Mortimer follows the first part of the script, but not the second. Explicitly associating his parents with deprivation—he is embarrassed by their chicken yard and blames them for his not having "a fine car or any money" (50)—his "ascent" is explicitly post-familial—he desires neither surrogate parents nor actual progeny (51)—and implicitly post-social, in that his desire for money is radically severed from any social order. He desires pleasure, not position.[9] For this reason, we cannot describe his career (in contrast to Thomas Sutpen's) as an ascent (which presumes mobility *within* a stable social order), but rather as an incoherent series of accumulations. This incoherence is not lost on Mortimer, whose desire to incarnate himself—to exist until "they would let him back into real life" (266)—assumes ever more extreme forms. He disfigures others because he is eroding: when, in a dream, "his own mirror told him he was an impos-tor in the body of Conway Twitty," he realizes "he was going to have to cut again" (255); as he muses later, "*Maybe I cut because I want them to have no face too*" (295).[10] When his confrontation with Peden goes awry and he is "thrashed on . . . very well" (270), he is "reduced . . . nearly to ectoplasm," which "terrified him. He had a nostalgia for himself" (298). He similarly codes his desire to inhabit the (tenuously) credible space of Eagle's Lake within a nostalgic scenario:

> He would become well known on the lake and finally a pride of the region when he became an elder, because you were colorful then and people liked to see you prosper. Get nostalgic about when times were colorful and wilder and better. Let go because of history and what you'd done for it. A picture of him shaking hands with the law. (277)[11]

Where, in *Never Die*, Fernando Muré rejects rehabilitation through nostalgia in order to "make a high mark for good," Mortimer imagines nostalgia as retroactively sanctioning his depravity. At this late stage in the narrative, Mortimer's nostalgia even extends to the parents whom previously he has "despised" (49): "Those good people. Not a finer man in the county than your postman daddy, what's his name?" (295). For their part, his parents (who have arrived unannounced on a visit from their home in southern Missouri) recognize Mortimer for what they have always tacitly known him to be, "an absence, or all things present at once . . . a dangerous nullity" (328–29). Their deferred epiphany punctuates Mortimer's last spoken words in the novel, which he (fittingly) repeats: "I exist, man" (328).

Because most of the novel's social pathologies are concentrated in Man Mortimer, his exile to prison in the novel's epilogue, neatly paralleled by the self-exile of Sheriff Facetto (who simply "ceased being" [335]), signals an act of social hygiene. This is not to say, however, that those pathologies are not widely diffused among the core group of characters who remain and who, throughout the narrative, have been mostly impotent to resist the boundary violations made by Mortimer and Facetto. Nearly everyone works for Mortimer or owes him money. Just as Facetto seduces Melanie Wooten, so Mortimer insinuates himself within the Eagle Lake enclave, forcing several characters to enact the drama of becoming "bootlicker to a phantom" (323). Given this pervasive impotence to resist Mortimer, it becomes difficult to identify precisely the formal logic by which the novel moves toward the epilogue's comic conclusion: if it is easy to see why Mortimer flourishes, it is more difficult to understand how the survivors endure. But endure they do and a comic conclusion (of a sort) it is,[12] complete with a wedding between Melanie and Harvard:

> John Roman and Max Raymond drew closer together, but
> Roman did not want anybody talking with him while he fished,
> and he did not like talking God at all. His wife Bernice was well.
> He loved God cautiously. He did not know how long this love
> would last.
>
> Harvard and Melanie were married by Peden on the plea-
> sure barge. Their marriage was that of pals after a fight and long

silence. It had become too late in time for fights, and often even memories. They clung. (336)

Even conceding Northrup Frye's observation that the society emerging at the end of comedy is based on ideals that are seldom defined or formulated because definition and formulation belong to the order that has been overcome (169), the opacity of the novel's conclusion presents a formal problem. In attempting to come to terms with the comedic space that emerges, I argue that it *offers* no terms—more specifically, that the recovery of credible space depends on the banishment of speech, which has all along been associated with performers such as Facetto, whom everyone agrees is "another fraud of vocality like Bill Clinton" (211). (Despite being rejected by Melanie for his "breathy dramatic pauses" and for treating the "community's nightmare as if it were some trivial dramatic work that had floated past a theatre workshop he was in" (335), Facetto performs one useful service before removing to a "far, far state": He demands that his deputy "[m]ake [Mortimer] quit talking" [336].) I want, in other words, to read a kind of allegory into Mortimer's confinement in Parchman Prison, "where he would not stop talking" (336), and the physical contact ("drew closer together," "they clung") that defines the novel's conclusion, which, in evacuating both speech and the intense, grounded pleasures characteristic of comedy, signals a kind of empty repetition or simulation of comedic form deployed against the regime of the simulacrum. Asceticism and reticence countervail the pathologies of pleasure and speech.

Hannah's critique of speech, then, parallels his broader critique of representations that substitute theme for space, nostalgia for history, stereotype for neighborliness, pornography for reciprocal sexual pleasure. In *The Theory of the Novel*, Georg Lukács describes the novel's world as a bifurcated one in which "the world of deeds separates itself from men and, because of this independence, becomes hollow and incapable of absorbing the true meaning of deed in itself, incapable of becoming a symbol through deeds and dissolving them in turn into symbols" (65). According to Lukács, the novel registers this loss by producing (in Lukács's metaphysical idiom) a "dissonance special to the novel, the refusal of the immanence of being to enter into empirical life" (71). In order to account for Hannah's critique of speech—the narrative's preference, as Max puts it, for "acts, not chats" (283)—we must first understand that, just as the novel's virtual economy intensifies Lukácsian reification, so its radical division of deeds and symbols ("acts and chats") amplifies Lukácsian dissonance to deafening postmodern levels. Because the sum total of the novel's givens preclude incarnation—whether understood as the reciprocal absorption of deed and symbol, the entrance of immanence into empirical life, or the Word made flesh—redemption (or more broadly, the formal resolution of the narrative's oppressive double-bind) can proceed only in hypothetical and contingent ways.

In this effort, animals and music help. Egan concludes his jeremiad with an injunction to "Shut up! Shut up! And talk to the animals. They have soul, they have art./Shut up and live with your gorgeous neighbors!" (149). Despite the paradox—it is a call for silence uttered aloud, just as Egan elsewhere denounces books ("a very mortal sin . . . not wrote by the Christly . . . a sign of present day hell" [72]) in a book—it is sound advice. As throughout Hannah's fiction, *Yonder Stands Your Orphan* imagines animals as humanity's radical Other commodified for inhuman ends: as Egan says, "they use a language we can't understand, so we kill them, tear them apart, even sell their parts for aphrodisiacs" (147). Animals *inhabit,* they do not speak: the relation is causal. The "only prophets" available (158), Ulrich and Carl Bob Feeney, speak for their silence: "They did not humanize animals. . . . They wanted to learn their language, and how indeed they kept going despite depression, despair, even suicide" (158). Dogs do not only endure, they prevail, living "huge lives before they die" (160), experiencing "ecstasy over the day" and "oneness with the infinite" (146). As Ulrich says, dogs "don't talk because they don't need speech. . . . Dogs are in space and time" (159–60).[13] The life of dogs thus inverts precisely the life of humans, colonized by speech, exiled from space and time, and distinctly suicidal. We must, however, recognize the pragmatic impasse which the lives of animals presents within the social field of the novel. If animals were, as Egan says, "*already there*" in the Garden of Eden, the world of the novel is radically postlapsarian; if animals "are Christ every day" (146), then the incarnation they embody remains inaccessible *per se.* At best, animals offer an example of silence, pleasure, and endurance that might, in some deeply refracted or hypothetical way, enable the practice of living with one's neighbors.

A parallel and equally "impractical" speechlessness is available in music—at least the sort performed by Mimi Suarez and, more centrally, the five "dark black" musicians at the church Raymond purchases. Their music, which they "had no interest in recording or selling," translates as "*Christ, we are your throat*" (284); Christ, in turn, cannot *say* anything. Again, the language of incarnation is marked by the absence of language, almost as if, to use Lukács's formulation, immanence of being can enter empirical life only as an exquisite hypothesis. Animals and music, then, offer cognate instances of redemption as pure form—redemption, that is, that cannot embody "content" lest it become transformed, through some inevitable momentum, into yet another vehicle of abject disembodiment. This is why the church, which Hannah has identified as the "only real hero" of the novel (Interview 262), must be a church without firm belief ("the Church of Open Doors, open for the lost and dead of all causes" [309]), just as the pleasure barge—the novel's other candidate as a credible, authentic social space—erupts into discord when Melanie Wooten interrupts its silent harmonies with a talky poem (180–82). As Egan suggests, credible space is contingent on "shutting up." This, in turn, renders the narrative relatively silent on the community that resists or at least survives the trend of culture and its various maladies of representation.

The broad pattern of contingent redemption—or, alternatively, incarnation as pure form—is repeated at the level of the individual:

> Max Raymond suddenly knew his vision would come at the end
> of his life and not a moment before. He was nearly blinded by
> the realization that he was a nuisance to both God and man. He
> repented. He would act. He felt expendable to a higher power
> and this was good. He was resigned but in no way sad. (311)

It is no coincidence that Raymond is on the receiving end of this deferred vision. Effectively orphaned by his mother, who prefers to attend to the "heathen orphans of the world" (89), Raymond becomes a saxophonist "who had somehow gotten good through pure want" (171). But his music is impure: a sonic ironist to his wife's pure music, playing "against her, mocking or blaming her for her gifts" (35), he is later rejected by the black musicians who are Christ's throat. Acutely attuned to the evil disembodied in

Man Mortimer, he is unable to resist it. Raymond is stylistically consonant with the novel and the culture it describes, a consonance that frames his repentance in a distinctive way, since what we recognize there is a curiously resigned and deflated version of what Flannery O'Connor once termed the "action of Grace in a territory inhabited largely by the devil."[14] Lacking any trace of the sublime, the language of redemption here signals the deferral of the pure, incarnated word, as if language itself cannot embody incarnation. Earlier, Raymond has explicitly named this desire in his poem:

These claims, What the Lord Wants Me to Do,
Greek, Greek to me.
I would like the straight Aramaic right from His lips.
. . .
Or just show up, why don't You? (243–44)

He gets, however, neither Christ nor His Word. His redemption is not epiphanic, but contingent; as a matter of the future conditional tense ("He would act"), it's still Greek to him. For this reason, redemptive acts— "What the Lord Wants Me to Do"—remain undefined except in the sense Raymond has recognized earlier in meditating on Christian militants who "cannot be Christian but are Christ's allies," who lack "visions," but war against "ambiguous fiends through history" (179).

In this boundary defense—albeit one sanctioned by Christ—lies the narrative's deep spatial logic. Revising O'Connor, we might say that the action of grace in a territory inhabited largely by devil is simply to banish the devil. For *Yonder Stands Your Orphan* is, at its core, the book of Man Mortimer, "the demon itself" (328),[15] and his expulsion, accomplished not through the law but through the "town's certainty that he was the killer [of Penny Ten Hoor]" (336), leaves the town cleansed, but inarticulate and imaginable only in terms of shared space. In an act of social hygiene roughly parallel to Mortimer's incarceration, the orphan's camp, thematically coherent to the point of insanity, has been "razed to the ground" (4). What remains is not a reimagined community—that is, a system in which speech and practice derive from, and in turn reproduce, some social archive—but a *retreat*: post-contractual, post-symbolic, post-familial, post-epiphanic. The law is not reconstituted as part of some utopian gesture, but exiled (in the form

of Facetto) as just another scene of empty performance. Coded territoriality, insofar at it involves the collective regulation of desire, remains inaccessible because it has been all along so uniformly undesirable. Desire itself is
mostly absent because it has circulated so monstrously as pornography. No
families remain, only neighbors and partners. For the exhausted survivors,
the narrative's utopian energies are dissipated lest the etymological paradox
of utopianism itself (as simultaneously "good place" and "no place") dissolve the only place they have left. In the epilogue's rather grim production
of locality lies, finally, Hannah's formal solution to the postmodern assault
narrative, the widely diffused story of the assault of the local by the global;
of place by tourism; of history by the museum; of the real by the simulacrum; of authenticity by mechanical reproduction; of coherent space by
time-space compression; of depth by surface; of value by consumerism.

In his reading of Lukács and the novel's "form problem," Fredric
Jameson identifies "the brute fact of contingency" as the "content" that
"a modernist aesthetics seeks to burn away, like slag, in order that some
'pure' work or form can emerge from the process" (36). *Yonder Stands Your
Orphan* inverts the scenario precisely: it is purity that cannot be assimi-
lated in the novel's messy domain, one dominated by cultural noise against
which "music" can be posited only as an "exquisite hypothesis," and against
which only silence can be brought to bear as a practical measure. This is
not to fault the novel for failing to provide an adequate resolution, but
rather to indicate the conditions in which it affords us, as Roland Barthes
says in another context, a "dizzy spectacle of *praxis* without sanction . . . a
Mosaic glance at the Promised Land of the real" (188). In an interview with
Dan Williams, Hannah describes being "shocked" and "staggered" by the
novel's "darkness," but also "struck" by the perseverance and endurance
of his survivors: "They just keep creeping on, keep fishing, keep having
their pleasure barges" ("Interview" 262, 63). These, of course, are acts, but
profoundly limited ones. Pleasure on these terms acts more directly as an
index of an ascetic space that has, by some minor miracle, been kept intact
from the world surrounds the fragile borders of Eagle's Lake,[16] a world in
which desire is rigorously embedded in an economy of artificial gratification and monstrous simulation, a world, finally, in which reality homesickness offers no cure. In a world condemned to mimicry, speaking is
decomposition; in a world wherein we cannot speak, we must be silent.

Notes

1. In labeling *Yonder Stands Your Orphan* as post-Oedipal, I mean to indicate a transition from the kind of "Anti-Freudian Plots" in Hannah's fiction described by James B. Potts, in which male characters "try to assert masculinity by mimicking larger-than-life figure, fearless, legendary figures such as Jeb Stuart (*Airships*), Hernando de Soto (*Ray*), and Geronimo (*Geronimo Rex*)" (238). Although I generally share Potts's view of the parodic and dissonant treatment of such quasi-Oedipal relationships, I would characterize Hannah's depiction of identity formation in his earlier work as fundamentally oriented along a Father/Son axis. For a reading of Geronimo Rex as a quest for the spiritual father, see Ken Millard's essay in this volume. In *Yonder Stands Your Orphan*, by contrast, the only quasi-Oedipal drama surrounds Sidney and Pepper Farté, "scions of a pusillanimous French line too lazy and ignorant to anglicize their name in a pleasant manner" (94). In this sense, the novel represents a departure from what Ruth Weston identifies as the "pervasive theme of initiation that accompanies the search for meaningful male adulthood in all of Barry Hannah's stories" (60).
2. See Schulz for a discussion of orphanhood as a trope by which female southern writers resisted the Oedipal dynamics of traditional southern culture.
3. The orphan's camp reproduces the long-standing fascination of utopian experiments with altering or reproducing family structure, a history that includes Marx's and Fourier's nineteenth-century attempts to detach sexual relations from marriage to more recent attempts to found new societies around a charismatic father figure.
4. This pattern is repeated throughout the text, notably in Melanie Wooten's desire to turn John Roman into "*Uncle Remus goes to war*" (26). Here, as in Mortimer's desire to figure himself as an object of nostalgia (see the discussion below), the commodification of human beings epitomizes the danger of "symbol" (26).
5. As Martyn Bone points out, Hannah cites Legba as apparently having control over the "zombified" Hare and Sponce (personal communication). In the Voudon pantheon, Legba is the spirit of thresholds—notably between the spirit world and the material world—although Hannah's reference to him apparently misidentifies him as implicated in zombification. As will probably be clear, Hannah's reference to "zombies" has less to do with Voudon than with the zombie of the popular horror film.
6. I should clarify that I am using "family" to refer primarily to a condition or *scene* of regulated, coded desire, not to a discrete social structure or institution. Although Hannah characteristically figures the former through the latter—most prominently in his troping of orphanhood as the lack of a coherent regulation of desire—the narrative offers neither nostalgia for the "traditional family" (as that term is commonly understood) nor a sociological critique of nontraditional family structures.
7. For a strong discussion of Hannah's deployment of the Civil War, see Martyn Bone's essay in this volume. Although Vicksburg figures centrally in "That Was Close, Ma," where the narrator laments "Oh Vicksburg, Vicksburg! I am, personally, the fall of the West" (*Bats* 345), I suggest that *Yonder Stands Your Orphan* deviates from what might be labeled the Jeb Stuart syndrome. In this syndrome, the Civil War is deployed as a quasi-Oedipal scenario, often with explicit erotic overtones. In *Yonder Stands Your Orphan*, the Civil War locates not so much a personal psychodrama as a collective narrative of dispossession and anxiety, a quasi-elegiac scenario that reproduces the structure of the family romance in aligning imagined history with the surrogate, idealized parent. Here, the thwarted recovery is not of a gratifying, heroic, and essentially masculinist experience (see Bjerre), but of a shared social space, a Lost Cause terrain

that evaporates under the pressures of what Vicksburg actually *is* in the novelistic present: an abject terrain of casino capitalism and pawn shop culture.

8. The third meditation on Vicksburg and the Civil War comes in Raymond's poem, where he imaginatively participates in his forebears' prayer to "give me Sherman, Grant or a lesser general": "*Ptoom and bummf*, hit square./This old mistress my rifle" (243). The poem goes on to imagine redemption in explicitly Christian terms, a shift that evacuates the redemptive potential of Mortimer and Booth's "clean head shot" scenario.

9. I should clarify this as an initial orientation, since position is finally what Mortimer does desire in his attempt to incarnate himself. Still, there is a crucial difference between Mortimer and precursor-characters such as Faulkner's Thomas Sutpen and Snopeses or Fitzgerald's Jay Gatsby in that these precursors are essentially conservative. Where the material self-objects of Faulkner's and Fitzgerald's characters are desired precisely because they are already valued by society, Mortimer's self-objects are desirable because he desires them. The free-floating nature of such desire, I suggest, attunes him to the economy of consumption that lacks a stable social grid.

10. The logic of Mortimer's maiming follows what Elaine Scarry calls analogical verification. According to Scarry, "when there is within a society a crisis of belief—that is, when some central idea or ideology or cultural construct has ceased to elicit a population's belief either because it is manifestly fictitious or because it has for some reason been divested of ordinary forms of substantiation—the sheer material factualness of the human body will be borrowed to lend that cultural construct the aura of 'realness' and 'certainty'" (14). Mortimer's perverse attempt to verify through the painful mutilation of bodily surfaces inverts the logic of the pornographic economy he commands, wherein the materiality of the body is reduced to pleasurable visual surfaces.

11. That Mortimer stages his rehabilitation with "the law" is appropriate, since Sheriff Facetto doubles Mortimer's anxious relationship to reality and eventual regression to nullity. See the discussion below.

12. For an alternative reading of the novel's conclusion as exhibiting a "new tone of desperation [which] is perhaps the most significant development in Hannah's thirty-year career," see Thomas Bjerre's essay in this volume.

13. Rick Bass calls Hannah the "the great dog-handler in modern literature" (v). Throughout Hannah's fiction, the treatment of animals serves as an ethical centrifuge dividing those who kick dogs and those who pet dogs. A humane regard for animals thus acts as an criterion of humanity itself, violated by both the excessively refined (Jeb Stuart in "Dragged Fighting from His Tomb," who counsels Captain Howard to "Use your weeping on people, not on animals" [*Airships* 54]) and the excessively brutal ("some blacks" and "white country people" who torture dogs in *Boomerang* [39], thereby signaling some innate human depravity). In *The Seeds of Time*, Jameson diagnoses the essentialist "ecological recovery of a sense of Nature" as existing in an antinomic relation with the antifoundationalist assumptions of postmodernity (46, 32–52). Hannah reproduces, I suggest, something of this antinomy in situating the use of Nature as both an index of cultural pathology and a potential "solution" that gestures opaquely toward the utopian.

14. For O'Connor, grace was an almost impossible subject for fiction: "We almost have to approach it negatively" (144). Although, as I argue, Hannah's reworking of "grace" is essentially negative—a matter less of incarnation than of escape—we should observe his radical departure from O'Connor's characteristically epiphanic conclusions, where visions ("Revelation") and the literal descent of the Holy Ghost ("The Enduring Chill") are narrative possibilities.

15. The formal problem of incarnation is doubled negatively in the figure of Mortimer, who is simultaneously the object of a nihilistic discourse (in which he is an empty "nullity") and an essentialist one (in which he incarnates evil).

16. The prologue, which apparently takes place after the events of the last chapter, indicates the spatial limitations of the resolution, since there, as we have seen, an economy of nostalgia and pornography is still operating.

Works Cited

Barthes, Roland. "Authors and Writers." *A Barthes Reader*. Ed. Susan Sontag. New York: Hill and Wang, 1982.

Bass, Rick. Introduction. *Boomerang/Never Die: Two Novels by Barry Hannah*. Jackson: UP of Mississippi, 1994. v-xi.

Deleuze, Gilles and Félix Guattari. *Anti-Oedipus: Capitalism and Schizophrenia*. Trans. Robert Hurley et al. Minneapolis: U of Minnesota P, 1983.

Faulkner, William. *Intruder in the Dust*. New York: Random House, 1948.

Frye, Northrup. *Anatomy of Criticism: Four Essays*. 1957. New York: Atheneum, 1968.

Hannah, Barry. *Airships*. New York: Knopf, 1978.

———. *Bats out of Hell*. New York: Grove, 1994.

———. *Boomerang/Never Die: Two Novels by Barry Hannah*. Jackson: UP of Mississippi, 1994.

———. "Interview with Barry Hannah: February 6, 2001." By Daniel E. Williams. *Mississippi Quarterly* 54.2 (spring 2001): 261–68.

———. *Yonder Stands Your Orphan*. New York: Grove, 2001.

Jameson, Fredric. *The Seeds of Time*. New York: Columbia UP, 1994.

King, Richard. *A Southern Renaissance: The Cultural Awakening of the American South, 1930–1955*. New York: Oxford UP, 1980.

Lukács, Georg. *The Theory of the Novel*. Trans. Anna Bostock. Cambridge: MIT, 1990.

Marcuse, Herbert. *Eros and Civilization: A Philosophical Inquiry into Freud*. 1955. New York, Vintage, 1962.

O'Connor, Flannery. *The Habit of Being*. Ed. Sally Fitzgerald. New York: Farrar, Straus, Giroux, 1979.

Potts, James B., III. "Barry Hannah's Anti-Myth Method: Anti-Freudian Plots and Fractured Fairy Tales." *Mississippi Quarterly* (2002): 237–50.

Scarry, Elaine. *The Body in Pain: The Making and Unmaking of the World*. New York: Oxford UP, 1985.

Schulz, Joan. "Orphaning as Resistance." *The Female Tradition in Southern Literature*. Ed. Carol S. Manning. Urbana: U of Illinois P, 1993. 89–109.

Weston, Ruth. *Barry Hannah: Postmodern Romantic*. Baton Rouge: Louisiana State UP, 1998.

Yaeger, Patricia. "Introduction: Narrating Space." *The Geography of Identity*. Ed. Patricia Yaeger. Ann Arbor: U of Michigan P, 1996. 1–38.

Interview with Barry Hannah

—*Daniel E. Williams*

October 13, 2005

Dan Williams (DW): *Well, Barry, how are your classes going?*
Barry Hannah (BH): I'm teaching the best graduate writing class I have ever taught.

DW: *Why is that?*
BH: Many thanks to our angel and loyal intercessor John Grisham, I think our program is starting to pay off. We have selective admissions, only a few very talented people. We have students from all over, from Michigan and California. But I also have a really rousing group of students now. Sometimes you just get a class to remember. You get everybody good. It's the good dice of time. I feel lucky, blessed.

DW: *How are you doing overall?*
BH: I'm good in my head. People are generally treating me better now that I'm a geezer. I'm having a good time, and I'm writing well. I think this book will get an anchor off my head. It's a novel about Ray's son, a flyer in Desert Storm. He's also the Ray from *Yonder*, and he's been estranged from his wife, Mimi Saurez. Though he's broken down financially, he's still a pilot, and he's also a lay preacher, a sincere

Christian, who is hiding from the IRS. There has been a string of church fires from Mississippi up to Missouri—mosques, temples, cathedrals, and small churches, all random fires. Ray's nephew is one of the arsonists, and he knows this but can't turn him in to the law. The fires have a strange effect on people, restoring some to spirituality and alienating others.

DW: *Tell me a little more about the book.*
BH: Well, there's a lawman, but he's also busted and a near felon. Ray's ministry is to the sick and needy, those who need help. I've tried to put real people into the novel. I have thrown away three novels, but I'll finish this one. It's set in Oxford, Richard Howorth, you, [Ron] Shapiro, even my doctor, the pain management dude out of Harvard med. Taking on Faulkner in his hometown. I have never done that before except in *Boomerang*, which is a different kind of book.

DW: *How is the writing going?*
BH: I hope the best writing I have ever done, but the work is slow. I hate revision, always have. And there have been health interruptions, but I make no excuses. This is one of those novels that takes a little longer. I don't want to repeat myself. This novel is a long adventure in the best way. I think about the novel with happiness, only sometimes as a chore. The work is backbreaking. Writing can be horribly tough. But I'm not always butt-tight about my own production as in former days.

DW: *What other kinds of projects have you been working on?*
BH: I wrote a piece on the Book of Luke, just ten pages long but tough work. I wrote it for *Paste*, a glossy rock and roll magazine out of Atlanta ["The Maddening Protagonist," *Paste* 19, (December 2005–January 2006)]. An old student of mine from Alabama is one of the editors, and he wanted something for their Christmas issue. He suggested something about the nativity, but I wrote further on Christ as he is depicted in Luke. It was a hell of a monster to write, but my old student said it moved him. Christ is nothing like the God in Job. He's much more a renegade ambassador of good will. Nowadays, as usual, there are too many mercenary Christians around, too many mystics for money. People aren't getting the straight stuff. More Christians are leaving the church out of disgust than out of apostasy. I like

a good sermon, but preachers rarely confess confusion. They tend to act like inerrant channels to God. Well, that's my mission statement.

DW: *You have been interviewed numerous times. What is the worst interview you ever had?*
BH: I can't remember a lot of the specific interviews, but there are types of interviews I despise. Those who want to put you into a bag and tie you up. They don't read you. They just want Barry Hannah to speak of the South, or to speak on the future of American letters. I just despise that type of lazy interview. I also hate the whole Faulkner thing, someone asking me what it's like to be an heir to Faulkner, or what it's like writing in the shadow of Faulkner. Then there's all the questions about the Oxford writing community. Oxford has been oversold as a writer-maker. It's a dumb fallacy, a chamber of commerce thing. People move to Oxford thinking it will help transform them into artists. It's just a gemlike flower of a big town.

DW: *Are there some interviews you like?*
BH: Writers sometimes offer good insights. I remember a series of interviews in the *Paris Review*, "Writers at Work," that was good. I read the Faulkner interview, and there were also interviews with Hemingway, O'Connor, and Styron. Interviews are an art form, and most are nowhere mediocrities feeding lines to other mediocrities. I did gain a lot from those old interviews, but not so much from interviews today. My cue comes from the animal world. My dog Nell sits on the couch in my office and inspires me, but not a lot of the people being interviewed today.

DW: *What was the worst question you were ever asked?*
BH: A lot of bad questions. I hate when an author is supposed to talk about his themes. Once someone asked me, "Aren't you always writing about unfulfilled males?" I think that's one of the worst questions I've had. Aren't we all unfulfilled? All art is about frustration. How can you write about fulfillment? How can you write about the Garden of Eden? You get a tableau, a still repetitive life.

DW: *What about some of the ways you have been tagged and identified? How do you respond to being labeled a "postmodern romantic?"*

BH: I don't know what post-anything means. Postmodern is a historical term referring to the period after World War II. I guess I am a romantic. It's a term that Ruth Weston used in a book she wrote about my fiction. She's a very nice, smart woman, but out of fear I have not read the whole book. I did pick up things from the modernists, Joyce, Faulkner, and Miller, the wild man. And Berryman and O'Connor. Folks like that who knew what they spoke and who followed their passions. My ideal narrative is when a man or woman just starts talking, like Mark Twain. I have no sense of structure. It's all idealized conversation, interesting voices. When you lose the naturalness in it, when you start putting literature in, you bomb. I outline in my head, but too much structure will destroy the good stuff in my head. I believe in the quest, the journey. I love to read biographies of those whose journeys have led to great or even sorry discoveries.

DW: *What don't you love to read?*
BH: College network poets. A lame group blurbing each other. No hint of the hunger of folks who need a new clear voice. They're just monkeys. I like to create modern fables as far as my limited talent will take me. I want something marvelous to come out of my fiction. I expect wild ecstasy when I'm writing. I insist on emotion, like the Romantics, like Wordsworth. Fiction ought to be exploratory. Writing is an act of discovery. T. S. Eliot wrote that old men should be explorers, old dry Tom. I love his poetry, but that high modernist method gets on my nerves. Old Tom was very wise, though.

DW: *Are there any questions that you wished you had been asked by an interviewer?*
BH: I wish I had been asked about my debts to those around me. I have never been able to give adequate tribute to my family, especially Dot, my sister, my wife, and pals in aiding my ambitions. I have had a beautiful education, all the literature and history I've read. I have had beautiful kinships. It helps if somebody is down the block or in the next room who gives a shit. I have read of many writers who are monsters of ingratitude, musicians too. I owe a big debt to music. Music was always there for me. Some of my pals are Bach, Dylan, Jimi Hendrix, and Mozart, ear perfect people. They stir me.

DW: *Any other debts?*
BH: Lately, Texas has had a huge influence on me, living with grad students like I did. They helped me in a lot of ways and were wonderful friends. There's a community of good spirits in San Marcos. I saw mainly the best in Texas. The Guadalupe River was beautiful, that cold green water. Fishing is always with me, always in my heart. I love Sardis Reservoir. I love to watch the waters and escape into their perfection, think of the savage food chain underneath.

DW: *Are there any questions that you would like to ask your readers?*
BH: I do that in my class. Most people can't tell you what they want. I'm always trying to find out what folks want. I always ask them where they want to go, how far they want to go. Ask them what books and music touched them the most. I want to find out what is inside of them even when they don't know. I want to know what passions direct them. These days I have almost a monastic life, but my motorcycle is close to the natural world. My motorcycle takes me to happy quietness in the country. I love the life of a motorcycle. I almost took flying lessons again. I went up a couple of times, and it was just lovely in the sky. It gave me that incomparable rush all over again.

DW: *Speaking of passion, a few years ago you had a remarkable near-death experience that profoundly influenced you. Not too long ago you published a beautiful essay ["Christ in the Room," Oxford American 48 (winter 2005), 70–75] describing this vision and how it personally affected you. How has this vision affected either you or your thoughts on writing?*
BH: I have a lot more humility now, a lot less hubris. I want to see Christianity work on a grand scale. It's also widened my subject matter. I have always envied doctors, those who care for the sick and needy, those who provide service and help. That's really Christ's message, service and help, and it's become a big subject in my life. I intend to help as many as possible. I don't fear death. I know nothing convincing about the afterlife, but I don't fear death. It's not the dying that's hard—it's the leaving. I don't have a tough dude's fearlessness of death. I have not been so tough. Suffering makes you stronger, but not when you're suffering.

Weakness is terrifying. Last year in the hospital I was an insane wimp. I refused to be left alone. I was afraid that I would fall off the cart. But Christ was not always strong. That cross scene is interesting. Those cruel-ass Romans. I watched Mel Gibson's *The Passion* [*of the Christ*]. It was not so anti-Semitic as it was anti-Roman. Christ felt betrayed by his father, and that's a human thing. He was killed by his Dad, and he felt this betrayal—"Why hast thou forsaken me?" When you are suffering, you're angry at everybody. There's no true empathy with anybody's pain. It was sobering that a man like the centurion, a man who had seen a lot of death and who had helped nail Christ to the cross, was the one who witnessed for Christ. He was a tough cookie. Maybe there is a little of the divine in all of us. I have never been laughed at for having had that vision of Christ, nobody has boycotted me that I know of. I think that many people are close to spiritual realities.

DW: *What's the best book that you haven't read but think you should read?*
BH: I don't read critical books of theory, and I don't read self-help books. Sometimes I like blissful ignorance. But I have never read Harold Bloom's *Where Shall Wisdom Be Found?* I had not read one word of Harold Bloom until his revised review of Cormac McCarthy's *Blood Meridian* came out. I know that he has a great mind and that he is a man of great breadth. And I know that he is fearless. In *Where Shall the Wisdom Be Found?* he talks about old age and the loss of friends. I have buried a lot of folks lately. Like Larry Brown. I didn't see a lot of him the past couple of years, but it was beautiful to have him around. He was an inspiring man. He took only one college writing course and taught himself. It's a great story.

DW: *How do you teach a writing course?*
BH: I believe in work and a stiff deadline. I think the couch critic's position is a third rate skill. I think that you have to be on time with your work, even if it's bad work. You have got to learn discipline. I got discipline up in Arkansas. Even as a drunk I wrote on time. I wasted too much time, but the discipline was such that I thought I was never a loser. I always believed I could come forth with something good and that things would be all right. Writing introduces you to the best people around,

but you have to have the discipline. We would explode if all we had was freedom. I could not imagine a life with full freedom. A good lesson to keep in mind is that nothing is ever lost. You can make up for blown time. Even if you were a wretch among wretches you can bring it on a page, and it's not wasted. For me it's been a lucky life. But for a Barry Hannah creative writing class I would have four short stories from four to twenty pages in length, two of the stories could be very brief, four to six pages. But one story a semester is not enough. You have to work. Also, stories should not be read past the deadlines. I don't give make-up work, and there's no extra credit.

DW: *Would you take the course?*
BH: Sure.

DW: *What about a course in Barry Hannah fiction?*
BH: I am flattered and grateful every time one of my books gets taught. I'm not even that successful, and I am truly humbled when I get taught. My self-importance has certainly not swelled. I am reminded every day not to get too swelled up. I can write some dreadful stuff.

DW: *When you have to fill out forms, questionnaires, and applications, what do you write when you come to the line, "Occupation?"*
BH: I always write "writer/professor." A long time ago I tried to ignore the fact that I had to teach, that I could not make enough money from writing. But over the years I have seen that it's possible to give much in the classroom and still be a good writer. Teaching has given me security and structure. Teaching is a high calling, a true art. Teaching and the creative life are now one and the same with me.

DW: *Writers are often asked who were the writers that influenced them. But who are the writers that you think you have influenced?*
BH: Good, overgenerous Michael Knight once said that I was an influence like Faulkner. I think I might have had some influence on the generation of Tom Franklin, writing pals and gals a generation behind me. It's the young and paperbacks that keep you alive.

DW: *What do you mean the young and paperbacks keep you alive?*
BH: Paperbacks are affordable, and young students keep me thinking, inspiring me. They don't get caught up in critical analysis. I hate every term applied to what we do, like literary fiction, or serious fiction. What we do is flinch from our lives, and rip back. I have a small but loyal fan base. I love it when a kid tells me how *Airships* changed his life. It seems to be the rallying book of my efforts, *Airships*.

Contributors

MELANIE R. BENSON is assistant professor of English at the University of Hartford, Connecticut. She has published articles in *Mississippi Quarterly* and *Pembroke Magazine* on writers such as William Faulkner, Frances Newman, James Weldon Johnson, and Louis Owens. She is currently completing a book-length postcolonial analysis of the discourse of quantification and calculation in twentieth-century U.S. southern fiction. Her current research focuses on Native American ledger art and other forms of cultural resistance.

THOMAS ÆRVOLD BJERRE is a Ph.D. student in the Center for American Studies at the University of Southern Denmark, Odense. His dissertation explores the influence of the traditional western on contemporary southern writers. His interview with Lewis Nordan appeared in *Mississippi Quarterly* in 2001, and he is a contributor to *Larry Brown: Voices of the South* (2006). He has also compiled a bibliography of Madison Jones's writings for *Madison Jones' Garden of Innocence* (2005). He is currently co-editing a special issue of *Mississippi Quarterly* on Lewis Nordan.

MARTYN BONE is assistant professor of American literature at the University of Copenhagen, Denmark. He is the author of *The*

Postsouthern Sense of Place in Contemporary Fiction (2005) and articles in *Journal of American Studies, Comparative American Studies,* and other journals. He is currently writing about literary representations of the U.S. South in transnational contexts by authors including Zora Neale Hurston, Nella Larsen, and Erna Brodber.

MARK S. GRAYBILL is associate provost for undergraduate studies and associate professor of English at Widener University, Pennsylvania. He has published articles in *CEA Critic, Critique, Southern Literary Journal,* and *Southern Studies.* Recently he published an essay on James Dickey's *Deliverance* in the collection *Upon Further Review: Sports in American Literature* (2004). He thanks Barry Hannah for not only giving him an interview when he was a struggling doctoral student, but also buying him breakfast.

RICHARD E. LEE is chair of the English department at the State University of New York's College at Oneonta. His recent publications include *Globalization, Language, and Culture* (2006); "'Crippled by the Truth': Oracular Pronouncements, Titillating Titles, and the Postmodern Ethic" in *The Postmodern Short Story: Forms and Issues* (2004); essays on cross-cultural pedagogy and business communication; numerous encyclopedia entries on British and African authors; and several articles on contemporary American short-story writers. He co-edited *The Dictionary of Literary Biography: American Short-Story Writers since WWII* (third series) in 2001, and is currently compiling another volume for this series, due to be published in 2007.

KEN MILLARD is senior lecturer in the Department of English Literature at the University of Edinburgh, Scotland. His publications include *Contemporary American Fiction* (2000) and *American Adolescence* (forthcoming). He is currently writing a book about contemporary fiction of the American West.

JAMES B. POTTS III is assistant professor of American literature at Mississippi College. He has published critical essays in *Southern Quarterly, Mississippi Quarterly, Journal of American Drama and Theater,*

South Carolina Review and other journals. He is currently completing projects on Alexander Solzhenitsyn, Cormac McCarthy, and James
Dickey.

SCOTT ROMINE is associate professor of English at the University of
North Carolina at Greensboro. He is the author of *The Narrative Forms
of Southern Community* (1999) and numerous essays on southern literature and culture. The essay in this volume is part of a larger project on
contemporary southern narrative entitled "The Real South: The Work of
Narrative in the Age of Cultural Reproduction."

MATTHEW SHIPE is a Ph.D candidate in American literature at
Washington University in St. Louis. He is currently completing his
dissertation on John Updike's short fiction.

DANIEL E. WILLIAMS is currently chair and professor of English
at Texas Christian University. He is the editor of *Pillars of Salt: An
Anthology of Early American Criminal Narratives* (1994) and co-editor of
*Liberty's Captives: Narratives of Confinement in the Print Culture of the
Early Republic* (2006). A specialist in early American literature, he also
teaches contemporary American fiction. From 1985 to 2003 he was Barry
Hannah's colleague at the University of Mississippi; in 2000, he taught
Ole Miss's first-ever Barry Hannah seminar.

Index

compared to Cormac McCarthy, xiii–xiv, 72, 80–81, 123–24, 128, 137; the Confederate States of America in his work, 23–24, 47, 49, 54, 73–74, 75, 77–79, 86, 87, 92–97, 110, 130, 133, 147–48, 149–50; heroism as a theme in his work, xiii, 46–63, 65, 72–83, 87, 92–99, 123, 126–27, 136, 146–47, 161, 177; identity in his work, 8–9, 18, 22–23, 57, 103, 142, 146–47, 156; intertextuality in his work, 10, 24, 87, 94; the Iraq war (1991) in his work, 97–98; the Korean war in his work, 106, 111; and literary parody, xiv, xv, 87, 92–99, 123–24, 128, 136, 150, 169; masculinity in his work, xii–xiii, 3, 4, 10–11, 46–63, 72, 77, 79, 87, 115–16, 117, 147, 152–53, 180n1; and metafiction, 15, 16, 20; music in his work, 4–5, 6, 13–14, 21, 28, 49, 57, 153–54, 162, 177, 179, 186; Native Americans in his work, xv, 6–7, 59, 130, 139, 141–58; and postmodernism, xii, xiv–xv, xvi, 8, 27, 29, 75, 79, 84–86, 97–98, 109, 110, 124, 125, 135, 136, 137, 137n3, 149, 150, 163, 167, 176, 179, 181n13, 185–86; and postsouthernism, xiv, 79–83, 87, 92–99, 141; public image of, x–xi, 86; race in his work, 6, 7, 93, 128, 144–45, 152, 156; "the real" as a theme in his work, xv–xvi, 9, 27, 30–31, 33, 35, 37–38, 44n10, 129–30, 134–35, 136, 154, 157, 162–82; redemption in his work, xiv, xv, 103–4, 113, 117–18, 162, 176–78; reviews of his work, ix–x, xi, xii, 73, 124; sex in his work, xiv, 4, 11, 14, 23, 32–33, 49, 53–56, 58–59, 63, 78, 113, 129, 132, 135, 147, 151, 152, 165, 171; the South in his work, xiii, xiv, xv, 3, 4, 16, 24–25, 46–47, 72–73, 81–83, 85, 92–97, 103, 108–10, 117, 130–31, 141–49, 152–57, 166–67; and the southern literary tradition, xiii–xiv, 65, 72, 79–83, 85–87, 109–10, 118n4, 124, 137n3; sport in his work, 51–52, 106–7, 118n3; and teaching, xvii, 183, 188–89; use of language, xi–xii, 5, 14, 15, 23, 24–25, 30–31, 73, 117, 123; the Vietnam war in his work, xiii, 23, 24, 51–52, 74–75, 95–97, 141–42; violence in his work, xiv, 4, 14, 23, 29–30, 32–33,

37–38, 46, 49, 53–56, 59, 63, 76–77, 102, 104, 107–8, 112, 113–14, 116–17, 118n3, 118n5, 118–19n6, 119n7, 131, 146, 152–53, 156; the West in his work, xiv–xv, 7, 98, 123–37, 143, 145–46, 148–57, 161; women in his work, xii, 49–51, 54–56, 58–59, 77, 113–14, 128–29, 132–33, 144–45, 147, 150–51, 152, 171; on writing, 183–84

Books: *Airships*, ix, x, xiv, 60, 61, 65, 73, 74–75, 87, 92, 180n1, 181–13, 190; *Bats Out of Hell*, xiii, 49, 60, 73, 87, 97, 180n7; *Boomerang*, ix, x, xi, xiv, xv, xvi, 86, 102–8, 112–18, 181n13, 184; *Captain Maximus*, xiii, xv, 49, 103–5, 113, 156; *Geronimo Rex*, ix, xi–xii, xv, 3–14, 28, 29, 58, 85, 87, 116, 141, 142, 143–48, 151, 152–55, 163, 180n1; *Hey Jack!*, xiv, xv, xvi, 102–18; *High Lonesome*, ix, x, xi–xii, xvi, 14–25, 54, 61, 108; *Never Die*, x, xi, xiv–xv, 61–62, 119n7, 123–37, 141, 142, 149–51, 161, 174; *Nightwatchmen*, x, xii, xvi, 26–43; *Power and Light* (limited edition), 73; *Ray*, ix, x, xiii, xiv, xv, 52–54, 61–62, 65, 75–77, 87, 95–97, 98, 102, 103, 105, 111, 118n2, 118n4, 118–19n5, 141–42, 152, 180n1; *The Tennis Handsome*, xi, xiii, 51–52, 58, 103–5, 107, 108, 113, 118n3; *Yonder Stands Your Orphan*, x, xiii, xv–xvi, 56–62, 81–82, 161–82, 183

Essays: "Christ in the Room," 82, 187–88; "Faulkner and the Small Man," 85–86; "The Maddening Protagonist," 184; "Mr. Brain, He Want a Song," 48

Stories: "The Agony of T. Bandini," 16, 23–24; "All the Old Hearkening Faces at the Rail," 60; "Bats Out of Hell Division," 73; "Carriba," 16; "A Creature in the Bay of St. Louis," 18–20, 22; "Dragged Fighting from His Tomb," 61, 74, 76–79, 87, 92–95, 96, 98, 99, 181n13; "Drummer Down," 16–17; "Even Greenland," 104; "Get Some Young," 24–25; "High Water Railers," 60; "The Ice Storm," 16, 22–23; "Idaho," 49; "Knowing He Was Not My Kind Yet I Followed," 74; "Ned Maxy,